"Preaching the Old Testament prophets is an intimidating task. So, I'm thankful for Andrew Hamilton. He loves the prophetic genre and has provided us with a guide that is both substantial and practical. . . . This book is worth reading and then using as a reference the next time you preach the prophets. You and your listeners will be better for it."

—Steven D. Mathewson,
author of *The Art of Preaching Old Testament Narrative*

"I am delighted to recommend Andy's book to preaching pastors and homileticians. His style makes him fun to read. But it's his content that puts him in my 'need to read' category. I especially benefited from reading his insights on how prophetic genre works and how to move from the prophets to *the* Prophet."

—Randal Emery Pelton,
Capital Seminary & Graduate School

"This is one of the best books I have encountered on how to grasp and communicate the scope and passion of the prophetic books of the Bible. While rich in content and overflowing with wisdom, it is delightfully easy to read, absorb, and put into practice. It will be enormously helpful to anyone determined to 'rightly handle the word of truth' that comes to us through the wild profusion and transforming power of prophetic speech."

—Christopher J. H. Wright,
author of *How to Preach and Teach the Old Testament for All Its Worth*

"Have any Bible books become as neglected as the Prophets? May this book change that! Our world desperately needs to hear the Prophets preached again. Where else can we get such a punchy presentation of how God really feels about sin and injustice or such a thrilling glimpse into the glorious hope of God's salvation plan? Hamilton expertly leads us into this collection of unique preachers, and his gracious guidance will unleash their preaching through us!"

—PETER MEAD,
leader of the Bible Teachers and Preachers Network,
European Leadership Forum

"The art of preaching prophecy demands balance, a different method of locomotion, and heightened awareness of one's surroundings. Dr. Hamilton takes us through concrete steps on how to preach the genre gracefully, even beautifully, without harming bystanders."

—JEFFREY D. ARTHURS,
Gordon-Conwell Theological Seminary

# HOW TO PREACH THE PROPHETS FOR ALL THEIR WORTH

# How to Preach the Prophets for All Their Worth

A Hermeneutical, Homiletical, and Theological Guide to Unleash the Power of the Prophets

ANDREW G. M. HAMILTON

*Foreword by Jeffrey D. Arthurs*

WIPF & STOCK · Eugene, Oregon

HOW TO PREACH THE PROPHETS FOR ALL THEIR WORTH
A Hermeneutical, Homiletical, and Theological Guide to Unleash the Power
of the Prophets

Wipf & Stock
An Imprint of Wipf and Stock Publishers
199 W. 8th Ave., Suite 3
Eugene, OR 97401

www.wipfandstock.com

PAPERBACK ISBN: 978-1-6667-3622-9
HARDCOVER ISBN: 978-1-6667-9426-7
EBOOK ISBN: 978-1-6667-9427-4

APRIL 27, 2022 2:33 PM

**To Ruth**
*La mia dolce metà.*

# CONTENTS

# ILLUSTRATIONS

## FIGURE

## TABLE

# Foreword

Jeffrey D. Arthurs

PREACHING THE PROPHETS is like ice skating—easy to do poorly. Your ankles cave in, you spend more time collapsing to your knees than gliding on your feet, and the skaters around you are in mortal danger! Ice skating can be a harrowing adventure because, well, it demands that we skate on ice, that slippery, hard, and unfamiliar substance. In the same way, when preachers turn to Haggai or Habukkuk, Micah or Malachi, they feel their footing give way. They long for the good old days of a series in Ephesians or Luke.

If John Stott's model of preaching is accurate (and I think it is)—standing between two worlds—then preachers soon discover that many difficulties attend the endeavor: the gap between ancient, Middle Eastern culture and modern culture is wide; the theology can be foreboding as it emphasizes judgment as well as hope; the language is often poetry—concise, cryptic, image-laden, and full of word play. And where is Christ? He makes important cameo appearances in the prophets, but the ancient oracles had only a shadowy understanding of Messiah.

This is where Andrew Hamilton steps in. He teaches us how to skate. The art of preaching prophecy demands balance, a different method of locomotion, and heightened awareness of one's surroundings. Dr. Hamilton takes us through concrete steps on how to preach the genre gracefully, even beautifully, without harming bystanders.

Is it worth the effort to learn how to preach the prophets? Yes. Without this major portion of God's holy word, our understanding of God, Christ, sin, and salvation will be stunted. Maybe that is why Jesus and the apostles preached the prophets.

So put on your skates, hang on to Coach Hamilton, and give it a whirl. With his instruction, and supported by the Holy Spirit, I'm sure you will stay on your feet.

# ACKNOWLEDGMENTS

Thanks be to God who has abounded in his grace to me. His grace has frequently been channeled through people who have lavishly poured into my life.

I begin by honoring those who first and most invested in my life. It is a privilege to call Mum and Dad the most godly, gracious, and generous people I know. They taught me to walk whilst showing me what walking with Christ looks like. They taught me to talk, filling my ears with words of encouragement. They taught me to read by reading Scripture together as a family. They taught me to think by being an ever-present sounding board. They taught me to trust, cheering me on whilst watching out for me all along.

I am grateful to colleagues and students at the Istituto Biblico Evangelico Italiano. Their input and feedback, in and out of the classroom, has enriched this work. A note of gratitude to colleague and friend Principal Daniele P. Pasquale for his encouragement. Roberta Giangiulio also merits special mention. Her generous and administrative help saved hours of my life.

I benefitted from being able to present some of this material to gifted preachers at "Workshop Predicazione" and the Preaching Network at the European Leadership Forum.

I am grateful to Dr. Arthurs and Dr. Pelton for their passionate and insightful teaching on preaching the literary forms of the Bible. Studying at Gordon Conwell Theological Seminary under the supervision of Dr. Arthurs has been one of the greatest privileges of my life. I have "stolen" all I could from his pastoral heart, scriptural insight, preaching expertise, and writing skill.

Finally, I am extremely grateful to my family. My children Isaiah, Hollie, and Joshua are my greatest fans and the best people to celebrate with at the end of any adventure. I cannot express in words my indebtedness to Ruth—the sweetest wife, loving mamma, patient proofreader, and best friend. I love you.

# PART 1

# WHY PREACH
# THE PROPHETS

# *Chapter 1*

## THE EXAMPLE OF JESUS AND THE APOSTLES

> "It was revealed to them [the prophets] that
> they were serving not themselves but you."
>
> —1 PET 1:12

WHEN WE TAKE OUR steps to enter the pulpit we are following in the footsteps of many great preachers of the past. Preaching has a long and strong history. We have all been shaped, consciously or unconsciously, by those who have gone before us. But what if you were the greatest preacher of all time? Preaching textbooks often, and appropriately, present Jesus as the ultimate preacher. Was Jesus shaped by the preachers that went before him? The Gospels shout a resounding yes. Tracing Jesus' words shows that not only was he shaped by those before him but that he took full advantage of their inheritance. It is well known that Jesus frequently quoted Moses (especially Deuteronomy) and David (the Psalms). What is often overlooked is how heavily he relied upon the theology, the approach, and even the language of the Old Testament prophets. If Jesus had a favorite prophet, it was undoubtedly Isaiah. Yet he did not just quote from Isaiah, but he also referenced, either by direct quotation or allusion, many of the other prophets. The apostles similarly relied upon the theology of the prophets, both in Acts and the Epistles, to teach core doctrines and to make key decisions. Jesus and the New Testament writers recognized the theological richness of the Old Testament prophets. This is the fundamental reason why the church cannot afford to neglect this significant portion of the canon. In this chapter we will explore how Jesus referred to the prophets to disclose his identity and to deliver some of his most memorable teaching moments. Then we will trace the impact that the prophets exerted on the New Testament writers.

## THE PROPHETS DISCLOSE THE TRUE IDENTITY OF JESUS

In recent years much attention has been given to connecting the Old Testament, including the prophets, to Christ. This connection unlocks the theological treasure chest of the prophets. Greidanus, who has been at the forefront of this endeavor, asserts: "Interpreters will miss the heart of the prophecy when they fail to link it to Jesus Christ."[1] In chapter 8 we will consider various hermeneutically responsible and canonically legitimate ways of connecting the Old Testament prophets to Christ. However, the relationship can also be viewed from the other direction. It is a two-way street. Connecting Christ *back* to the prophets is also necessary to gain a fuller understanding of his identity and mission. Therefore, we can both agree with Greidanus's assertion and yet be tempted to invert it. Interpreters will miss the heart of the identity and mission of Jesus Christ when they fail to link him to the prophets. The prophets enable us to fully appreciate the story and the promises that Jesus Christ fulfilled. Jesus himself invited us to journey *back* to comprehend his true identity.

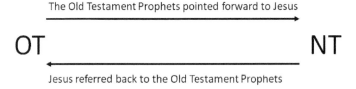

The Old Testament Prophets pointed forward to Jesus

OT          NT

Jesus referred back to the Old Testament Prophets

### Son of Man

Jesus' favorite title for himself was "Son of Man." He used this title eighty-two times across the four Gospels. Jesus did not coin this title, but he

1. Greidanus, *Modern Preacher and the Ancient Text*, 258.

derived it primarily from an Old Testament prophet. Daniel uses the term in a staggering description of a glorious vision: "Behold, with the clouds of heaven there came one like a son of man, and he came to the Ancient of Days and was presented before him. And to him was given dominion and glory and a kingdom, that all peoples, nations, and languages should serve him; his dominion is an everlasting dominion, which shall not pass away, and his kingdom one that shall not be destroyed" (Dan 7:13–14). This vision did not go unnoticed and was used in Jewish literature during the intertestamental period.[2] Jesus chose to use this loaded title to reveal his identity. This title confirms the humanity of Jesus.[3] However, this vision discloses Jesus' divine nature. Yahweh, and only Yahweh, coming in judgment and riding the clouds as a chariot is a common Old Testament image (Ps 18:10–13; 97:2–4; 104:3; Isa 19:1; Nah 1:3). Therefore, paradoxically, Jesus' self-identification as the Son of Man reveals his divinity more than his humanity. Nowhere is this more evident than in the climactic moment of the final interrogation of Jesus by the high priest. The council was increasingly frustrated because of their inability to find a definitive and reliable testimony against him. The turning point takes place when he claims to be the Son of Man that will come with the clouds of heaven (Mark 14:62). The high priest reacted by tearing his garments and accusing him of blasphemy. All doubts vanished regarding who Jesus was claiming to be when he identified himself as the Son of Man described by the prophet Daniel.

By using the title Son of Man Jesus also shows he has the credentials to inaugurate the kingdom of God. Daniel's vision of the Son of Man takes place in a context where earthly kingdoms are portrayed by four frightening and seemingly uncontrollable beasts. The situation appears hopeless until Daniel is given a vision of the Ancient of Days sitting on his throne. In an effortless, swift move, the Ancient of Days destroyed the most ferocious beast and stripped them all of their dominion (Dan 7:1–12). The next vision is "an enthronement oracle,"[4] a coronation. The Son of Man is presented before the Ancient of Days and receives dominion over the indestructible, universal, and eternal kingdom (Dan

2. Especially in the apocryphal books of 4 Ezra and Similitudes of Enoch.

3. This is true in Daniel's vision of "one like a son of man" but it is especially true when we consider the way this title is used in another Old Testament prophet. Son of Man is a designation that is frequently used in Ezekiel and in this context the title does not seem to have a technical connotation; rather it simply means "human being."

4. Moyise, *Jesus and Scripture*, 27.

7:13–14). This ceremony establishes that the Son of Man has the right to inaugurate the kingdom of God and thus informs many, perhaps all, of the instances in which Jesus uses this title. Wright highlights that these Son of Man sayings fall into three basic categories. First, there are those occasions in which Jesus used the title when he spoke with authority over sin, sickness, and nature. Second, there is the category in which these sayings are used in relation to his rejection, suffering, death, and resurrection. The third and largest category of these sayings presents the Son of Man eschatologically coming in glory and acting as judge on behalf of God. Wright then concludes: "Taken together, these three categories are remarkably comprehensive as a way of encapsulating how Jesus saw his own identity as well as how he envisaged his immediate and more long-term destiny."[5] Why is Son of Man Jesus' favorite title? What did he want us to know by using it? How should it influence our understanding of his identity and mission? We cannot even begin to answer these questions without Daniel. The title Son of Man is tightly tethered to Daniel's prophecies, and it is there we fully grasp its significance.

## Messiah

A title that also decisively contributed to revealing the identity of Jesus, but one that he was much less keen to use, was the title "Messiah." The term Messiah is linked to the Old Testament practice of anointing people to signal that they had been set aside and equipped by God for a special service for God. Prophets (1 Kgs 19:16), priests (Exod 28:41), and especially kings (1 Sam 9:16; 16:13; 1 Kgs 1:34) were often anointed. Through the promises and prophecies, the messianic expectations grew of an ultimate Messiah, a son of David (2 Sam 7:1–17), that would come to deliver and restore Israel. The Old Testament prophets often spoke of this hope of deliverance that would be brought about by Yahweh through a royal figure (Isa 9:1–7; 11:1–5; Jer 23:1–6; Ezek 34:17–31; Dan 9:25–26, etc.). The messianic hopes escalated during the intertestamental period because of the political status of Israel under the authority of foreign nations. By the time Jesus came along, when Israel languished under the authority of Rome, the longings for a Messiah were intense. Yet Jesus did not capitalize on these longings. He never used the term Messiah directly about himself. There seems to be an intentional, and to some extent

---

5. Wright, *Knowing Jesus through the Old Testament*, 150.

mysterious, elusiveness. Why was Jesus elusive? Why was he reluctant to use the term Messiah? The most probable explanation is that the term Messiah had become impregnated with flawed connotations. The people were waiting for a Messiah that would restore the nation. They wanted a political and military leader. Jesus did not want to be straitjacketed into this understanding (misunderstanding) and therefore stayed clear of the term Messiah.[6] Despite this lack of explicit self-appropriation of the term Messiah, Jesus hinted that he was the Messiah by quoting the prophet Isaiah (Luke 4:18). He never denied his identity as the Messiah when asked (John 4:25), even in a hostile environment (Mark 14:6). He interrogated the disciples about his identity and blessed Peter when, the quick-to-answer apostle, recognized him to be the Messiah (Matt 16:15–17).

More than the words of Jesus, his actions pointed back to the messianic prophecies and thus accredited him as the Messiah. The sheer volume of prophecies fulfilled by Jesus prove he was the long-awaited Messiah. The prophets offered specific prophecies about the place (Mic 5:2) and miraculous nature of his birth (Isa 7:14). They preannounced that his ministry would begin in Galilee (Isa 9:1–2) and that he would be preceded by a forerunner (Isa 40:3–4). They also predicted he would be welcomed with great joy as a king in Jerusalem (Zech 9:9), yet he would be betrayed for thirty pieces of silver (Zech 11:12–13). All these prophecies help us recognize Jesus of Nazareth as the Messiah. The greatest concentration of messianic prophecies is found in the prophets. Therefore, how can we expect to fully understand the identity of Jesus "Christ" (Greek equivalent of the Hebrew "Messiah") without consulting the prophets?

## Servant of Yahweh

Delving into the prophets, in this case Isaiah, helps us capture another side of Jesus that he recalled in order to reveal his identity. Jesus is the "Servant of the Lord" or the "Suffering Servant" in Isaiah. He linked his ministry to the servant songs (42:1–9; 49:1–13; 50:4–11; 52:13—53:12) and to other related passages in Isaiah. At the very beginning of his public ministry Jesus read from Isaiah 61:1–2 and identified in himself the fulfillment of these prophecies (Luke 4:17–21). He referenced the same passage again when responding to the delegation that John the Baptist sent to inquire regarding his identity (Luke 7:22). Although, strictly speaking,

---

6. Wright, *Knowing Jesus through the Old Testament*, 145.

Isaiah 61:1–2 is not one of the servant songs, the connection between this passage and the mission of the servant of the Lord as described in Isaiah 42:7 is unmistakable. Furthermore, Jesus revealed that he was the servant of the Lord, not just with his words, but also with his actions. Matthew is keen to help his readers see Jesus as the servant of the Lord. Matthew not only records the clear allusion to the servant of the Lord at the baptism (Matt 3:17; Isa 42:1), but he also includes several quotations from the servant songs in the context of Jesus' healing ministry (Matt 8:17; 12:15–21). Jesus also declared himself to be the servant of the Lord to his disciples on the night of his arrest by quoting the servant song in Isaiah 53 (Luke 22:37). He identified himself as the servant of the Lord from the beginning to the end of his life. Therefore, to comprehend the significance of his teaching, healing, and especially his death, Jesus is inviting us to look back to the prophet Isaiah and pay attention to the description of the servant of Yahweh. This is where it gets tricky.

Looking back, we will find ourselves asking the same question that the Ethiopian eunuch wrestled with regarding the identity of the servant of the Lord: "Who is the prophet talking about, himself or someone else?" (Acts 8:34). Within the four servant songs (Isa 42:1–9; 49:1–13; 50:4–11; 52:13—53:12), Isaiah appears to fluctuate between applying this title both to the nation of Israel and to a specific individual. This ambiguity is clearly seen in the second servant song, where the servant is unambiguously identified as corporate Israel (Isa 49:3), and yet the servant is also called to act for Israel (Isa 49:5–6). How can this be? Who is the prophet talking about? Israel was certainly called to be the servant of the Lord and to fulfill a peculiar service for the Lord. The elect nation, however, did not entirely fulfill its calling as the immediate context of servant songs shows (Isa 42:18–24). Therefore, the Lord raised up another servant, the ultimate Servant, who would perfectly fulfill his calling on behalf of Israel and for Israel (Isa 49:5–6). Jesus is the ultimate servant of the Lord who: carried out his ministry with tenderness (Isa 42:3; Matt 12:18–21), is the light for the gentiles (Isa 42:4; 49:6; Matt 12:21; Luke 2:32), endured suffering (Isa 50:6; Matt 26:67), is exalted (Isa 52:13; John 12:32), carried our sorrows (Isa 53:4; Matt 8:17), willingly sacrificed himself (Isa 53:7; Acts 8:32), and suffered for the sins of many (Isa 53:12; Mark 10:45).

Jesus relied upon the prophets to disclose his true identity as the Son of Man, the Messiah, and the servant of the Lord. These three images woven together provide a formidable portrayal of the Lord Jesus. The Old Testament prophetic background is fundamental to fully understand and faithfully preach the good news of Jesus. There are depths to our understanding of the identity and mission of Jesus that can only been achieved by receiving the teaching of the Old Testament prophets. No wonder the risen Savior considered it a priority to open the minds and melt the hearts of the disciples to understand how the Old Testament Scriptures spoke about him (Luke 24:27, 32, 45–47). As the two anonymous disciples journeyed to Emmaus the Lord came alongside and took them on a much greater journey. They journeyed back to Moses and traced the trail of the prophets to see how they had spoken about Jesus. Our view of Jesus will remain impoverished unless we are willing to do the same.

## THE PROPHETS SHAPED THE TEACHING OF JESUS

Jesus considered preaching to be of upmost importance. He began his ministry by preaching in Galilee (Mark 1:14). On more than one occasion Jesus revealed that he was sent by the Father and he came with the purpose of preaching (Mark 1:38; Luke 4:18, 43). Jesus is frequently referred to as "Teacher" and "Rabbi" (Matt 8:19; Mark 5:35; Luke 6:40; John 1:38). Therefore, it is not surprising that, like other rabbis, Jesus taught in synagogues (Mark 1:21–28; Luke 4:14–21). He also proclaimed the good news of the kingdom in towns (Matt 9:35), by lakes (Mark 4:1), and on mountainsides (Matt 5:1), using a plethora of visual aids and rhetorical devices to effectively communicate to the crowds. He gripped his listeners because he preached with unique authority and grace (Mark 1:21–22; Luke 4:22). All these elements demonstrate that preaching and teaching were not peripheral aspects of Jesus' ministry. He was certainly more than a preacher, but he was not less than a preacher. Indeed, he was an extremely effective preacher who preached with authority, creativity, clarity, compassion, and passion.

We preachers take notice that such an effective preacher borrowed some of his most memorable images/expressions from the prophets: spring of living water (Jer 2:13; 17:13; John 4:14; 7:38), vine/vineyard (Isa 5:1–7; John 15:1–11), born again (Ezek 36:25–27; 37:1–14; John 3:3–6), fig tree (Jer 8:13; Mark 11:12–25), fishers of men (Jer 16:16; Matt 4:18–19), bride and groom (Isa 62:4–5; Matt 9:15), light of the world (Isa 60:3; John 8:12), hear but never understand (Isa 6:9–10; Mark 4:12), cup of God's wrath (Jer 25:15; Luke 22:42), den of robbers (Jer 7:11; Mark 11:17), harvest (Joel 3:13; Matt 13:39–40), sheep (Mic 2:12–13; John

10:3–4), shepherds (Ezek 34:1–24; John 10:11), etc. The prophets hold the copyright for most of these images. Admittedly some of them are not used exclusively by the prophets but are key biblical themes that appear throughout the canon. Their use by the prophets, however, enriched and expanded their significance. Jesus was aware of this. His use of the language of the good shepherd (John 10) is a prime example. The imagery of the shepherd appears across the biblical genres from historical books to the Psalms (Psalm 23 being the best-known example), yet the prophets developed it most fully. The prophets portrayed kings and leaders in Israel as shepherds and the people as their flock. They frequently exposed the leaders as worthless shepherds who, instead of caring for their flock, exploited and devoured them (Ezek 34:8–10; Zech 11:16–17). In contrast to these worthless shepherds, the prophets present Yahweh as the good shepherd that will gather and protect his sheep. He will gather the scattered sheep after the exile (Jer 31:10), and even carry the lambs in his arms (Isa 40:11). The use of the shepherd imagery becomes even more intriguing because on the one hand the Lord declares himself to be the ultimate shepherd for his people (Ezek 34:11, 15; Mic 7:14; Zech 10:3), yet he also promises to send a ruler from the house of David, born in Bethlehem, to be the ultimate shepherd (Ezek 34:23; Mic 5:4; Zech 11:4). Jesus is clearly alluding to, and leveraging, the theology of the prophets when he declares himself to be the Good Shepherd par excellence.

Jesus uses each of the above images in a specific way, and exploration of the Old Testament background helps us understand them.[7] On some occasions Jesus *quotes* directly from the language of the prophets to explain what was taking place in his day (e.g., Matt 13:14–15) or what will take place in the future (e.g., Matt 24:15–31). On other occasions he uses the terminology of the prophets, therefore *alluding* to their original context, but developing their message in an innovative and surprising way (e.g., John 15). On still other occasions Jesus does not use the language of the prophets per se, yet the careful reader will detect subtle *echoes* (e.g., John 4:35–38). For those that regard echoes as too tenuous, Moyise provides a helpful musical analogy: "Music critics do not confine their comments to the loudest instruments of the orchestra. It is often the subtle sounds at the very brink of hearing that determine the quality of the performance. And echoes can be quite loud if you are standing

---

7. In order to undertake such explorations, it is worth consulting Beale and Carson, *Commentary*.

between two mountains."[8] As Hays has successfully demonstrated, the words of Jesus resound with echoes of the Old Testament Scripture.[9] The sheer quantity of quotations, allusions, and echoes testify that Jesus considered the teaching of the prophets to be essential for his disciples. Jesus is endorsing the importance of the message of the Old Testament prophets.

## Wind, Spirit, and Breath

One place where this endorsement becomes explicit is in the conversation with Nicodemus (John 3). The "born again" conversation is also an excellent example of the importance of subtle allusions and echoes. You know the story. The prominent teacher of Israel comes to Jesus at night. He is taken aback by Jesus' declaration of the necessity to be "born again/from above" (3:3). Nicodemus is puzzled by these words, as is evidenced by his clumsy question about the impossibility of being reborn physically (3:4). To help Nicodemus understand, Jesus restates his main idea, enriching it with language from the Old Testament. This language unlocks the meaning of this puzzling expression (3:5–7). Jesus clarifies that to be "born again" means to be "born of water and the Spirit." This is an allusion to Ezekiel (36:25–27), where the prophet explains the need for God's intervention to remove the heart of stone and give a heart of flesh. This language of giving a new heart, a heart that beats for the Lord, is described by the prophet as being sprinkled by clean water and as being given a new spirit. Despite this allusion, the expert of the Jewish Scriptures failed to make this connection. Am I being unfair to Nicodemus? Is it unrealistic to expect Nicodemus to make the connection with these few words? Perhaps this would be unfair if this was all that Nicodemus had to work with. However, Jesus provided other important clues that connected his words to the prophet Ezekiel. The play on words with wind/spirit[10] (John 3:6–8) is a clear reference to the same section of the book of Ezekiel (37:1–14). This memorable play on words is not original to Jesus but is derived from the remarkable vision of the valley of dry bones that is given to Ezekiel. This dramatic vision uses another play on words with breath/wind/spirit which all translate the single Hebrew word "*ruah*" (equivalent

8. Moyise, *Old Testament in the New*, 8.

9. Hays, *Echoes of Scripture in the Gospels*.

10. *Pneuma* is the Greek word for both "spirit" and "wind."

of Greek "*pneuma*" in John 3), which is repeated ten times in this section (Ezek 37:1–14). The Spirit of the Lord transported the prophet into a valley full of dry bones and instructed him to prophesy over the bones. As the prophet followed the instructions, he heard a rattling sound and saw the bones coming together and being covered by flesh and skin. A second time the Spirit invited the prophet to prophesy: "Thus says the Lord God: Come from the four winds, O breath, and breathe on these slain, that they may live" (Ezek 37:9). Ezekiel prophesied and saw the valley of corpses live and stand like a great army. It was an awesome sight, a scene worthy of any horror movie, but it is also awesome in what it symbolized. The dry bones represented the house of Israel during the exile. The exiles felt dead, without hope. They said: "Our bones are dried up, and our hope is lost; we are indeed cut off" (Ezek 37:11). The purpose of the vision was to renew the hope of the exiles; comparing the bringing back to life of dry bones to the restoration of Israel after the exile. This restoration was not just physical but also spiritual. The Lord declared: "I will put my Spirit within you, and you shall live, and I will place you in your own land" (Ezek 37:14). The scope of this vision, however, goes beyond anything that Israel experienced in the postexilic period and points to a much greater regeneration. A regeneration that would be a miraculous act of the Spirit of God. A regeneration that would be like a heart transplant replacing a heart of stone with a living, soft heart for the Lord. A regeneration that would not just involve emotions but a transformation of the entire person.[11] A regeneration that would involve giving new life by the Spirit of God to the deep spiritual deadness in the heart of man. A regeneration that would be like a new birth. With this in mind, returning to John 3, it is easy to understand why Jesus transported the well-versed Nicodemus to the prophecy of Ezekiel. The language of new birth, water, wind, the sound of the wind, and spirit were all clues. Nicodemus, however, fails to tune in to the vision of the prophet Ezekiel (John 3:9). The teacher fails, as the blunt response of Jesus attests (John 3:10). Carson comments:

> Jesus' response projects the blame in sharp focus: Nicodemus, in his role as Israel's teacher, should have understood these things. The article with this expression (lit. 'the teacher of Israel') suggests he was a recognized master, an established religious authority. 'You are the Reverend Professor Doctor, and do not

11. "Heart" in Hebrew is an idiom for the whole inner person, including what we would today describe as "mind" and "will."

understand these things?' Nothing could make clearer the fact that Jesus' teaching on the new birth was built on the teaching of the Old Testament.[12]

This scolding retort, and the entire exchange, demonstrates how highly Jesus regarded the teaching of the prophets. In John 3, Jesus is standing on the shoulders of the prophets to deliver the centerpiece of his teaching on the doctrine of regeneration.

## THE PROPHETS IMPACTED THE NEW TESTAMENT CHURCH

The reliance upon the prophets was not exclusive to Jesus but is pervasive throughout the New Testament. From the birth of the New Testament church the apostles considered the Old Testament prophets an indispensable part of God's revelation. This emerges plainly in Paul's description of the nature and purpose of Scripture in 2 Timothy 3:14—4:2. We must remember that when Paul uses the terms "Holy Scriptures" and "all Scripture" he is referring to what is now called the Old Testament. Therefore, Paul is convinced that the church needs the Old Testament since it is God-breathed, able to lead to salvation through faith in Christ, and profitable in equipping believers for very good work. Based on this conviction Paul called Timothy to preach the Old Testament, including the prophets, to the church.

The first text that is the basis for the first sermon recorded in the book of Acts, Peter's sermon at Pentecost, is drawn from an Old Testament prophet (Acts 2:16–21). Peter preached from the prophet Joel to proclaim the new era that had dawned through the death and resurrection of Jesus of Nazareth, the Messiah. To prove that Jesus was indeed the suffering Messiah, the apostles, once again, relied on the prophets. They called the prophets as key witnesses to demonstrate that what had taken place had been preannounced and was part of God's plan of salvation (Acts 3:18, 24; 8:32–33; 10:43). Stephen's theologically significant summary of Israel's history is predictably loaded with quotations and allusions from the Old Testament. The majority simply serve the purpose of retelling the story. There is however one quotation, from the prophet Isaiah (Acts 7:49–50), that has the specific purpose of reminding the people that what the Lord wants is not an impressive building like the

12. Carson, *Gospel According to John*, 198.

temple but a life of humble obedience. The writings of the prophets, on this occasion the prophet Amos, were also a key reference point at the very delicate conference in Jerusalem when deciding about the inclusion of the gentiles into the new covenant community (Acts 15:15–18). This was a make-or-break moment for the early church. James, and the other conference participants, made this decision based on the message of an Old Testament prophet. The book of Acts also ends with the often cited, and, sadly, frequently fitting, words of Isaiah regarding the unresponsiveness, hardness, and blindness of the people to the word of God (Acts 28:26–27). From the beginning to the end of the book of Acts many of the key moments and speeches in the early church were drawn from the quiver of the prophets.

The prominence of the prophets continues in the Epistles. The Epistles are saturated with quotations, allusions, and echoes from the prophets. Without attempting to survey all these instances it will suffice to note the influence that the prophets had in the formation of some key doctrines. For example, Paul's thesis that salvation is by faith and not by works, in both Romans and Galatians, is rooted in Habakkuk: "the righteous shall live by faith" (2:4). A concentration of prophetic quotations also appears in Paul's discussion of the mystery of election in Romans 9–11. Paul uses the symbol of an olive tree to describe the unfolding plan of God for Jewish Christians (the root of the olive tree), gentile Christians (branches cut off from a wild olive tree and grafted onto the cultivated olive tree), and the unbelieving Jews (natural branches currently cut off from the cultivated olive tree but capable of being grafted back on). Paul describes these three groups and builds his argument following the prophetic blueprint. He begins by quoting Hosea to show that the inclusion of the gentiles is part of God's unfolding plan (Rom 9:25–26). He relies upon Isaiah to demonstrate that many of those who considered themselves God's people, Israel, have stumbled and become blind (Rom 9:33; 10:21; 11:8) apart from a remnant (Rom 9:27–29). However, the prophets also enable Paul to anticipate and hope that this blindness is only temporary and that these natural branches will be grafted back in (Rom 11:25–27). Paul's interpretation of the intricate present situation of the church and his anticipation of the plan of God for the future derives from a careful study of the prophets.

Peter, too, in both of his Epistles, strongly endorses the testimony of the Old Testament prophets. He asserts that the prophets, by the Spirit, prophesied about the grace and salvation in Christ (1 Pet 1:10–12). Peter describes this as a service that they were carrying out for our benefit. They were serving us. The searching, the visions, and the oracles of the prophets were not only for their immediate audience but for every generation of the people of God. Furthermore, in his second epistle, we see that Peter's confidence in the prophetic writings is such that he boldly argues that they are "more fully confirmed" than even his own experience of the transfiguration (2 Pet 1:16–21).

The ongoing importance of the prophets is also evident by considering how much the book of Revelation is saturated with Old Testament prophets. Although John does not use direct quotations, Revelation is full of allusions and echoes from the Old Testament. John expects us to tune in to hear these echoes and see that he is singing off the same hymn sheet as the Old Testament authors. Alongside the Psalms, most of these echoes come from the world of the prophets, specifically from Isaiah, Ezekiel, Daniel, and Zechariah.

## WE NEED THE PROPHETS

The unanimous witness of Jesus and the New Testament writers therefore establishes the importance of the Old Testament prophets as a crucial part of the word of God for the church. Jesus and the New Testament writers viewed the Old Testament prophets as a key part of their Bible. Their testimony is too strong to be ignored. If Jesus and the apostles did not hesitate to affirm the prophets' authority, to make key decisions based on their message, and to preach from them, neither should we.

Furthermore, the New Testament writings are impregnated with theological concepts and images whose meaning cannot be fully understood without knowledge of the Old Testament prophets. The New Testament is not rootless, but rather is rooted in the Old Testament, which includes the rich soil of the prophets. If we eradicate it from this soil, we are in danger of not only having a partial understanding of key doctrines of the Christian faith but also of having an incomplete appreciation of the person and work of Jesus. Thus, we cannot afford to neglect this major part of the Old Testament. As we have seen, the following New Testament concepts are only comprehensible when we take heed of the prior revelation that we find in the prophets: Son of Man, Messiah, servant of the Lord, good shepherd, new birth, prophet, kingdom of God, salvation, new covenant, and day of the Lord. Therefore, when the prophets are silenced the church experiences two related and overlapping problems. First, it does not receive nourishment from this crucial part of the Old Testament. Second, even the nourishment it assumes it is receiving from the New Testament is lacking key ingredients. The church cannot afford to be malnourished. As we enter the pulpit today, standing on the shoulders of those that went before us, we must not forget the prophets.

# *Chapter 2*

# THE VALUE OF THEIR MESSAGE

> "Therefore I testify to you this day that I am innocent of the
> blood of all of you, for I did not shrink from declaring to
> you the whole counsel of God."
>
> —ACTS 20:26-27

TO CONTINUE TO EXPLORE reasons why we should preach the Old Testament prophets, we will dive into their message and see their value for the church. In the previous chapter we saw that Jesus and the apostles commended the prophets to us. In this chapter we will begin to flick through the pages of the prophetic books to gain a first-hand appreciation of their work. We will do this for a dual purpose. First, gaining an appreaction of the value and relevancy of their message will fuel a desire to preach the prophets. Second, surveying the overall prophetic message will serve us well in preparation for preaching this important part of Scripture. Before launching into this survey it is important to affirm that whilst the Old Testament prophets did not deliver their message directly *to* us, nonetheless their message is *for* us. Indeed the prophetic literature, together with the rest of the Old Testament, is part of the word of God for the church.

## TOTA SCRIPTURA

Recognizing the Hebrew Scriptures as part of the word of God for the church is an important premise because a commitment to preach the Old Testament will only emerge when it is viewed as a legitimate and essential part of the Christian Bible. Not everyone agrees that the Old Testament should be considered on par with the New Testament as God's special revelation for the church. Some ministers have a defective view of the Old Testament and this is one of the reasons why they fail to invest time and effort into preaching the prophets. What are the various ways in which the Old Testament is viewed today? According to Greidanus there are four contemporary positions.[1] Some consider the Old Testament to be sub-Christian, meaning that most of the Old Testament ought to be rejected apart from a few gems that still have value. Others view the Old Testament as non-Christian, claiming that the Tanakh[2] ought to be viewed as a complete and independent work and not as part of Christian revelation. A third view, which is much more common within the church, is that the Old Testament is pre-Christian, meaning that it is not entirely and intrinsically a Christian message unless it is connected to the New Testament. Achtemeier holds to this view: "Apart from the New Testament, the Old Testament does not belong to the Christian Church and is not its book. The Old Testament is the word of God to Israel."[3] The final view, which is the one I advocate, is to consider the nature of the Old Testament as Christian and a crucial part of God's progressive revelation to the church. Preachers who do not hold to this high view of the Hebrew Scriptures will inevitably reduce the Old Testament to a substandard illustration database and will tend to discount it as suitable material for Christian preaching. Kaiser is correct when he affirms that, "our teaching and preaching will always remain stunted if we fail to see that God has a wholeness to his Word that embraces both testaments in one unified, single plan."[4] This high view of the Old Testament corresponds with Paul's view of the Old Testament. As we mentioned in the

1. Greidanus, *Preaching Christ from the Old Testament*, 39–46.

2. "Tanakh" is the acronym that is used to identify the Old Testament. The acronym is formed by combining the initial letters of the three major sections of the Hebrew Bible: *Torah* (Law), *Nevi'im* (Prophets), and *Ketuvim* (Writings).

3. Achtemeier, *Preaching from the Old Testament*, 56.

4. Kaiser, *Preaching and Teaching from the Old Testament*, 38.

previous chapter, Paul is adamantly convinced that the church needs the Old Testament Scripture (2 Tim 3:14—4:2).

This is why as preachers we will want to preach Ezekiel as well as Paul, Jeremiah as well as Peter, the Minor Prophets as well as the Gospels. The Old Testament books, including the Prophets, are part of the word of God for the church, therefore anyone who is committed to preaching "the whole counsel of God" (Acts 20:27) must preach the Prophets. The reformers expressed this commitment with the slogan *"Tota Scriptura."* This slogan is the other side of the coin of the better-known slogan *"Sola Scriptura."* Sola Scriptura* is the refusal to add anything to Scripture since Scripture alone is the only source of special revelation. *Tota Scriptura* is the refusal to subtract anything from Scripture and therefore the commitment to embrace the entirety of God's special revelation in the entirety of Scripture. The reformers demonstrated this high view of Scripture in the pulpit. Apart from Revelation, Calvin preached on virtually every book of the Old and New Testament. He preached the staggering number of 343 sermons on the book of Isaiah, 174 sermons on the book Ezekiel, and seventeen sermons on Zephaniah.[5] That is what *Tota Scriptura* looks like in practice. Many of us maintain this high view of Scripture, of all of Scripture, on paper (especially in our doctrinal statements), but fail to demonstrate it in the pulpit. If we truly believe that the prophetic books are part of the word of God for the church, then it is our responsibility to make sure that the unique message of the prophets is reaching this generation of believers. The fundamental reason, therefore, for preaching the Old Testament prophets, alongside the desire to imitate the example of Jesus and the apostles, is the recognition that their words recorded in Scripture are nothing less than the inspired words of God for the church. The message of the prophets is part of God's message to the church. With this premise in mind we are now ready to survey and appreciate the message of the prophets. We will begin our survey by understanding the role that the prophets played within the covenantal relationship between the Lord and his people. We will then explore what the prophets reveal about us and about God and see why this is a message that needs to continue to resound from our pulpits today.

5. DeGreef, *Writings of John Calvin*, 95.

## COVENANTAL RELATIONSHIP

Let us begin, then, by understanding the role that the prophets played in the relationship between the Lord and Israel. This is important for us in order to grasp the theological richness of their message. The more we understand the theological world of the prophets the better we will be placed to see the relevance of their message for us today. The concept of covenant framed the theological world of the prophets.The relationship between the Lord and his people was a covenant. A covenant is essentially an agreement or a treaty between two or more parties. Covenants were not exclusive to Israel but were common across various Near Eastern cultures. Scripture presents multiple covenants that vary in scope: individual, national, and universal. Within the framework of the Old Testament the most prominent covenant is the Mosaic covenant that the Lord established with the nation of Israel at Mount Sinai. The Lord brought the people of Israel out of slavery in Egypt and entered into a covenant agreement with them. This was a treaty that had all the typical elements of a legal contract.[6]

| Hittite Suzerein Treaties | Exodus (Mount Sinai) | Deuteronomy |
|---|---|---|
| Preamble: Introduces the parties | "I am the Lord your God" (20:2a) | The Lord and the people of Israel (1:1–5) |
| Historical Prologue: Summary of the key elements of the relationship between parties. | "who brought you out of the land of Egypt, out of the house of slavery" (20:2b) | From Mount Sinai through the wilderness to the plains of Moab (1:6—4:49) |
| General Stipulations of the Treaty | Moral law: Decalogue (20:3–21) | The Decalogue and the basis of the law (5–11) |
| Specific Stipulations of the Treaty | Civil and Ceremonial Laws (20:22—23:19) | Exposition of laws that emerge from the Decalogue (12–26) |
| Deposit: How and where the Treaty will be kept | Ark of Covenant in the Tabernacle (25:16, 21) | Written on Large Stones in the Promised Land (27:1–3) |
| List of Witnesses | Moses, Aaron, Aaron's sons, and seventy elders (24:1–2) | Heaven and Earth (30:19) |
| Rewards and Sanctions | Blessings and Curses (Lev 26) | Blessing and Curses (28) |

*Table 1: Parallel between Covenant and Treaty*

6. Rata, "Covenant," 99.

## Covenant Enforcers

This covenant, or treaty, is the basis for understanding the relationship between the nation of Israel and the Lord. How did the people of Israel do in upholding their side of the agreement? Sadly, not very well, and this is why the prophets were needed. The record of the Old Testament shows that, apart from a few brief positive spells, the people of Israel continuously and willfully violated the terms of the agreement. The proof of this flagrant violation was that the people were not enjoying the blessings that the Lord had promised but were enduring the curses he had threatened (Lev 26; Deut 28). Instead of experiencing prosperity, plenty, and protection, they were experiencing drought, danger, and defeat. These sanctions, however, were not just punishments but also functioned as wake-up calls for the people to repent of their rebellion. The people of Israel, however, snoozed through these wake-up calls. The Lord therefore intervened by sending the prophets to confront the people of their covenant violations, warn them of the sanctions that they would experience, and plead with them to live by the terms of covenant. The prophets were covenant-enforcement mediators.[7] They did not come with an innovative message but came to reinforce the existing message of the Mosaic covenant in an innovative way. Even the future events that they predicted were primarily the contextualized and detailed actualizations of the list of blessings and curses that had been previous revealed.

## Beyond an Agreement

However, we must resist the temptation as New Testament believers to reduce the relationship between the Lord and Israel, and the consequent role of the prophets, as a cold legal agreement with stipulations and sanctions. If we do so we run the risk of both misunderstanding the theology of the prophets and failing to grasp its pertinence for us. The covenant certainly was a treaty with a legal dimension, but it was much more than that. The covenant was also a bond. It established a profound and intimate relationship between the Lord and his people similar to the relationship between a father and his children, or a husband with his wife. The core of the covenant is expressed with the central formula: "I will take you to be my people, and I will be your God" (Exod 6:7). This is the heart of the

7. Fee and Stuart, *How to Read the Bible*, 184.

covenant. The Lord was committing himself to the people of Israel and, in turn, expected them to be committed to him. This language is resumed in the New Testament to speak about our relationship and commitment to the Lord. Therefore, while there are differences between the old and new covenants, there is enough continuity for us to greatly benefit from the prophets' message and ministry. It is a gross misrepresentation to depict the relationship between the Lord and the old covenant people as a mere legal agreement that has little to do with the relationship of love that characterizes the new covenant. Even with Israel, from the very beginning, the language of love was preeminent over the legal language. The Lord chose Israel not because they deserved it but because he was fulfilling his promise given to the patriarchs (Gen 17:8). The Lord set his love upon Israel (Deut 7:6–8). He brought them out of Egypt and made them his treasured possession (Exod 19:5–6). This is love language, not mere legal language. The bond between the Lord and Israel was not based primarily on a cold legal agreement but on a profound intimate relationship. The legal framework was an important and necessary corollary, but the language of love, treasured possession, and being chosen surpasses any legal agreement. However, a strong relationship inevitably implies mutual commitment, and this is where the law played an important part. The Mosaic covenant, therefore, is best understood as a deep bond between the Lord and Israel that is consolidated in a legal framework. This implies that covenant violations were not just the breakdown of a legal contract, but much more importantly, a breakdown in relationship.

This understanding of the Mosaic covenant as an intimate relationship helps us better comprehend the role, message, and passion of the prophets, and their importance for us many centuries later. We described the prophets as covenant-enforcement mediators, and this is apt. However, we should not think of the prophets as disinterested attorneys acting as cold public prosecutors dispassionately listing the many violations of the people. The Lord sent the prophets to be his representatives, to warn and plead with the people. The prophets' passion therefore mirrored the Lord's passion for his people. The stakes were high, so the prophets used heartfelt, captivating language (and at times bizarre actions) to persuade the people to repent and trust in the Lord. This language of the prophets continues to echo down the centuries and call covenant people today, in this case us, to repent of our sins and trust in the Lord.

## Taking Your Children to Court

To help us preachers further understand the theological world of the prophets, the nature of the Mosaic covenant and the role of the prophets as covenant-enforcers, it is worth making a brief stop in the first chapter of the prophetic writings. The opening scene of Isaiah captures this combination between the legal and the relational dimensions of the Mosaic covenant. These dimensions shape the content and the tone of the prophetic message. If we don't grasp them we will struggle to preach well from the prophets. Isaiah can shed some light for us by trasporting us into a courtroom drama. The importance of this trial is established by the importance of the witnesses that are summoned: heavens and earth (1:2a). The Mosaic covenant was a significant agreement, and an agreement on this scale required creation itself as a witness (Deut 4:26; 30:19; 31:28). By calling creation to come into the courtroom it is immediately clear that the Lord is indicting the people of Israel because they have violated the terms of the covenant. However, it is not just a legal affair, it is much more personal than that because of the filial relationship between the judge and those sitting in the dock. The children of Yahweh are the guilty party. The ones whom the Lord had lovingly reared and brought up, rebelled against him (1:2b). No wonder the language is loaded with strong emotions. For the prophets, sin was certainly violation of God's law, but it was more than that. Sin was (and is) personal and relational. The rebellion of the children of Yahweh is serious and absurd. Even an ox and a donkey know their owners, yet the children of Yahweh have forsaken and despised their Lord (1:3–4). They are ungrateful children that have rebelled against a loving father. They have turned their back on the Lord. They have shut the door in his face. You can feel the pain and indignation in this accusation. The extent of their sinfulness and rebellion is captured by the stark image of sickness and of raw wounds that cover an entire body: deep, infectious, and widespread (1:5–6). Consequently, they attracted God's judgment: cities burnt, the country left desolate, and even the great city of Jerusalem reduced to a shaky shed (1:7–8). Considering the extent of their rebellion the prophet remarks that it is an act of God's grace that Israel did not experience the same fate as Sodom and Gomorrah (1:9). In this courtroom drama the Lord is acting both as a judge and a grieving parent. As a judge, he rightfully condemns the people of Israel for violating his law. As a father, he grieves because it is his own rebellious children he is condemning.

## THEIR MESSAGE

Having grasped the nature of this covenantal relationship we are now better placed to understand the message of the prophets and see why it is a message we still need to hear today. But is it even possible to talk about the message of the prophets? Does not each prophet have his own message? Yes and no. We can talk about the *unified* message of the prophets because, although each prophet had specific emphasis, they shared common core themes. The prophets can be thought of as a formidable choir, where their unique voices blend to form one powerful tune. A tune that the prophets refused to change. A tune that is repetitive and therefore can easily get stuck in our heads. A tune that was originally composed for Israel but that the church also needs to hear. The prophets composed a tune that will both knock us down by confronting us with the horror of our sin, and yet also cause us to soar on wings like eagles by trusting in the greatness of God. These themes, the decadence of the human heart and the greatness of God, are the main themes of the prophetic message. They emerge directly from the covenant and are embedded in the formula, "I will take you to be my people, and I will be your God" (Exod 6:7). Through the covenants, old or new, God has committed himself to humanity and expects us, specifically his people, to be committed to him. The prophets affirm God's steadfast faithfulness in maintaining his commitment to his people and expose their stubborn infidelity in upholding their commitment to God. To appreciate the significance of the prophetic message for us, we will scan some of the pages of the prophetic literature, paying attention to these two aspects: the sinfulness of the human heart and the greatness of God. We will begin with what the prophets say about our sinfulness.

## The Horror of Our Sin

What the prophets say about us is not flattering. They lay bare the horror of our sin. The prophets tell us that we are corrupt from head to toe (Isa 1:6), that our hearts are deceitful (Jer 17:9), that our good deeds are worthless (Isa 64:6), and that our sinfulness is perpetual (Jer 2:32). They help us to take sin seriously. The prophets lived in a spiritual and moral climate in which sin was downplayed. Adherence to religious rituals masked idolatrous and rebellious hearts. The prophets' task was to expose the sinfulness of the people and to warn them of impending judgment. Large sections and, in some cases, entire books are occupied with the announcement of upcoming judgment upon Judah, Israel, or the surrounding nations. The prophets boldly confronted the people with the ugliness of their sin. They were sent to get under the people's skin. They were good at it. In their day, their message of sin and judgment was unpopular but much needed. In our day, their message of sin and judgment continues to be unpopular but is still much needed. The prophets do not allow us to downplay the seriousness of our sin. They describe sin in all its horror. For this reason, it is not always easy and certainly not comfortable to read the prophets' description of the human condition. Nonetheless, a sober and precise diagnosis of what our hearts are like, which is what the prophets offer, is still needed today.

The prophets don't speak about sin abstractly but unmask specific sins and call the people of God, individually and collectively, to repent. From the very outset Isaiah denounces the three areas of covenant violations, three categories of sins, that marked Israel during the prophetic period: idolatry (1:21), social injustice (1:15), and religious ritualism (1:13).[8] Today these sins continue to plague not just our society but also the church. Therefore the prophets' message about sin, and these sins in particular, continues to have direct bearing on the lives of New Testament believers.

## Idolatry

The first and major category of sin that characterized the people of Israel during the prophetic period was idolatry. Idolatry, more than the other two categories of sin that the prophets denounced, may initially appear irrelevant to us today. Not many of us are tempted to sacrifice a goat to Molech. Nevertheless, idolatry can manifest itself both in an obvious form, as it did in the days of the prophets, and in a subtle way, as is the case today. Idolatry has changed its skin, but not its disposition. It is still as dangerous as ever. For this reason hearing the prophets passionately condemn idolatry is important for us as it will help us guard ourselves from potential idols in our lives. Let us thus allow the prophets to help us feel the seriousness of idolatry before unmasking some subtle ways in which idolatry can manifest itself today. The prophets identified idolatry as the ultimate rebellion against Yahweh. Idolatry was not seen simply

8. Hays, *Message of the Prophets*, 63–68.

as a violation of the law of Moses but as a personal rejection of the Lord himself. By turning to other gods Israel was abandoning Yahweh. It was a breakdown of the very heart of the covenant relationship: "I will take you to be my people, and I will be your God." That is why, although the prophets did not shy away from charging the other nations with idolatry, their primary focus was with the covenant people. Israel's struggle with idolatry started from day one (Exod 32) and accompanied them throughout their history. The problem became even more acute during the prophetic period. After its separation with Judah, the Northern Kingdom of Israel immediately chose the direction of disloyalty to Yahweh. They even had their idolatrous hotspots where they built golden calves (Amos 4:4–5; 5:5–7; Hos 8:5). This problem, however, was not just found in these epicenters but rather was pervasive throughout the land. Idolatry spilled to Judah. The prophets, especially the preexilic prophets,[9] continuously rebuked the people and reminded them that loyalty to Yahweh was incompatible with participation in worship of foreign gods (Isa 2:8–9; Jer 2:20–28; Ezek 8:1–18; Hos 4:10–19; Amos 5:26; Mic 1:5–7; Nah 1:14; Hab 2:19–20; Zeph 1:4–6). The prophets highlighted the folly of worshiping idols by ridiculing both the idols themselves and the idol worshipers (Isa 41:22–24; Jer 10:5). The prophets mocked the idols not for the sake of entertainment but to cause the people to see the error of their way and bring them to repentance. Idolatry was and is no laughing matter. Indeed, it was the reason for the deportation of both the Northern and Southern Kingdom.

## Temple Tour

This is abundantly clear in the book of Ezekiel, where we are brought on a tour of the temple with the prophet (Ezek 8). This temple tour serves the purpose of demonstrating that the pervasiveness of idolatry was such that it had even invaded the temple. The sacred place constructed for the worship of Yahweh was now occupied with an idol at its gates (8:5–6), walls covered with drawings of idols (8:10), a woman burning incense to a foreign god (8:14), and men with their backs to Yahweh worshiping the sun (8:16). The tour ends with the Lord declaring that this idolatry will

---

9. The preexilic prophets are those that lived and ministered before (and sometimes during) the Babylonian exile (586 BC). The prophets that are therefore excluded from this category are: Haggai, Zechariah, and Malachi.

drive him away from his sanctuary, and this takes place a few chapters later (10:18–19). It is hard for us to grasp the full significance of this departure. It signaled a dramatic breakdown of the covenantal relationship between the Lord and his people. The presence of the Lord had left the temple. A few years later the temple would be destroyed, and the people of Judah deported. How could this happen? How could the Lord abandon his temple? How could the Lord allow for his temple to be destroyed by Nebuchadnezzar? How could the covenant people of God be deported from the promised land? There is a one-word answer to all these questions: idolatry. Once again, however, the prophets were not delivering new information, as this trajectory and outcome had already been delineated, and in a sense predicted, in the sanctions of the covenant in Deuteronomy 28. The people had dramatically violated the legal stipulations of the covenant, and, therefore, judgment was inevitable.

## IDOLATRY AS ADULTERY

The prophets, however, help us to see that idolatry was and is much more than simply violating covenant conditions. They didn't primarily condemn idolatry by referencing a specific law (e.g., Deut 5:6–10), rather they portrayed idolatry as unfaithfulness to Yahweh. The people have abandoned their God. The Lord departing from the temple was a consequence of this shattered relationship. For this reason, several prophets resort to the fitting metaphor of an adulterous wife to describe Israel.[10] Israel's idolatry is compared to the inexcusable adultery of a disloyal wife that devastates her "marriage." The marriage imagery helps us to feel the hurt that the Lord felt because of idolatry.

The first prophet (chronologically) to use this metaphor was Hosea. Hosea's own dreadful marriage becomes a metaphor to illustrate the dreadful marriage between the Lord and Israel. Hosea's wife behaves like a whore (Hos 1:2; 2:5). This behavior mirrors the spiritual adultery that the people of Israel were committing. Isaiah agrees and states outright that "the faithful city has become a whore" (Isa 1:21). Idolatry is ugly and hurtful. The prophet Jeremiah also leverages the broken marriage motif to shame the people of Judah. He calls them a donkey in heat (Jer 2:24). Ezekiel's longest oracle (Ezek 16) is also based on this infamous

10. It may be even more fitting when we consider that sexual promiscuity was a typical part of the worship of foreign gods.

metaphor. The prophet uses shockingly strong, violent, and sexual language to illustrate how horrendous idolatry is in the eyes of the Lord.

We need to hear this message. We need to see idolatry how the Lord sees idolatry. We may not build golden calves or be tempted to worship Baal or Molech. Nonetheless our hearts are still perpetual idol factories.[11] Paul doesn't delimit idolatry simply to the actions of our hands but also includes the desires of our hearts (Col 3:5–6). He defines covetousness as idolatry. This implies that the battle against idolatry takes place in the arena of our hearts. This is also reflected in what Jesus considers to be the first and greatest commandment: "You shall love the Lord your God with all your heart and with all your soul and with all your mind" (Matt 22:37). The prohibition, "you shall have no other gods before me" (Exod 20:3) is thus included and stated positively in this summary as loving the Lord our God with all our being. Anything, therefore, that gets in the way of this total devotion to the Lord can be idolatry. This broader yet deeper understanding of idolatry as anything or anyone (including ourselves) that replaces God in our hearts implies that what the prophets said about idolatry should challenge us deeply. We continue to elevate people, things, and experiences to the level of matching or even replacing God. With our mouths we declare our allegiance to God, but we fail to demonstrate it with our lives. Our hearts are more often consumed with family, friends, fun, fitness, and fortune rather than with a passion for the glory of God.

*More Justice, Less Ritualism*

The other two areas of sin in which we have much to learn from the prophets, areas which characterized the prophetic period, are social injustice and religious ritualism. The prophets often tackled these two categories together. The people thought the Lord might turn a blind eye on their unjust systems because of the abundance of their sacrifices. The Lord sent the prophets to warn his people that the exact opposite was taking place. The Lord was turning a blind eye to their many sacrifices because their hands were marred with injustice (Isa 1:15). Social injustice was no small matter for the prophets. It was another demonstration of the broken relationship between the Lord and his people. If idolatry

---

11. Calvin, *Institutes*, 97. Modern-day adaptation of Calvin's famous quote: *Hominis ingenium perpetuam, ut ita loquar, esse idolorum fabricam* (*Institutes* I.11.8).

displayed the breakdown of the vertical dimension of the covenant, then social injustice displayed the breakdown of the horizontal dimension of the covenant. Both idolatry and social injustice are demonstrations that the people had abandoned the Lord and were not fulfilling their role as covenant people. The people's commitment to the Lord included treating others with love and justice. Moreover, the values that the people of Israel lived out were meant to reflect Yahweh's character. This is what it meant for the covenant people of Israel to fulfill their role as "a kingdom of priests and a holy nation" (Exod 19:6). The prophets were inviting the people to be true to the covenant. Not a new message, but a strong reminder of the values and the commitment that the law prescribed. Such is the level of predominance of this theme in the prophets that, for many, "prophetic preaching" has become synonymous to preaching on matters of social justice.[12] Most of the prophets, sooner or later, confronted and warned the people of social injustice.

Isaiah regularly spoke of the Lord's concern for the poor (58:6–7) and exposed the people for their lack of justice and righteousness (10:1–2; 5:1–7). Isaiah also made it clear from the outset that treating others justly and fairly was much more important than empty ritualism. The Lord's message through the prophets was that the Lord did not, and would not, accept sacrifices tarnished by rampant evil and injustice. Not only did the Lord not accept this hypocritical ritualism, he also adds that it had become a "burden" and "hateful" in his eyes (1:12–15). How could the Lord be pleased with the offerings, solemn assemblies, and prayers of the people when their daily lives were marked by iniquity and injustice? Or to modernize the question: How can the Lord be pleased with our tithes, our worship gatherings, and prayers when we fail to love our neighbors? The Lord was not, and is not, interested in meaningless exuberant rituals, but in meaningful, benevolent lifestyles. What the Lord required was clear: "Wash yourselves; make yourselves clean; remove the evil of your deeds from before my eyes, cease to do evil, learn to do good; seek justice, correct oppression; bring justice to the fatherless, plead the widow's cause" (1:16–17).

---

12. See Tisdale, *Prophetic Preaching*, and McMickle, *Where Have All the Prophets Gone?*

## Hiding in the Temple

Jeremiah also tackled the themes of social injustice and empty ritualism. The prophet declared that the Lord practices steadfast love, justice, and righteousness on the earth. Therefore, anyone who claims to know the Lord must reflect the Lord's character by caring for the poor and the needy (9:24; 22:16). Caring for the vulnerable in society was a demonstration of truly knowing the Lord, who has a soft spot for the downtrodden. The problem, however, is that their actions reveal that the people do not really know the Lord. They think they know the Lord, but their idolatry and lack of care for others proves the contrary. The people of Judah think they can work the system and therefore benefit from the Lord's covenant blessings without having to live out their covenant responsibilities. Jeremiah addresses the folly of this approach in one of his memorable oracles, the so-called "Temple Speech" (Jer 7). He positioned himself at the entrance of the temple and unleashed a stern rebuke to all who entered. The temple was considered, and called, "the Lord's house" (7:2), as it represented the Lord's presence on earth. The people of Judah considered the temple to be invulnerable. It had become a talisman that would ensure they would not be decisively defeated by the Babylonians. The presence of the temple, for the people, guaranteed the Lord's protection. They felt safe in the temple. Jeremiah exposed the folly of this way of thinking. The biggest problem for the people was not the strength of the Babylonian army but the imminent judgment of God because of their covenant violations. This was one of the consequences of having the Lord in their midst. Absurd to consider yourself safe simply because you were hiding in the temple (7:8–11). This ploy was not going to be successful, as the story of another sacred place, Shiloh, demonstrated. Shiloh was the place in the Northern Kingdom where the tabernacle had first been placed when Israel entered the land. Although once a sacred place it had now become desolate because of the judgment of God for the iniquity of the people of Israel. The same fate awaited the temple. The Lord would treat the temple in Jerusalem in the same way unless the people repented of their sin (7:12–15). The key to enjoying safety, therefore, was not to hide in the temple but to "amend their ways" by executing justice by ceasing to oppress the vulnerable, and by no longer chasing after foreign gods (7:5–7). The sacredness of the temple meant nothing unless there was justice in society.

## Cows, Cannibals, and a Court Case

This theme continues and intensifies in the Minor Prophets. The prophets give us an insight into God's heart for the downtrodden and challenge us as preachers to call the people of God today to reflect God's heart for the helpless. The prophets were not afraid to raise their voices to speak on behalf of the voiceless in society, and neither should we. The prophecies of Amos and Micah, for example, are saturated with colorful and strong pronouncements in this area of social justice. Amos's prophecy is poignant not only because of the message that he delivered but also because of who he was. Amos was not a professional prophet but a shepherd and a farmer (1:1; 7:14–15) sent from the countryside of Judah to the affluent people of Israel to condemn them for their neglect and oppression of the poor (2:6–8). An example of Amos's colorful and strong language is found in his comparison of the women of Samaria to cows (4:1) because of their self-indulgence built on oppressing the poor. Amos was a brave prophet. This language of calling them "cows," although it may not be politically correct, was aimed at helping the people to see the gravity of their actions so that they would repent and escape God's judgment (4:2–3). The countryman prophet was clear that the rampant social injustice would bring about the day of the Lord, a dark day for them (5:18–20). No amount of religious festivals, of burnt offerings or songs would prevent God's judgment. They are not a pleasing aroma but a stench to the Lord (5:21–23). The Lord wants the people of Israel to replace the constant flow of meaningless religious rituals with a constant flow of justice and righteousness. This is the meaning of what have become the most memorable words of Amos: "But let justice roll on like a river, righteousness like a never-failing stream" (5:24).

Micah also uses strong language. He resorts to the language of cannibalism to describe the behavior of the leaders toward the nation. Those that were tasked with embracing justice and caring for the nation instead are devastating and devouring the people (3:1–3). The judgment of the Lord will therefore be severe and inevitable (3:9–12). Therefore, the Lord brings the people to court because of their injustice. It is another lawsuit oracle (6:1–8). Creation is again brought in as the covenant witness, the people of Israel are summoned as the guilty party, and the Lord himself acts as the public prosecutor (6:1–2). The scene is set. The Lord has an indictment against his people. We are expecting a long list of accusations. Yet, as the Lord takes his stand there is a surprising turn of events. As the Lord looks to his people that have so clearly violated the covenant, his heart seems to melt with love and compassion for them. The Lord transitions from being a formal public prosecutor to a loving husband, passionately attempting to win back his estranged wife. The cold, distant, heartless language of a public prosecutor gives way to the warm, intimate, heartfelt language of a husband seeking to win back his wife. He calls them with affection: "O my people" (6:3, 5). The Lord goes further still and takes his people on a journey down memory lane (6:3–5). He mentions some events, places, and people that bring back to memory some of the special times that the people experienced with the Lord: Egypt, Moses, Aaron, Miriam, Balak, Balaam, Shittim, and Gilgal. Linked to each of these locations is a special story that will tug at their heartstrings. A question emerges spontaneously because of this journey down memory lane: "With what shall I come before the Lord, and bow myself before God on high?" (6:6). The next series of questions shows that Israel still doesn't get it. They continue to miss the point as their solution is to propose to offer ever-increasing extravagant sacrifices (6:6–7). The prophet reminds the people that the Lord has already told them what he requires from his people with the famous summary: "to do justice, and to love kindness, and to walk humbly with your God" (6:8).

This sample of the prophetic literature shows how much the prophets disliked empty ritualism, and how much they cared about matters of justice. The concept of justice, for the prophets, is much more than mere retribution. The biblical concept of justice does not just envision punishing evil but involves actively fighting for what is good and right. To "do justice" you need to engage with, and for, the victims, the poor, the weak, and the vulnerable. You need to fight for justice for those who are unable to fight on their own. The theme of social justice, however, was not just one of the hobby horses of the prophets. The prophets were not social activists, but they were messengers of the Lord, bringing his message to his people. Their concern for justice was rooted in the Lord's heart for widows, orphans, foreigners, the poor, and the oppressed. This inevitably means we cannot simply dismiss their message as irrelevant for us today. Their message for the people of Israel became part of the word of God for the church. If the church wants, as it ought, to reflect on how to respond to issues of social justice, then the prophets must be consulted. We must allow Scripture, rather than our culture or political affiliation, to guide our understanding, values, and actions relating to this area of social justice. The Old Testament prophets have a strong voice that will challenge and sensitize the church. Faithful preachers who are committed to preaching Tota Scriptura will refuse to silence the prophets on this issue. Their voice is too loud.

Why is it important for us to listen to their voice? Why should we as preachers make sure that our people today hear the message of the prophets on this matter of social justice? Jesus answers these questions for us by narrating a story of a rich man that ended up in the place of torment because he showed utter contempt for a poor man that he saw on a daily basis (Luke 16:19–31). The rich man did not hear, or at least did not listen to, the message of "Moses and the *prophets*" (Luke 16:29, 31). He did not share the Lord's burden for the poor because he did not pay attention to the message of the prophets. If we want our people to share the Lord's burden for the poor then we need to echo the message of the prophets. The prophets may not answer all of our theological questions regarding the right relationship between social justice and evangelism,[13] but they will certainly give us a burden for the needy. Amos will make it harder for us to simply step over the "Lazarus" living in our neighborhood. Micah will cause us to rethink our shopping habits that actively contribute to fueling injustice systems. Isaiah will expose our hypocrisy in intentionally drowning out cries for help by singing worship songs.

The message of the prophets on sin is strong and, at times, disturbing. Being compared to a whore, a donkey in heat, a fat cow, or a carnivore is certainly not pleasant. Yet we often need this type of harsh rebuke to recognize the seriousness of our sin. A sober view of our ourselves is needed in an era where the church, as well as society, is tempted to dilute the seriousness of sin.

## The Greatness of God

As well as giving us a sober view of humanity, the prophets also offer a glorious view of God. The prophets are radically God-centered. God is

---

13. The discussion regarding the right relationship between involvement in social justice and evangelism is ongoing. However, I think the majority of Evangelicals agree with Piper's summary statement in Cape Town at the Lausanne Congress on World Evangelization: "Could Lausanne say—could the global church say—for Christ's sake we Christians care about all suffering, especially eternal suffering? I don't want you to choose between these two truths . . . If there rises in your heart a resistance to the phrase 'especially eternal suffering,' or if there rises in your heart a resistance to the phrase 'we care about all suffering now,' then either we have a defective view of hell or a defective heart" (Lausanne Movement, "Bible Exposition," 17:38–19:14).

the primary character throughout the prophetic literature. Therefore, by preaching the prophets we are giving our people a front-row seat that enables them to admire the majesty of God. This is much needed today. It is too easy to be influenced by society, and to end up with a terribly distorted view of God. For many in our society, God is reduced to a slighly less cheery Father Christmas, or a slighty less excentric genie of the lamp. The prophets help us to reject and refute these distorted notions and enable us to gaze at his majesty. Such is the abundance of the descriptions of God in the prophets that any attempt to provide a summary will inevitably be incomplete. No list and explanation of attributes could adequately describe the One who is indescribable. Nevertheless, the contribution of the prophets is significant because within their literature God is not only the main character, but also the primary Speaker. "Thus says the Lord" is the frequent refrain of the prophets. The Lord, within the prophetic literature, is presented in a variety of ways: Husband, Father, Sovereign, Holy One, Creator, Shepherd, Judge, and Savior. This list is not exhaustive. Together these descriptions provide a wonderful view of the greatness of God. What is surprising is not only the variety of descriptions but also that some of them are in tension with one another. The prophets show us that in God we find "an admirable conjunction of diverse excellencies."[14] It is worth exploring some of these tensions to capture the awesome depiction of God that we see in the prophets, and to continue to grow in our understanding and estimation of their message.

### Sovereign and Shepherd

The first pair of diverse excellencies we can admire in the prophets is the Lord as both Sovereign and Shepherd. The description of the Lord as our Shepherd is greatly loved. It conveys the protection and provision that we experience in the Lord. The Lord is the Shepherd that tenderly cares for us. This beautiful description is further enhanced by another description of the Lord that we see in the prophets. The Lord, as well as being our caring Shepherd, is also the Sovereign King. In the deepest and darkest uncertainties in life, the prophets reassure us that we can rest in the tender care of the Supreme King. This is a truth that is worth pondering and preaching.

---

14. Beautiful "Edwardian" expression that he used to describe the Lord Jesus as the Lion and the Lamb (Edwards, "Excellency of Christ," 5:537).

## SOVEREIGN OVER THE NATIONS

The prophets stressed the sovereignty of God even in the midst of their tumultuous lives. The geopolitical scene in their day was extremely volatile. Several superpowers were keen to take control of the Fertile Crescent.[15] The Assyrians, then the Babylonians, and finally the Persians managed to dominate the Near Eastern world. The nation of Israel needed to tread carefully to avoid ending up squashed by these superpowers. Furthermore, Israel was also surrounded by other smaller nations. These nations were both a constant threat and an opportunity to form allegiances. Like a complex chess game, the nation of Israel needed to make the right move at the right time to not end up in a checkmate position. Within this complex and hazardous context, the Lord sent the prophets to reveal that all these great nations were pawns that he moved according to his master game plan (Isa 14:26–27; 46:10; 55:11; Jer 29:11). All the geopolitical events were the outworking of the sovereign will of God. The great and powerful nations were simply instruments in his hand. The Assyrians are likened to an axe (Isa 10:15) and the Babylonians to a sword (Ezek 21:9–10) in the Lord's hand. The nation of Israel may have been surrounded by several superpowers, but ultimately there was only one Superpower. This was the interpretive key that the prophets used to explain the complex geopolitical situation. The other cultures believed that behind the clashing of nations there was the clashing of the gods of the nations. The common belief was that the stronger god determined the military victory. Therefore, when the Babylonians conquered Jerusalem, Nebuchadnezzar took utensils from the temple in Jerusalem and brought them to the temple of his god (Dan 1:2). He was convinced that the Babylonian gods were stronger than the God of Israel. The prophets disagreed. The victory of the Babylonians over the people of Judah was not a consequence of the strength of the Babylonians gods, but it was the Lord using the foreign nation to judge the people of Judah for their sins. Yahweh gave Jehoiakim, king of Judah, into the hands of Nebuchadnezzar (Dan 1:2). All the narratives, dreams, and visions throughout the book of Daniel reinforce that it is the "God of heaven" that "changes times and seasons;

---

15. The Fertile Crescent is a region in the Middle East shaped (unsurprisingly) like a crescent. This area, which arches from the Persian Gulf to Northern Egypt, was the home of important ancient civilizations: Babylonians, Assyrians, Egyptians, Sumerians, and Phoenicians. For this reason, it is often called the "Cradle of Civilization." It was a sought-after region because of its agricultural and commercial potential.

he removes kings and sets up kings" (2:21). None of the prophets divert from this strong conviction of the sovereignty of God even in the darkest days for the people of God. On the contrary it is especially in those dark days that the prophets double down on this conviction. This is a conviction that believers need today. When the results of our latest blood test are upsetting, when we can't get ahold of our teenage daughter, when we are handed a dismissal letter, or even simply when our anxieties make it a struggle to get out of bed, we need to know that the Lord is Sovereign.

## THE CHARIOT AND THE OMNIS

The mesmerizing description that the prophet Ezekiel sees is an example of the importance of knowing that the Lord is sovereign in the midst of dark days. Ezekiel, as well as being a prophet, was a priest (1:3). At the age of thirty (1:1) he would have been due to start his service in the temple; however, he found himself living far from Jerusalem among the deported in Babylon. Talk about a prohibitive commute. No doubt having reached the age of service in the temple and finding himself hundreds of miles away from the temple was a hard and hurtful experience for the priest. In this context the prophet is given a staggering vision of God. Amazing truths about God emerge from this vision. It is a vision of a glorious chariot. In Ezekiel's day it was typical to see depictions of kings (and gods) in chariots ready to conquer their enemies. These representations conveyed the strength and the authority of the monarchs. The more impressive the chariot and the beasts towing it, the more impressive was the power of the one riding the chariot. There would have been many of these depictions in Babylon. Yet this chariot that Ezekiel sees goes way beyond anything he would have seen in Babylon. The scale of the chariot was breathtaking, the materials were borderline indescribable,[16] and the chariot was towed by four staggering, living creatures. On top of this remarkable chariot there was a sapphire throne. A staggering vision! One thing is sure: whoever was riding this chariot was much more powerful than any king or any god of any superpower. Ezekiel was reminded of the Lord's omnipotence.

Moreover, there was another fundamental difference between this chariot and other chariots of his day that would have caught Ezekiel's

---

16. The prophet is stretching his language to try to describe what he sees. Note the many times, in this first chapter, he uses the expression "in the likeness of."

attention. The other chariots were rigid and very limited in their movements because of their wheel structure. Changing direction rapidly and sharply was not their strong point. Maneuvering a U-turn was a real challenge. In contrast, the chariot that Ezekiel sees is described as having intersecting wheels ("wheel within a wheel" 1:16) that appear to be multidirectional. Much is made in the vision of the ability of this chariot to move with great ease in all directions. The prophet sees a mobile throne. The message is clear. The Lord is sovereign not just in Jerusalem, but also by the Chebar Canal in Babylon. There is nowhere where this throne cannot reach. The very fact that Ezekiel saw this awesome vision whilst in Babylon is a demonstration of this. This vision conveys that there is nowhere, not even Babylon, that is outside the Lord's reach. Ezekiel was reminded of the Lord's omnipresence.

It is worth lingering on one more aspect of this vision, and in particular one more detail concerning the wheels. We are told that the rims of all four wheels were full of eyes all around (1:18). This is an important detail because, as well as highlighting the pervasive nature of the presence of the Lord, it also establishes that the Lord sees and knows everything. Nothing escapes his attention. He sees what is taking place in the most secret room in the temple and what is taking place in the headquarters in Babylon. Ezekiel was reminded of the Lord's omniscience.

This vision greatly impacted the prophet. In a day when the dark clouds seemed to have gathered on the nation of Judah and on the life of the exiled priest, Ezekiel saw a vision of this glorious chariot coming from this great bright cloud (1:4). This vision communicated to the prophet, and through him to the people, that the Lord was sovereign. Moreover, this vision comunicates to us today, and through us to our people, that the Lord is still in control today. When we feel at the mercy of the storms of this life, this vision of God in Ezekiel is the anchor that our souls need.

The Lord revealed himself in this remarkable way to the people of Judah when they needed it most. In the days when the people were deeply aware of their powerlessness, they were reminded of the Lord's power. The people, therefore, knew that they were not in Babylon by chance or because the Babylonians had a stronger army but because of the sovereign will of the Lord. The Lord was still in control. Furthermore, it was exactly because the Lord was in control that they were in exile in Babylon. The Lord had drawn Babylon as his sword and had wielded it against his own people because they had violated the terms of the covenant. Whilst humbling, this also infused hope in the people. Their present and their future were in the hands of their God, who is also sovereign over every nation.

None of the other prophets had a vision quite like Ezekiel's. Nevertheless, all the prophets shared this view of the absolute sovereignty of God. This is clear not just by the many oracles that celebrate the sovereignty of God but also by the titles they used. The titles "the Lord Yahweh" and "Lord of hosts" each appears over 200 times across the prophetic literature. Both titles reinforce the notion that Yahweh is in a category of his own and that his rule is absolute.

## SHEPHERD OVER HIS FLOCK

The Lord, according to the prophets, is not just the sovereign King but also the attentive Shepherd. The shepherd imagery is frequent throughout the Prophets. The association between a king and a shepherd may appear strange to us, but it was a common association back in the days of the prophets. Kings and leaders were often described as shepherds to underscore their responsibility to care for, and protect, the people. The prophets resorted to the shepherd motif to highlight the failure on the part of the leadership in Israel. The leaders in Israel were classified as "bad shepherds" who were unjust, lazy leaders that took advantage of their flock rather than caring for them (Jer 10; Ezek 34; Zech 11). In contrast to these "bad shepherds," the Lord himself promises that he will step in to shepherd his flock. The Lord will rescue, gather, feed, heal, and strengthen his sheep (Ezek 34:12–16). He will rule over them with justice (Ezek 34:16). The unjust and lazy shepherds will be replaced with the just and passionate shepherd. Ezekiel further develops the shepherd motif, creating an ambiguity between the Lord himself being the shepherd (34:15) and the Lord promising that his servant David will be the shepherd (34:23). As noted in the previous chapter, Jesus beautifully and perfectly solves this ambiguity (John 10). The main reason why the prophets leverage on the shepherd language is to portray the Lord's compassionate protection and provision for his people. The Lord is the caring Shepherd that will gather the scattered flock (Jer 31:10) following the exile, and will even carry the lambs in his arms close to his heart (Isa 40:11). It is hard to think of a better image to convey protection and tenderness. What comfort!

Yet this image becomes even better when we allow the prophet Isaiah to remind us that the hands that are keeping us safe (Isa 40:11) are the same hands that can hold the oceans or measure the heavens (Isa 40:12). The Shepherd that is gathering his flock among the nations is also the Sovereign Lord for whom all the nations are but a drop in a bucket (Isa 40:15). This combination of the authority and power of the sovereign King with the compassion and protection of the tender Shepherd would, per excellence, bring comfort to those who trusted in the Lord (Isa 40:1).

This rich view of God continues to comfort the people of God today. The Assyrians, Babylonians, and Persians have been replaced by other key players. Nevertheless, it is still easy to be alarmed by what we see across the international scene. Yet the prophets remind us that the Lord is in control. We can also get alarmed by what we see around our own personal scene. We often face obstacles that are too high for us to overcome. We carry burdens that are too heavy for us. We encounter problems that are too difficult for us to solve. We meet challenges that require more patience and more long-suffering than we can produce. Life, at times, is simply too much for us. We know this and we feel this. In these moments, when the clouds become darker and thicker, we need a clear view of the One who is sovereign over every nation and yet is tenderly holding us in his arms.

## Judge and Savior

Another tension we see in the prophets is that the Lord is presented both as Judge and Savior. This paradox is a key element of the message of the prophets. Indeed it is a key element of the gospel. For good reason the metanarrative of the Bible is often referred to as salvation history, or the story of salvation. The prophets were part of this story, and so are we. To understand our role and to play our part in this great story, we need to recognize that the Protagonist of this story is both Judge and Savior. The prophets can help us fathom this mystery.

### THE JUDGE WILL JUDGE

The prophets portray God as the ultimate judge. Perhaps this is the dominant role attributed to God in the prophetic literature. Numerous large sections and, in some cases, entire books are occupied with the announcements of upcoming judgment upon Judah, Israel, or the surrounding nations. These announcements are calling the people to repent.

The prophets plead with the people to return to the Lord so that they will avoid God's judgment. The judgments that the prophets describe are the covenant curses that had been introduced as far back as Deuteronomy 28. These judgments are vivid, significant, and escalating. The prophets warned the people of famine, drought, foreign invasion, and ultimately of being kicked out of the promised land. During the time of the prophets (800–450 BC), the people experienced the full force of the judgments that had been threatened. The implicit, and often explicit, background to the oracles of judgments is that God is the ultimate judge of Israel and the nations. God will intervene and judge. The day of the Lord will arrive.

Knowing the Lord is judge was a double-edged sword for the people of God. Knowing there is an ultimate judge that will condemn the people of Israel for their idolatry, injustice, and hypocrisy was a daunting thought. Knowing there was an ultimate judge that would also condemn the foreign nations that had oppressed Israel was a comforting thought. One of the books in which we see this dynamic at play is the book of Habakkuk. The book is a passionate exchange between the prophet and God. The prophet wrestled with the problem of evil. He struggled to reconcile what he was seeing around him with what he knew to be true of the Lord. Have you ever had a similar struggle? Many believers today share Habakkuk's struggle to reconcile the evil and injustice they see in this world with their knowledge of the goodness and justice of God. How can we solve this conundrum? Habakkuk helps by guiding us in a profound reflection on how God exercises his justice. The prophet poses two questions (laments!) to the Lord and then listens twice to the Lord's answer. In his first lament (1:1–4), the prophet complains that God is not intervening as a judge to condemn the people of Judah. The Lord has gone soft on sin, according to the prophet. Justice is perverted. The Lord's answer is astounding (1:5–11). The Lord is sending the Babylonians as his agent of judgment upon the nation of Judah. This solution is simply unbelievable for the prophet (1:5). Far from being soft on sin, the Lord is about to judge his people through the Babylonian army. The judgment is going to be swift (1:8), violent (1:9), and unstoppable (1:10). The Lord is going to judge his people for their iniquity and wickedness. This is a frightening prospect for the prophet and the people. This shocking revelation of God's intention to judge Judah using the Babylonians produces Habakkuk's second lament. How can the Lord use such a brutal nation as an instrument of his judgment? How can the Lord use the evil Babylonians to judge those that are "more righteous" (1:13)? How can the Lord use a more wicked nation to punish a less wicked one? This is the essence of the prophet's complaint. This is a strong and reasonable complaint, and the prophet is determined to get his answer (2:1). The Lord answers, assuring the prophet that the ultimate Judge will punish all the wicked at the right time. This judgment may appear slow in arriving (2:3), but it is nonetheless certain and therefore can be written down (2:2). The Babylonians will be judged for their greed, iniquity, and idolatry (2:6–20). It is an answer worth waiting for. To know that the Lord will judge is a grave concern and a great comfort for the people.

## Gracious Threats

The sheer volume of oracles of judgment can make reading the prophets tough. Many preachers avoid the prophets exactly because they are reluctant to announce judgment. They wonder how this emphasis on judgment can go hand in hand with the other aspects of the character of God (grace, love, mercy, compassion). The scale, severity, and certainty of judgment appear to leave little room for grace. However, these preachers fail to grasp the purpose of the oracles of judgment as passionate and compassionate calls to repentance. The oracles of judgment are warnings, threats. The desire of the Lord (and often of the prophets) is not to unleash his judgment, but rather that the threat of judgment would bring about a radical repentance in the hearts of the people. Viewed with this perspective, even the announcements of judgment are demonstrations of the grace of God. He is pleading with his people. He is inviting, begging them to repent so that he can "repent" of the judgment he had threatened.

This willingness of the Lord to relinquish judging his people is also true in many of the oracles in which this clause is not explicit. Many oracles seem to present God's judgment as something that will happen no matter what. It appears the opportune time for repentance has run out. In some cases, it does appear that the Lord is saying through the prophet that time is up and that God's judgment is now unavoidable. Jeremiah appears to reach this moment in his ministry. The people of Judah go from being clay that can still be changed (Jer 18) to a hardened clay jar that now can only be broken (Jer 19). However, there are other times where, although there is no explicit clause, the door (or at least a window) of repentance is still open. An obvious example of this is Jonah. He reluctantly delivers a very short pronouncement of judgment upon the great city of Niniveh (3:4). No hint of the opportunity to escape this judgment. Yet, as we discover, the people do repent of their sin and the Lord does relinquish the judgment he had threatened. Furthermore, we read that this comes as no surprise to Jonah (4:1–3) and that this was the reason why he was hesitant (to use an understatement) to go to Niniveh. The warning of judgment carried an implicit call to repentance. The same is true for many other oracles of judgments. The purpose of these oracles is certainly to announce the judgment of God but also to issue a gracious and passionate call to repent.

However, we must not fall into the other extreme of interpreting the oracles of judgment as empty threats. Sadly, the people did not respond in repentance to these oracles and therefore they faced the judgment that had been predicted. The Lord's patience, although abundant, ran out and judgment fell upon the people. The day of the Lord arrived.[17] This was a key concept that the prophets used to announce God's dramatic and decisive intervention in history. The prophets warned the people that the day of the Lord, the day of reckoning, would arrive. What day were the prophets talking about? According to Amos (5:18), the day of the Lord was when the Assyrians invaded Samaria and took the Northern Kingdom away to exile. According to Zephaniah (1:7, 14), the day of the Lord was judgment on Judah by the hand of the Babylonians. According to Jeremiah (46:10), the day of the Lord was the destruction of Egypt by the hand of the Babylonians. According to Isaiah (13:6, 9), the day of the Lord was the judgment upon Babylon by the hand of the Persians. According to Obadiah (15), the day of the Lord was the judgment upon Edom. According to Joel (3:14), the day of the Lord is the final day of vindication of God and his people. Evidently, for the prophets, the concept of the day of the Lord is not just restricted to a one-off episode in history but signals God's decisive intervention in various moments in history. Perhaps it would be better to speak of days of the Lord. Nevertheless, there is an intrinsic connection between these days since the decisive interventions of judgment by the Lord in history provide a preview of the ultimate day of judgment. The judgments against Samaria and Jerusalem therefore point to a greater day of reckoning, where the full force of God's wrath will be unleashed on those that are not in Christ. In view of this, it is obvious there is still a need to hear the prophets' passionate and compassionate call to repentance.

17. At times the prophets replace the expression "the day of the Lord" with similar terminology like "the day," "that day," or "the great day."

## THE SAVIOR WILL SAVE

This call to repentance, however, is only possible because the Lord is not just the Judge but also the Savior. Indeed, even the day of the Lord for the prophets was not just a day of judgment but also a day of salvation (Zeph 3:9–20). In the same way that the prophets dreaded a decisive and dramatic intervention of the Lord in history to judge, they also longed for a decisive and dramatic intervention of the Lord in history to save his people. This is a key part of the message of the prophets. Judgment was not, or at least did not have to be, the last word. Beyond judgment there was salvation. The prophets described a new era, an era of ultimate blessing in which the people would experience the Lord's salvation. This day was possible because the Lord is not only the Judge, but he is also the Savior. With the same certainty that the prophets announced that the Lord would deliver them into the hands of foreign nations they were also convinced the Lord would then rescue them. Indeed, if we consider a helicopter view of the three major prophets, we can typically see three great sections: warning of judgment upon Israel and Judah, oracles of judgment toward the nations, and a promise of restoration. The same pattern can be seen across the Minor Prophets, especially when we consider them as one book (and there are good reasons to do so).[18] The Book of the Twelve has warnings of judgment for Israel and the nations, and then a promise of salvation. The Lord is at least as committed to salvation as he is to judgment.

---

18. The current trend in Old Testament scholarship is to treat the twelve minor prophets as one unified book: The Book of the Twelve. The main reasons are: In ancient lists of the Old testament books (Sirach, Josephus) they are considered one unit; the Book of the Twelve is considered one book in Judaism; they were collected together in one scroll; the books with a historical subscription are organized in chronological order and there are evident connections between the end of some prophets with the beginning of the subsequent prophet (e.g. Joel 3:16 & Amos 1:2; Amos 9:12 & Obadiah; Hab 2:20 & Zeph 1:7). For further reading, see Nogalski and Sweeney, *Reading and Hearing the Book of the Twelve.*

| | Isaiah | Jeremiah | Ezekiel | Book of the Twelve[19] |
|---|---|---|---|---|
| Oracles of Judgment for Judah and Israel | 1–12 | 1–29 | 1–24 | Hosea, Joel, Amos, Micah, Habbakuk, Zephaniah |
| Oracles of Judgment for the Nations | 13–23 | 46–51 | 25–32 | Obadiah, Jonah, Nahum |
| Oracles of Salvation | 40–45 | 30–33 | 33–48 | Haggai, Zechariah, Malachi |

*Table 2: Patterns in the Prophetic Books*

The relationship between judgment and salvation is strong. The prophets present salvation as a reversal of the judgment that the people would experience. This is crystal clear in the central portion in Jeremiah (30–33), the so-called "Book of Consolation." In the first part of the book the Lord had announced the judgment that the people of Judah would experience. In this central part of the book the Lord anticipates that, following this judgment, there would be salvation, where he would overturn and undo all the judgments the people would experience. Just as the Lord would send the people into exile he will now regather and bring them back to the land. Just as the Lord predicts Jerusalem would be destroyed, now the Lord promises Jerusalem would be rebuilt. The people who were under foreign domination would now experience freedom. The salvation the Lord promises would more than overturn the judgment.

| Judgments Announced | Judgments Overturned |
|---|---|
| Jerusalem Destroyed (6) | Jerusalem Rebuilt (30:18) |
| Reduced Population (6) | Increased Population (30:19) |
| Exile (25) | Return (30:3) |
| Wounds (15) | Healing (33:6) |
| No Celebration (7) | Celebration (30:19) |
| Broken Covenant (11) | New Covenant (31:31–33) |
| Judgment for Sin (25) | Forgiveness (31:34) |

19. I'm not suggesting, for example, that the minor prophets listed in the category "oracles of judgment for Israel and Judah" do not also include oracles announcing judgment on other nations (Hab 2:5–10) or oracles of salvation (Zeph 3:9–20). I'm simply highlighting that, in terms of emphasis, the minor prophets can be viewed in these three macro categories.

| Judgments Announced | Judgments Overturned |
|---|---|
| Terror (25) | Peace (32:37) |
| Prostitute (2) | Virgin (31:4) |

*Table 3: Jeremiah: Judgments Announced and Overturned*

The message of the prophets therefore enables the people to look to the future with hope and anticipation. This anticipation was born in part by the language and the images the prophets used. The strategy they used to convey the greatness of the Lord's intervention in the future was to use the great events of the past as paradigms to enlarge expectations for the future. This future restoration was going to be like, only better than, great events and experiences of the past (e.g., a new creation, a new exodus, a new pilgrimage, a new covenant, a new Davidic king). Understanding this strategy of using what the Lord has done in the past as a model for what he will do in the future is the key to interpreting and preaching the oracles of salvation. Of particular importance is the image of a new exodus. The exodus out of Egypt is celebrated throughout the Old Testament (particularly in the Psalms) as the great salvation event, the key moment that differentiated the nation of Israel from all the other nations. Against all odds, the Lord demonstrated he was more powerful than the gods of Egypt and delivered his people. The exodus became the paradigm of God's salvation. The remarkable message of the prophets is that what awaits the people in the future is even greater than the exodus—the salvific event per excellence. A new and better exodus. It is "The Exodus 2.0." In the original exodus the people were brought out of Egypt, in the new exodus the people will be gathered from all the nations (Isa 43:5–6). The first exodus was primarily the deliverance of Israel, the new exodus will extend to the gentiles (Isa 11:10–16; 19:19–25). This language does not necessarily reveal with precision the details of what will take place, but it does convey the emotional load of this great salvation. Remembering God's redemption in the past enabled the people of God to look to the future with hope in the anticipation of deliverance and therefore encouraged them to trust in the Lord in the present. This summary captures the essence of the prophets' message about salvation and highlights its relevance for us. The prophets are calling us today to trust in the Lord. We do this by remembering God's great redemption, a greater redemption than the one the prophets remembered, and by looking forward to God's final deliverance, a greater deliverance than the prophets imagined.

## SALVATION BELONGS TO THE LORD

One aspect of the message of the prophets that is clear is that salvation comes from the Lord, and only from the Lord. This is a constant refrain of the prophets (Isa 43:3; 45:21–22; 49:26). The Lord himself declares via the prophet that the title of Savior can be attributed exclusively to him: "I, even I, am the Lord, and apart from me there is no savior" (Isa 43:11). The insistence that only the Lord was able to save was necessary, because the people of Israel were consistently tempted to trust in other nations or in idols for their salvation. The kings of Israel were continuously exploring the opportunities to form allegiances with other nations, thinking this was the way to remain safe or to gain deliverance. The prophets denounced this foolish thinking and repeated that ultimately salvation would not come from foreign nations (Isa 20:5–6; Hos 14:3). This was one of the purposes of the oracles of judgment against the nations. This was a way of indirectly warning the people of the foolishness of relying on other nations for their salvation. The prophets were even more direct when it came to idols. As we have seen, the prophets didn't just denounce the foolishness of trusting in idols, they mocked this strategy. Isaiah humorously describes the foolishness of carving an idol with your hands and then asking the idol to provide salvation (44:20). The idols are powerless when contrasted with the powerful Arm of the Lord that can truly deliver salvation (Isa 33:2; 51:5). This unique ability to save was, at times, also certified by foreign rulers. The book of Daniel is the strongest example. In at least two incidents salvation seemed unlikely. Shadrach, Meshach, and Abednego were thrown in the fiery furnace and came out unharmed. Daniel himself was fed to the lions, and yet was left untouched. The conclusion of both incidents saw the foreign kings of great empires recognize that "no other god can save in this way" (3:29) and that the God of Israel alone "rescues and saves" (6:27). Salvation is a prerogative that belongs exclusively to the Lord.

Although the Lord alone can save, the prophets do anticipate that this salvation will be brought about through his agent, the coming Messiah. Isaiah says that God's salvation will come by the servant of the Lord (Isa 49:6). Jeremiah announces that the people of Judah will be saved thanks to the "righteous branch" (Jer 23:5–6) and the "Shepherd" (Jer 36). Micah and Zechariah also speak about a coming Davidic king that will bring salvation (Mic 5:2; Zech 9:9). Therefore, the announcement of salvation and this new age of restoration includes all the messianic prophecies.

This also helps us to understand the nature of the salvation that the prophets spoke about. As we know, the Messiah of Israel came to save his people from their sin and offer eternal life. Although the prophets did not have the full picture, they could see enough to realize that the salvation that would be brought about by the sufferings of Christ was much more than deliverance from a foreign nation. They predicted the gracious salvation of our souls that would be accomplished through the sufferings and subsequent glories of the Messiah (1 Pet 1:10–12). Therefore, similarly to their view of judgment, the prophets' understanding of salvation certainly included political and national connotations. The people looked forward to the day in which they would be delivered from captivity and brought back to the promised land. Nevertheless, because going into exile was God's judgment upon them, salvation included a strong spiritual connotation. The prophets, and through them the people, looked forward to a day of peace and forgiveness. A day in which they would not only be saved from foreign nations but from their sin (Ezek 36:29; 37:23) and the wrath of God (Joel 2:32; Zech 1:18). The prophets did not just announce a temporary salvation, but rather an eternal one (Isa 45:17; 51:6).

So, is the Lord the Judge or the Savior? Both! This is the beauty of this great story of salvation, the beauty of the gospel. The prophets remind us of the seriousness of our rebellion and warn of impending judgment. The prophets, however, also reveal the Lord's heart and provision for saving his people from his righteous judgment. We are saved from a judgment that we deserve because we are offered forgiveness that we don't deserve—a salvation that was purchased by God's great agent of salvation. The prophets therefore help us to see and appreciate all we have in Christ. It is now our turn to play our part in this great salvation story and proclaim this good news of forgiveness in Christ.


## A UNIQUE VOICE

We have concluded this brief tour of the message of the prophets. The purpose of this tour was to enrich our understanding and boost our appreciation of the message of the prophets. We have certainly flicked through pages of great literature, and when you do this it is then hard to put the book down. Furthermore, we have flicked through great literature that the Lord inspired for the good of the church. I hope this flickthrough has triggered in you a desire to read carefully and preach faithfully the prophetic books.

As we have seen, the clear commission to preach the Old Testament Scriptures comes directly and unmistakably from the word of God itself. This task is not fulfilled by simply preaching the odd psalm or a favorite narrative, but it involves preaching the various genres found in the Old Testament, including the Prophets. This commitment to Tota Scriptura, however, is not an inconvenience or an unpleasant task but a delightful duty. We are privileged to have the opportunity to preach from such fascinating literature with such a powerful message. The prophets have a unique voice that contributes decisively to giving us a clearer view of God, and a clearer view of ourselves. The church needs to hear and respond to the beauty, depth, and relevance of the prophetic message. Through the prophets, God speaks to us today.

# *Chapter 3*

# THE GENIUS OF THEIR RHETORIC

> "And he said to me, 'Son of man, eat whatever you find here.
> Eat this scroll, and go, speak to the house of Israel.' . . . Then
> I ate it, and it was in my mouth as sweet as honey."
>
> —EZEK 3:1, 3B

FOR PREACHERS THERE IS another strong incentive that motivates us to preach from the prophetic books—the prophets were great preachers, and it will do us no harm to spend time in their company. We have a lot to learn from the prophets and their rhetoric. Preaching from the prophetic books is like taking part in an advanced homiletics class. It is a steep learning curve that will sharpen and improve the efficacy of our preaching. In this chapter I will briefly consider the reasons why it is legitimate to describe the prophets as preachers. I will then take a stand in defense of rhetoric before analyzing the genius of the prophets' rhetoric and drawing out some tips we can glean from them. However, before we do any of this, let me tell you how I first noticed that the prophets were masterful communicators.

## HAVE YOU READ MY BOOK?

For as long as I can remember, preaching has fascinated me. I started thinking about preaching long before I ever read a book on the subject.

I observed, from a young age, that most preachers had the superpower of slowing down time. Most sermons appeared to be agonizingly long. However, I also noted that this was not true of all sermons and all preachers. Some preachers were different. Some preachers were magnetic and even though they probably preached long sermons, time seemed to fly. This was my experience when I listened to a Scottish preacher that visited our church most years. He spoke with passion, clarity, and gravitas (the Scottish accent contributed to this). Several decades later, I still remember key sections of his sermons and I still hear the thick Scottish accent. One sermon I remember was a vivid description of what it might look like to spend eternity with all the saints at home with the Lord. The preacher began and finished by describing the joy of contemplating the beauties of Christ. However, in the central part of the sermon he led us to imagine some of the other encounters we might have. He imagined a conversation with the apostle Paul, discussing the theology of Romans. He then imagined the thrill of hearing, firsthand, various heroes of the faith retelling their adventures: Abraham, Joseph, Moses, Joshua, David, the disciples, Timothy, Augustine, Luther, William Carey, etc. Then, he said, you introduce yourself to another man and discover that it is Ezekiel. The prophet turns to you and simply asks: "Have you read my book?" The Scottish preacher expertly paused and allowed the penny to drop. It dropped. We were guilt-tripped. I imagine that many of us went home and quickly read the book of Ezekiel. The idea that one day we might meet Ezekiel was a strong enough motivation to read his book. But is it a strong enough motivation to preach his book? Perhaps not! There are better reasons to preach Ezekiel that simply the desire to avoid an awkward conversation. However, what I couldn't help but notice when reading the book of Ezekiel was his communication. Ezekiel was a terrific communicator. He went to remarkable lengths to deliver God's message to God's people. I have since discovered that this was not a trait that belonged exclusively to Ezekiel, but rather that the prophets, as a category, were masterful communicators. We have a lot to learn from them. Spending time with the prophets is like spending time with an experienced, passionate, and gifted preacher. We become better preachers simply by listening to, and learning from, them.

## THE PROPHETS AS PREACHERS

As preachers we can learn from the prophets because there is a noticeable degree of continuity between their ministry and our ministry. Preaching has a long history. Preaching, understood as the task of declaring the word of God, can be traced back to the patriarchs in the Genesis account. Enoch and Abraham are referred to as prophets (Jude 14; Gen 20:7). Peter refers to Noah as a herald or preacher of righteousness (2 Pet 2:5). In the Torah narrative we encounter Moses. Despite his initial objections (Exod 4:10–16), the Lord called and equipped Moses to be a preacher. Of course, Moses was more than a preacher since he was also the leader, the divinely appointed lawgiver, and the mediator between God and his people. Yet Moses should and ought to be viewed also as a preacher. The book of Deuteronomy can be properly viewed as the three final sermons preached by Moses to the people of God.[1] In these sermons we find Moses' faithful exposition of the law that had been previously given, coupled with a strong dose of exhortation and application. These crucial elements of preaching can be seen in sermons that Moses preached over 3,000 years ago. Christopher Ash presents a strong theological case for preaching from the book of Deuteronomy alone. He successfully argues: "Deuteronomy is the mandate for the people of God to assemble under the preached word of God, or to be more accurate, the written word preached."[2] The Old Testament prophets fulfilled this mandate as evidenced by their ministry. Moses was the protoprophet that established the paradigm for subsequent prophets. The prophets were preachers that exhorted the people of God to be faithful to the terms of the covenant. Of course, the prophets were more than "mere" preachers. No preacher today can claim their sermons come directly and immediately from God in the same way the prophetic oracles came from God. We preach with authority, but it is a *borrowed* authority that only extends insofar as we are faithful to the written and inspired word of God. Scripture is inerrant, but we are not, and our people know it too well. Furthermore, the role of predicting the future was another facet of the role of the prophets that we don't have as preachers. Nevertheless, it is also true that the basic task of the Old Testament prophets was to boldly proclaim the word of God to their listeners, exhorting and pleading with them to respond in obedience.

1. The three speeches/sermons in Deuteronomy are usually identified as: Historical speech (1:6—4:43), legal speech (4:44—26:19), and prophetic speech (27–30).

2. Ash, *Priority of Preaching*, 23.

This is the same task preachers have today. Therefore, although it would be improper to consider the Old Testament prophets to be just preachers since their words (more precisely, some of their words) became Scripture, it is perfectly adequate to consider them fully fledged preachers. Carlson, whilst not neglecting the obvious differences, highlights the many parallels between the prophets of old and preachers today:

> Preachers have the same essential ministry as the prophets: we speak the word of God to God's people. We also have a similarly framed message: we apply the Lord's previous redemption and promised hope to present life situations. Furthermore, both prophets and preachers carry out their glorious ministry by the same essential means: the Spirit of the Lord is upon us.[3]

We can learn a lot not just from what they said (i.e., their message) but also from how they lived (i.e., ministry) and how they communicated (i.e., their method).

The prophets are great examples for us because they were fully committed to the task and art of communication. They were extremely effective communicators who used a wide range of figures of speech and rhetorical techniques to persuade their listeners. Various approaches have been employed to evaluate the rhetorical genius of the prophets.[4] The prophets pass all the rhetorical tests with flying colors. To give us an appreciation of their rhetorical brilliance and to inspire us to learn from them we will look at the prophets' rhetoric through the lens of the three classic elements of persuasion: ethos, logos, and pathos. But before we do that, it is worth pondering if it is appropriate for preachers to use rhetoric in the proclamation of the word of God. Is there a place for rhetoric in the pulpit? Is there not a risk of highlighting the form and neglecting the content? Is this not relying upon "lofty speech" and "earthly wisdom" rather than upon the power of God (1 Cor 2:1–5)? These are legitimate questions that are worth considering.

---

3. Carlson, *Preaching Like the Prophets*, 59.

4. Block, for example, looks at Ezekiel's rhetoric through the lens of the five canons of rhetoric: invention, arrangement, style, memory, and delivery (Block, "Preaching Ezekiel," 169–70).

## In Defense of Rhetoric

Rhetoric certainly gets a bad rap. Admittedly, too often rhetoric is used to mask inadequate content or, worse again, to perpetuate a deceitful message. This was certainly the case in Corinth where false teachers with great rhetorical prowess tempted the church. In his second epistle, Paul calls them "super-apostles." They followed the approach of the Edenic serpent and used cunning words to tempt the church away from their devotion to Christ (2 Cor 11:3–6). Barnett comments: "Paul sees *words*—erroneous in content but smooth of delivery—as Satan's instrument to seduce the church from her loyalty to Christ."[5] These smooth orators were altering the message of the gospel and leading the church off track. Paul, therefore, is keen to distance himself from them by exposing this improper use of rhetoric. This does not, however, mean that Paul did not recognize the value of carefully crafting his words to convince his listeners/readers of his message. Paul was eager to persuade the church in Corinth to respond to his message, and he was not against using rhetoric to reach this goal. On the contrary, even in his correspondence with the Corinthian church, Paul himself employs rhetorical techniques to carry forth his argument. The ultimate and decisive evidence is Paul's beautiful poem of love (1 Cor 13). According to Morris, it is "the greatest, strongest, deepest thing Paul ever wrote."[6] Therefore, what Paul was criticizing was not the use of rhetoric per se, but the improper use of rhetoric to mask, manipulate, or misguide.

As preachers we should think of rhetoric not as something which is intrinsically good or intrinsically bad but as a neutral tool that can then be used for good or for bad. Rhetoric is like a knife that can be used by a criminal to stab or by a surgeon to cure. This was crystal clear for Augustine and he made a good case for it:

> Since rhetoric is used to give conviction to both truth and falsehood, who could dare to maintain that truth, which depends on us for its defense, should stand unarmed in the fight against falsehood? This would mean that those who are trying to give conviction to their falsehoods would know how to introduce their subject to make their listeners favorable, interested, and receptive, while we would not; that they would expound falsehoods in descriptions that are succinct, lucid, and convincing, while we would expound the truth in such a way as to bore our

---

5. Barnett, *Second Epistle to the Corinthians*, 502 (italics original).

6. Morris, *Tyndale New Testament Commentaries*, 176.

listeners, cloud their understanding, and stifle their desire to believe; that . . . pushing and propelling their listeners' minds toward error, they would speak so as to inspire fear, sadness, and elation, and issue passionate exhortations, while we, in the name of the truth, can only idle along, sounding dull and indifferent. Who could be so senseless as to find this sensible?[7]

The prophets certainly were not so senseless. They knew and used the power of rhetoric to proclaim the only message that would cure the people of God. They were great surgeons.

## ETHOS

Ethos is the listener's perception of the character and integrity of the orator. When listening to an orator it makes a world of difference if we think the speaker truly believes what he is saying, lives in accordance with the ideas he is expressing, and cares for the well-being of his listeners. Our intentional or intuitive evaluation of the ethos of a speaker determines their credibility, their power of persuasion. For Aristotle, ethos was the most decisive element of persuasion. Leith considers this assessment to still hold true today: "The ethos appeal is the first among equals . . . the foundation on which all the rest is built."[8]

This seems to be true universally, but it is especially true when it comes to preachers. The perceived integrity, holiness, and devotion of a preacher is a crucial factor in preaching. The preacher's character and lifestyle matter. I have greatly benefited from imperfect sermons—delivered in a stumbling manner, but preached by godly men—that have been deep and powerful. I have also had the experience of listening to exegetically precise and technically polished sermons that have been shallow and powerless. What determines this difference? One factor is certainly the preacher's ethos. I'm not saying exegetical precision and effective delivery are not important. I'm simply observing that these aspects cannot compensate for the lack of godly character. The messenger is not more important than the message, but the messenger and the message are intrinsically linked to the extent that the credibility of the messenger will affect the credibility of the message. Paul knew this well. One of his longest epistles (2 Corinthians) is an apologia of his life and ministry

7. Augustine, *De Doctrina Christiana*, 197.

8. Leith, *Words Like Loaded Pistols*, 48.

to establish the credibility of his message. Paul frequently leaned on his lifestyle to accredit his message: "You know what kind of men we proved to be among you for your sake" (1 Thess 1:5). Paul was keen to highlight his credibility because he knew the power of ethos.

## A Credible Bunch

How did the prophets do from this point of view? Did they practice what they preached? Are they a credible bunch? To fully answer these questions, it would be necessary to create a profile for each prophet. This, however, would be hard to achieve, considering the limited biographical data we have. The focus of the prophets was on the message they had received from God rather than on their lives. Even the autobiographical information they include, such as Jeremiah's frustrations and Hosea's marriage drama, is not motivated by egocentric self-referencing but by a desire to contribute to the overall message of the book. Despite these difficulties, a survey of the prophetic books allows us to identify some common characteristics of the prophets' lifestyles.

The first unmissable characteristic of the prophets was their perseverance in times of difficulty and opposition. They had the hard task of delivering a hard message to hard hearts. Being a prophet was not the right career choice for the faint-hearted. They had to swim against the tide. Of all the prophets Jeremiah is the one who most allows us to see the struggles the prophets endured. Consider some of the difficulties he experienced. His message was met with outright rejection (7:1—8:3). He experienced opposition from those in authority (1:19). He competed against false prophets who delivered a false message of hope that tickled the ears of the people (28:1–17). He was a lonely and isolated voice (1:18). He was mocked and beaten (20:2). He ended up in prison and in a cistern (37:11—38:13). He was forced to go places against his will (43:1–7). He was betrayed by the people who were meant to be closest to him (11:18–23). His career seriously impinged on his personal and family decisions (16:1–4). Being a prophet was tough! No wonder he tried to resign (20:8–11).

Not all the prophets experienced all these difficulties, but these give an idea of the climate in which they ministered. Despite these hardships the prophets persevered. Even Jeremiah withdrew his resignation and ministered for more than forty years (1:2–3). The prophets demonstrated remarkable courage, longsuffering, and determination. Their commitment to the Lord, and to the message that he had entrusted to them, was remarkable. They never diluted their message. They fearlessly confronted the people with their sin. They were men of God delivering the message of God. They blazed the trail that as preachers we must walk. We will be tempted to give up. We will be tempted to please men rather than please God. We will be tempted to water down some parts of Scripture. We will be tempted to be discouraged because of the lack of results. Shall I continue with the temptations we face as preachers? Yet, like the prophets of old, we must resist such temptations and persevere with courage to fulfill the task the Lord has given us.

*Job Interviews*

The prophets, however, were not superheroes. They were not perfect or invincible, and they knew it. They were not slow to admit their weaknesses. Many of them felt inadequate for the calling they had received. They were honest and humble about their limitations. We see this in their job interviews, the calls the prophets received.

Isaiah, for example, became deeply aware of his unworthiness when confronted with the holiness of God. Isaiah (6:1–8) sees the Lord sitting on a throne high and lifted up. It is a dramatic scene. The intensity of the moment is heightened by the actions and the voices of fiery angelic beings who proclaim the utter transcendence and the absolute purity of the Lord (6:2–3). This vision of the holiness of God causes the prophet to recognize by contrast his own sinfulness (6:5). Isaiah knows at once that he is lost, unworthy. In the previous chapters he had denounced the unworthiness of others, but now, before the majesty of God, the prophet confesses his own misery. He is a prophet with unclean lips. That is like being a painter with a dirty paintbrush. He is utterly unfit to serve God.

Jeremiah also reacted humbly to the Lord's call. The Lord revealed to Jeremiah that he had formed him and set him aside to be a prophet to the nations from before his birth (1:4–5). Jeremiah had every reason to feel special and fully equipped for the task of being a prophet. Yet his response to God's call denotes humility. The prophet sees himself as young and unfit for the job (1:6).

Ezekiel's humility, unlike Isaiah's and Jeremiah's, is not seen in his words but in his body language. Ezekiel does not say anything. The great vision he witnessed left him literally speechless. His only reaction was to fall on his face (1:28). This was his reaction to the vision of the glory of God. Even when the Lord invited him to stand, he did not get on his feet on his own (2:1). Flat on his face perhaps seemed like the only appropriate position before the glory of God.

Isaiah, Jeremiah, and Ezekiel were all deeply aware of their unworthiness to carry forth the important ministry with which they had been tasked. The prophets' honesty and humility, however, did not flow into self-pity, but rather a healthy dependence on the Lord. The recognition of their limitations caused the prophets to have no option but to rely on the strength the Lord would provide. The Lord was keen to expose the inability of the prophets so that the prophets would learn not to rely on themselves but on him. The Lord was equipping his messengers. He was shaping their character and strengthening their ethos.

## Ready to Work

Following their verbal or nonverbal confession of being unworthy, the Lord takes the initiative to assure the prophet he is the One who can sanctify, sustain, and strengthen them.

We left Isaiah as a self-professed unworthy prophet. "Woe is me" (6:5) was Isaiah's hopeless cry. Yet these words of doom were not his last words. In this atmosphere of hopelessness Isaiah experienced the grace of God. The Lord sent a seraph to touch the prophet's mouth with a burning coal from the altar (symbolizing the Lord's provision). This touch personally, instantaneously, and efficaciously applied God's grace to the prophet (6:6–7). Isaiah was cleansed and equipped to serve the Lord and become his messenger. The taste of God's grace transformed Isaiah's words from "woe is me" to "here I am! Send me" (6:8).

We left Jeremiah explaining that he was unsuitable to be a prophet. The two major problems for the prophet were that he was without authority because of his youth and he was inadequate because of his inability to speak. The Lord does not deny these limitations but promises to equip the prophet so he will overcome these weaknesses. Jeremiah will have all the authority he needs because it is the Lord that is sending him (1:7a). He therefore will have authority over nations and kingdoms. The rise and fall of the nations will depend on Jeremiah (1:10). The Lord empowered Jeremiah with abundant authority. The Lord will also solve the other problem by putting his words in Jeremiah's mouth (1:10). Jeremiah is worried he won't know what to say, and the Lord simply instructs him to say what he commands (1:7b). Problem solved! The prophet can now get to work (1:17), knowing that even if he encounters strong opposition the Lord will make him invincible like a fortified city (1:18–19).

We left Ezekiel flat on his face. The Lord, by his Spirit, sets Ezekiel back on his feet. Again, the Lord does not forget the prophet's frailty. As a matter of fact, the Lord calls the prophet Ezekiel in this instance, and throughout the book, "son of man." The use of this title highlights the prophet's humanity and thus, also, his fragility. However, this weak man can be encouraged because the Lord is on his side. He has nothing to fear (2:6; 3:9). Furthermore, the Lord quite literally fed the speechless prophet with the words he needed (2:8—3:3).

This combination the prophets had of an awareness of inadequacy and a reliance on the Lord's provision is an essential mark of a godly and effective preacher. If we enter the pulpit with a sense of superiority, feeling fully adequate for the high calling of preaching, we can be sure the stench of our pride will not just assault the noses, but also the ears, of our listeners. On the other hand if we tiptoe into the pulpit with a crushing sense of inadequacy and fail to trust in the Lord then we will utter weak and powerless words. These words may reach ears but will certainly not transform hearts. Both these approaches, pride and despair, are recipes for disaster. Preaching is a high calling. Too high for any of us. Yet we are commissioned by God in Christ to proclaim the holy word of God to the people of God (2 Cor 2:16–17). This conviction allows us to walk into the pulpit feeling entirely unworthy yet also knowing we have been made adequate in Christ. This combination of humility and faith that we see in the prophets is the ideal recipe for a robust preaching ministry. If, like the prophets, our lives are characterized by these virtues, then they will *radiate through* in our preaching and will ignite our words. This is the power of ethos.

## A Burden to Carry

Another important part of evaluating ethos is determining whether speakers are gripped by what they are saying. Do they really believe what they are saying? Or are they simply cold professionals delivering someone else's message? Does their message come from deep within? The weird instruction given to Ezekiel to eat the scroll gave him the words to say, but it also gave him a burden to carry. The Lord's message to his people needed to be internalized by the prophet. The Lord's message, in a sense, became Ezekiel's message. Or, to see it from another perspective, we can say the prophets cared for what the Lord cared for. They were not just spokesmen for the Lord, they were fully consumed by their role. The Lord's message to his people had become like a fire within their bones that they could not contain. That is why resignation wasn't really an option for the prophets despite Jeremiah's attempts (Jer 20:9).

This personal involvement is inevitable because the prophets were not just given words from the Lord but a burden from the Lord. This is the meaning of the word translated "oracle" (Heb. "*massa*"). An oracle was not just a speech to read but a burden to carry. The prophets felt the weight of what they were proclaiming. That is why it was not easy to silence the prophets. The false prophets attempted to silence Jeremiah to no avail. Amaziah, the idolatrous priest of Betel, attempted to send Amos back to the countryside in the south to no avail. Amos's answer was brilliant (7:14–15). He essentially said he wasn't really a prophet but a simple herdsman and a dresser of sycamore figs. However, he couldn't simply return to his day job because the Lord had sent him to prophesy against the people of Israel. Amos couldn't simply pack his bags and leave. It was not just a matter of turning the prophetic tap off and on.

The prophets were longsuffering, honest, humble, trusting, and trustworthy. They had all the right credentials. They had great ethos. What about us? Are we of the same pedigree? I suspect many of us fall short, so it will do us no harm spending time with these great preachers of the past. They will shape our character, and this in turn will sharpen our ministry. The prophets will teach us to both "watch our lives and our doctrine closely" (1 Tim 4:16). To leverage the persuasive power of ethos, both areas need our attention. As the Puritan pastor Richard Baxter explained: "It is a palpable error of some ministers, who make such a disproportion between their preaching and their living; who study hard to preach exactly, and study little or not at all to live exactly."[9] Preaching is, after all, "truth through personality."[10]

---

9. Baxter, *Reformed Pastor*, 63–64.

10. Brooks, *Lectures on Preaching*, 5.

## LOGOS

When we think about oral communication, especially preaching, we rightly tend to emphasize the content of the message. Aristotle called it logos. Logos is the verbal intellectual argument, including the way the arguments are crafted logically. In the previous chapter we identified the core message, the logos of the prophetic books. Before becoming written books, these messages were oral communications delivered in a specific time and place. What we have in the prophetic books, therefore, is, as Chalmers highlights, a collection of their "greatest hits."[11] For us preachers it is worth considering how they structured and communicated their logos so that we can learn from the greatest sermons of great preachers.

Of course, in doing this we will soon be reminded of the distance that separates us from the prophets. They lived in a different world. This will inevitably mean we will experience difficulties in understanding their message. We often need to work hard to grasp their logos. The language and the rhetorical strategies adopted by the prophets can initially appear puzzling. Luther, for example, said the prophets had "a queer way of talking."[12] However, when we endeavor to understand and explore their methodology we soon realize there was genius in their madness. The difficulties we experience in understanding their communication are not due to their inefficiency as communicators but rather to cultural and linguistic gaps. The prophets were great communicators. The people understood the prophets all too well. The problem was not that the people struggled to understand what the prophets were saying; they understood what the prophets were saying but didn't like it. The prophets were crystal clear, and this is the basic mark of any communicator worth their salt. What can we learn from the prophets about how they conveyed their message? Can we steal any of their secrets?

## Start Big!

Start big! Start strong! Start well! The prophets teach us the importance of a good introduction. It is hard to overstate the importance of a strong introduction in oral communication. Essentially all preaching and public speaking textbooks agree on this point. The consensus is that a good

---

11. Chalmers, *Interpreting the Prophets*, 146.
12. Luther, cited in Von Rad, *Old Testament Theology*, 2:33.

introduction is a crucial element in effectively conveying your message. It was important back in the days of the prophets, and it remains important today. Perhaps its importance is rising. Robinson suggests that "when people come to church, they come with clickers [remote control devices] in their heads. If you do not get their attention fast, they may be off to the menu for dinner, to a baseball game in the afternoon, or to some conflict they are having at work."[13] So, what is the best approach to keep the people from changing the channel?

The prophets show us there is more than one way to grab the ears of our listeners. A quick survey of how they start their books proves this: Isaiah surfaces a need (Israel are guilty and on trial), Ezekiel shares a breathtaking experience (vision), Hosea uses a personal story (adulterous wife), Amos opens with a vivid image (roaring lion), Joel begins with a devastating current event (the locust invasion), Habakkuk sets up tension (evil and injustice), Zephaniah starts with a shocking statement ("I will utterly sweep away everything"), and Malachi begins with a question ("How have you loved us?"). A similar survey could be carried out by identifying the introductory strategy of the single oracles. The prophets knew how to capture the attention of the people.

## Preach Like a Sniper

The introductions for the prophets, however, were not simply attention-grabbers. They properly introduced the main theme the prophets wanted to address. This is another area of excellence of the ancient preachers—they always had a clear and coherent main theme. Listening to a sermon, or even a speech, that does not have a clear main theme is often frustrating. Sermons need a gravitational center: Robinson's famous big idea![14] When we attempt to cover many different themes, we fool ourselves into thinking we are being highly effective due to the volume of information we are delivering. This is not the case. Listeners' minds will struggle to cope with the overload of fragmented information. Even if our minds can cope, our hearts cannot cope with a high volume of stimuli without becoming immune. This concept was first explained to me using an illustration of the effects of a single nail versus a bed of nails. Our instinct would suggest that the more nails we use the more chances there are to penetrate through a

13. Robinson, *Biblical Preaching*, 120.
14. Robinson, *Biblical Preaching*, 17–20.

hard shell. However, you can lie on a bed of nails with little or no effect. In contrast one nail well angled will penetrate a hard shell. The point is that a sermon with multiple ideas will most likely lose its efficacy, whilst a sermon built around a well-crafted central idea will pierce through hard hearts. Robinson uses a different illustration: "A sermon should be a bullet, not a buckshot. Ideally each sermon is the explanation, interpretation, or application of a single dominant idea supported by other ideas, all drawn from one passage or several passages of Scripture."[15]

The prophets' oracles may have multiple images, illustrations, or sections, but these serve the purpose of developing a key idea. Their oracles have a gravitational center. Therefore, whilst it may be difficult to grasp all the nuances of what the prophets are saying, it is hard to miss their main point. We can quickly identify the main thrust of their oracles. Consider, for example, the prophecy of Joel. The task of interpreting the book of Joel is not without its challenges: unknown dating of the book, relationship between the locust invasion (1:1–20) and the army invasion (2:1–17),[16] and pinpointing the fulfillment (or fulfillments) of future prophecies (2:28–32).[17] Despite these interpretative challenges, it is not difficult to recognize the main thrust of each oracle. The first oracle describes a devastating locust invasion that ought to push the people to repentance (1:1–20). The second oracle describes the day of the Lord as the invasion of a powerful army that may yet, however, be averted by returning to the Lord in repentance (2:1–17). In the third section of the

---

15. Robinson, *Biblical Preaching*, 17.

16. The relationship between these two invasions can be understood in at least three ways: 1) The locust invasion (1:1–20) functions as a warning and forerunner of a military invasion (2:1–17) that is yet to come. 2) The same locust invasion (1:1–20) is described a second time but with more intensity (2:1–17). 3) The locust invasion (1:1–20) is the description of an actual military attack using metaphorical language that is then represented (2:1–17) and identified as armies coming from the north (Assyrians or Babylonians).

17. Peter famously quoted this passage and announced its fulfillment in the day of Pentecost (2:17–21). However, some elements of this passage, those often linked to judgment (blood, fire, columns of smoke, darkness, etc.), did not take place on the day of Pentecost and, according to some interpreters, will be fulfilled at the return of Christ. Other interpreters consider these to be prophetic symbolism of judgment that don't necessarily refer to a specific fulfillment. The relationship between near- and long-term fulfillment, the possibility of multiple fulfillments, and the right understanding of metaphorical language all come into to play and will influence our interpretation. We will return to these important interpretive challenges in the next few chapters.

prophecy the Lord promises a future restoration where the Lord will give his people freedom, land, and an abundant experience of his Spirit (2:18–32). The book concludes with a further message of comfort by contrasting the judgment against the nations with the glorious future for the people of Judah (3:1–21). Understanding all the nuances and the rich imagery of each oracle of Joel is tough. Grasping the core of each message, however, is easy because the prophet in each oracle had one big idea he was developing.

Admittedly one of the reasons why it is easy to spot the main idea of the prophetic oracles is because of the limited number of themes the prophets dealt with: sin, judgment, and restoration. Nevertheless, the fact that we can group together oracles in these categories is proof that it is easy to identify the specific themes the prophets were addressing in the specific oracles. If these are clear for us, they were crystal clear for their listeners. The prophets teach us that if we want to hit the bullseye of the listeners' hearts we should load our sermons with a bullet, not a buckshot.

## Crystal-Clear Preaching

What other strategies did the prophets use to enhance their clarity? Carlson provides an answer by carrying out an interesting study. He compares the principles that Sunukjian[18] prescribes to enhance oral clarity with the practice of the prophets.[19] Carlson suggests that four out of the six principles Sunukjian prescribes are identifiable in the prophets: restate critical sentences, consistently use the same key language or phrasing, use rhetorical questions to transition from one major movement to the next, and present each new point in a deductive manner.[20] Carlson is applying the best standards of current homiletics to the prophets to see how they match up. Although there are times when this matching feels

18. Sunukjian, *Invitation to Biblical Preaching*, 268–99.

19. Carlson, *Preaching Like the Prophets*, 92–109.

20. The other two principles are: give a mini-synopsis of the point of any verse before you read them and use physical movements to mark off major units or concepts in the message. The first one was not applicable to the prophets because both the prophets and their listeners did not have the same access to Scripture as we have today. Concerning the second one, we don't know for sure how the prophets used physical movements or gestures in their delivery. My guess is that, considering how invested they were in their message and how there were instances in which they use dramatic physical actions in their delivery (Isa 20:1–2; Ezek 12:1–7), this was part of their arsenal as preachers.

contrived, the overall results are impressive. The prophets demonstrate that they would be consistently at the top of any preaching class when it comes to oral clarity. They knew what they wanted to communicate and structured their sermons to give their listeners every chance to grasp what they were saying.

Without a doubt the prophets knew what they were doing and the direction they wanted to take in their communication. They were good pilots. Their take-off (introduction) was impressive, their destination (main theme) was clear, and their flight plan (development) was effective. What else is missing? What else should be part of a good sermon? The landing! The goal of a sermon is not merely to give information but to bring about transformation. It therefore needs to be applied. Robinson states: "Like an able lawyer, a minister asks for a verdict. Your congregation should see your idea entire and complete, and it should know and feel what God's truth demands of it."[21] Application is the delicate but necessary landing of the expounded truth into the listeners' lives. Demanding a verdict can be uncomfortable. In a sense, it is confrontational. It transforms the listening experience from a passive stance to an active response. The prophets, however, never shied away from calling the people to a response. They never left their listeners in doubt about what the Lord demanded of them. Moreover, they often first discarded inappropriate or unsatisfactory responses (Isa 1:11–15; Mic 6:6–7) before explicating what the Lord demanded of his people (Isa 1:16–20; Mic 6:8). The clarity of their message removed all excuses.

There were times when the prophets did not include overt, specific instructions of application. However, even in these occasions the people were not left in the dark regarding what the Lord required of them. Even in the absence of an explicit application there was a strong implied application. The many oracles of the coming judgment contained an implied application to bow their heads before the Lord and repent of their sin. The many oracles of salvation contained an implied application to lift their heads out of the current circumstances and trust in the Lord. Carlson comments: "Since the prophets are rhetorical masters of irony, it is ironic that one of their more common types of specific and relevant application is the implied application. . . . The implied application is still specific and relevant because the charge or accusation which implies the correct

---

21. Robinson, *Biblical Preaching*, 128.

response is specific and relevant."[22] Jonah's mini-sermon in Nineveh is a good example. "Yet forty days, and Nineveh shall be overthrown!" (Jonah 3:4). The application is not stated but implied. Arguably the force of an implied application may have been even stronger than an explicit one. The people generated the appropriate response to the prophetic word on their own and therefore felt a stronger compulsion to obey. However, the truth of the matter is that it was the prophet who was whispering this application to their heart. This was part of the oratorical brilliance of the prophets. At times a whisper is louder than a shout.

When considering their logos, we see that the prophets had engaging introductions, an unmissable main idea, effective strategies that enlighten and develop their message, and a hard-hitting application. It might give our preaching a shot in the arm to log a few hours of flight time alongside such skilled pilots.

## PATHOS

The third aspect of classic rhetoric is pathos. Chapell defines pathos as, "The emotive features of a message, including the passion, fervor, and feeling that a speaker conveys and the listeners experience."[23] This aspect tends to receive less attention than the other two in preaching books. In some cases it is seen negatively as an attempt to mask a questionable ethos and/or to overcompensate for a weak logos.[24] Arthurs, however, makes a strong case for "promoting" pathos and recognizing its importance without demoting logos and ethos.[25]

> The old dichotomy between logic and emotion, the head and the heart, does not reflect how humans actually make decisions. . . . Pathos is primary in human decision-making because God made us to respond to emotional appeals, and he himself uses pathos. He motivates us through awe of his immensity, fear of

22. Carlson, *Preaching Like the Prophets*, 126.

23. Chapell, *Christ-Centered Preaching*, 34.

24. For example, we often see an unethical use of pathos during election campaigns when politicians eloquently present a long list of promises with great *pathos,* knowing all too well that they will not be able to fully deliver these promises once in office. Similarly, and closer to home, most of us have had the painful experience of listening to a preacher who had clearly not done his homework and was trying to compensate for the lack of content with a *passionate* delivery.

25. Arthurs, "Pathos Needed," 591–95.

his holiness, confidence of his goodness, and joy of his grace. Pathos is crucial, not incidental, to God's communication.[26]

The prophets seem to agree.

## Upgrade Needed

The prophets gave much importance to the emotive dimensions of what they are saying. As we observed in the previous chapter, the message of the prophets was repetitive. It is not an exaggeration to claim that the general prophetic message could be summarized in a just a few brief pages. Yet, we have page after page with oracle after oracle. Why did they use so many different oracles to deliver essentially the same message? Why so repetitive? A big reason for the abundance of oracles was to convey the emotive force of their message. Pathos! The prophets were keen to persuade the people not just with logic and the truthfulness of their argument but also with emotion and passion. They were keen to reach and move the hearts of their listeners in order to bring about transformation. Cicero observed: "Mankind makes far more determinations through hatred, or love, or desire, or anger, or grief, or joy, or hope, or fear, or error, or some other affection of the mind, than regard for truth, or any settled maxim, or principle of right."[27] Again, there is no need to put pathos in contraposition with logos or ethos, and instead to simply see the importance of considering the emotive dimensions of our preaching. The prophets are excellent role models for us and show us how to utilize all these aspects of rhetoric.

## Metaphors, Poetry, and Parallelism

Perhaps the primary trait of their speech was the abundant use of metaphors. They employed metaphors not just to illustrate cognitively what they were saying, but also, and perhaps primarily, to convey the emotional weight of their message. Their metaphors were carefully chosen for this dual purpose. Consider, for example, Amos's metaphor of a shepherd rescuing an animal (or pieces of an animal) from the mouth of a lion. "As the shepherd rescues from the mouth of the lion two legs, or a piece of an

26. Arthurs, "Pathos Needed," 591–92.
27. Cicero, *Cicero on Oratory and Orators*, 131–32.

ear, so shall the people of Israel who dwell in Samaria be rescued, with the corner of a couch and part of a bed" (Amos 3:12). The language is strong, vivid, and emotive. It is hard not be to be moved! Israel is compared to an animal torn to shreds by a lion. Undoubtedly both the prophet and his listeners were deeply impacted by the vividness of this language.

The prophetic literature in general is saturated with poignant metaphors. The prophets describe blessing as new wine dripping from mountains (Amos 9:13), Israel as a desolate vineyard (Isa 5), idolatry as adultery (Jer 2), the Lord as a hunter (Hos 7:12), and the consequence of the impurity of the priest as dung on their faces (Mal 2:3). The list could go on. Appreciating the arresting and emotive metaphors of the prophets is a key to understanding their message. According to Sandy, the density of metaphors was the "secret" and the distinguishing feature of the prophets' rhetoric. Sandy is enthusiastic about the prophets' lavish use of metaphors. He lists the fundamental functions of metaphors in communication: they create a visual image, speak to the right side of the brain, invite interaction, add elegance and originality, convey abstract ideas, influence how we think, express ideas compactly, increase memorability, and increase the power of persuasion.[28] The prophets loved metaphors and were experts at using them. It was their weapon of choice for piercing hard hearts.

The prophets' pathos can be seen in more than their masterful use of metaphors. They used language creatively and poetically. Poetic language is well-suited to convey emotion. This is the big advantage of poetry over prose. The prophets' choice of poetry was not primarily aesthetic but pragmatic. They were not seeking to mesmerize the people with the artistic elegance of their poetry, rather they were seeking to persuade the people by tugging on their heartstrings. Their use of poetry was not to garner admiration but to cause transformation.

In addition to metaphor, another key characteristic of Hebrew poetry is parallelism. We often think of parallelism primarily as repetition. This is a shallow comprehension of this important device. The interplay between parallel lines is much more significant than mere repetition. Alter observes that just as language resists true synonymity since small wedges of difference exist between closely akin terms, so "literary expression abhors complete parallelism."[29] Even when parallel lines *seem* to be

---

28. Sandy, *Plowshares and Pruning Hooks*, 60.

29. Alter, *Art of Biblical Poetry*, 10.

saying the same thing, they are never entirely synonymous. Indeed the small wedges of difference that exist between the corresponding lines are the crux of parallel constructions. Fokkelman agrees and explains that the equivalence in a parallel construction "serves as a foundation for observing and enjoying differences. The similarity becomes the background against which disparity announces itself."[30] Thus the key to grasping the function of parallelism is to pay attention to the interaction between parallel lines.

When we do this, we discover that "the characteristic movement of meaning is one of heightening or intensification . . . of focusing, specification, concretization, even what could be called dramatization."[31] Thus the essence of parallelism is not to restate but to complete, emphasize, intensify, and heighten the idea that is being expressed.[32] We see an example of this intensification dynamic in Isaiah's use of parallelism (Isa 41:8-10):

> But you, Israel, my servant,
> Jacob, whom I have chosen,
> the offspring of Abraham, my friend;
> you whom I took from the ends of the earth,
> and called from its farthest corners,
> saying to you, "You are my servant,
> I have chosen you and not cast you off";
> fear not, for I am with you;
> be not dismayed, for I am your God;
> I will strengthen you, I will help you,
> I will uphold you with my righteous right hand.

Consider, for example, the intensifying effect of Israel being called not just God's servant but also God's chosen people and "the offspring of Abraham, my friend." Each parallel line is upgrading the privileged status of the people of Israel and allowing the people to experience more and more intensely the Lord's care for them. Similarly, the parallel instructions to "not fear" and to not "be dismayed," coupled with the reasons for these instructions, are not mere restatements but important reinforcements. The final parallel structure is threefold. The assurance that the Lord will "strengthen," and "help" is heightened with the final line "I will uphold you with my righteous right hand." The accumulative effect of these three lines, together with greater length, concreteness, and the specificity of

---

30. Fokkelman, *Reading Biblical Poetry*, 78.
31. Alter, *Art of Biblical Poetry*, 20.
32. Kugel, *Idea of Biblical Poetry*, 51–54.

this final line, helps us feel the strength of the Lord's promise. The use of parallelism thus transforms these beautiful words into a shower of comfort for the people of God. Clustering together these promises enables the listener (or the reader) to not just understand these promises but to feel and believe them.

A similar effect is created when the prophets cluster together not just lines but also metaphors. Metaphors are placed one after the other to create an even stronger escalating effect. This grouping together of metaphors is, in a sense, a combination of parallelism and metaphoric language—a parallelism of metaphors. Consider, for example, the various images (metaphors and similes) Isaiah brings together in his opening oracle (1:1–9) to describe the wickedness of Israel: rebellious children (v. 2), foolish animals (v. 3), disrespectful subjects (v. 4), widespread sickness (vv. 5–6), a desolate land (v. 7), a booth in a vineyard (v. 8), and Sodom and Gomorrah (v. 9). The effect of grouping together is that you don't just understand the horror of sin, you feel it. When confronted with our sin, we tend to put up our defenses. We don't want to feel guilty and, therefore, we hide behind excuses. Grouping together multiple images that show us the seriousness of our sin is a potent strategy to break through our defenses. We may resist the first or second image but the *accumulative force* of all these images of the horror of sin will eventually leave us defenseless. With metaphor after metaphor the prophets are bringing us to our knees like an expert boxer who, jab after jab, wears down his opponent.

## Emotional Rollercoaster

Emotions mattered for the prophets. Their message was clear, and their application was evident; now it was necessary to infuse some power and strength into this clear message. The prophets were not interested in tickling the people's intellect; they wanted the people to feel the full-blown punches they were delivering. To do this they often structured their oracles to deliver their message with maximum emotional effect. This was a deliberate and highly effective strategy. Amos's opening oracle is a masterclass. The Lord is introduced as the lion that roars from Zion (1:2). It is a roar of judgment. The prophet then announces the Lord's judgment upon all of Israel's neighboring nations: Syria (1:3–5), Philistia (1:6–8), Tyre (1:9–10), Edom (1:11–12), Ammon (1:13–15), Moab (2:1–3), and

Judah (2:4–5). The announcement of judgment is given to all these nations with the same formula: "for three transgressions of . . . , and for four, I will not revoke the punishment" (1:3, 6, 9, 11, 13; 2:1, 4.). The judgment that will fall on Israel's neighbors is therefore presented as both deserved and inevitable. It is not hard to imagine the people of Israel, to whom Amos was delivering this prophecy, rejoicing, and perhaps even celebrating as they heard the announcement of coming judgment upon their neighbors and rivals. This was good news. Finally, the Lord was going to judge these evil nations. They probably thought: "We need more prophets like this country chap from the south." This enthusiasm, however, was short lived when the prophet delivered his longest and strongest judgment. The final judgment was forcefully directed to the nation of Israel (2:6–16). The Lion had encircled its prey. They were trapped. The same people that had agreed with and celebrated the judgment on their neighbors now could not but accept the judgment that was upon them for the same sins. If anything, they were even more culpable than the other nations because they were God's covenant people. Their cheer for the judgment upon the other nations had been turned into a cry of distress for the judgment that awaited them. The prophet Amos led the people on an emotional rollercoaster to then deliver his knockout punch with maximum force. Amos employed what Alter considers to be a typical element of prophetic poetry, "a rhetoric of entrapment."[33] Have you ever attempted this strategy? Have you ever led your congregation to point their finger of judgment upon society in general, or categories of people in society, or even their colleagues and neighbors, to then turn that finger of judgment upon themselves, showing how they too are guilty of the very same sins they despise others?

Or to ask a more general question: Do you give thought to the emotional dimension of your preaching? Arthurs counsels us to give serious thought to it: "From the earnest pleading of Charles Spurgeon, to the pastoral warmth of Jack Hayford, to the exuberance of E. V. Hill, effective preachers represent God—his ideas and emotions. When preachers use pathos (and logos and ethos), they handle the Word skillfully."[34] Arthurs goes on to suggest that without an upgrade of pathos our sermons risk being like Ralph Waldo Emerson's lectures, which he himself described as: "Fine things, pretty things, wise things, but no arrows, no axes, no

---

33. Alter, *Art of Biblical Poetry*, 180.

34. Arthurs, "Pathos Needed," 592.

nectar, no growling, no transpiercing, no loving, no enchantment."[35] The prophets can teach us to do better and use our ethos, logos, and pathos for the good of the people and for the glory of God. In chapter 7 we will consider how to enjoy, explore, and exploit the language and rhetoric of the prophets when preaching the prophetic literature.

## PREACHERS EXPECT TO BE HEARD

The Old Testament prophets were exceptional preachers. They preached with courage, clarity, and conviction the word of God to the people of God. Some of their sermons became part of the canon of Scripture and therefore are accessible to us today as the written word of God. Preachers today have the responsibility of taking on this preaching mantle and declaring the word of God (including the Prophets) to the current generation. Another solid reason to preach the prophetic literature is that preachers will learn from the prophets how to combine faithful exposition with creative and effective proclamation. After all, the prophets were preachers, and preachers expect to be heard.

35. Arthurs, "Pathos Needed," 592.

# PART 2

# How to Preach the Prophets

# Chapter 4

## HANDLE THE PROPHETS WITH CARE

> "Do your best to present yourself to God as one approved,
> a worker who has no need to be ashamed, rightly handling
> the word of truth."
>
> —2 TIM 2:15

IN THE PREVIOUS CHAPTERS we identified solid reasons to preach from the Old Testament prophets. As preachers we should feel both the duty and the desire to preach the prophets. However, this desire is and will be insufficient if we lack the know-how. As preachers our task is to discover and proclaim the *meaning* of the biblical text—what God intended to reveal through the Old Testament prophets by the words and grammar he inspired. Preaching the prophets, therefore, requires the ability to interpret the prophetic literature correctly. Preaching prophetic literature is hard. Most preachers feel much more at ease unpacking the intricate arguments of the Pauline Epistles or following the thrilling adventures of biblical narratives rather than exploring the prophetic books. The world of the prophets is a world full of interpretative challenges. In this chapter we will explore this world of oracles and visions. To achieve this, we will first need to find our footing in this unusual environment of the prophetic genre. Then we will identify a decalogue of guidelines to follow to avoid taking wrong turns in, what is for many of us, uncharted territory.

Before we do this, some preliminary comments about genre and how it influences interpretation are in order.

## GENRE AND INTERPRETATION

We struggle to interpret the prophets because we are not familiar with the prophetic genre. We have the equivalent to epistles, narratives, and psalms in contemporary cultures, but we don't have the equivalent to the prophetic genre. Unfamiliarity with this genre inevitably leads to difficulties in interpretation. The plethora of different interpretations of biblical prophecies, with the many theological battles that have thus ensued, confirms that many of us struggle to rightly handle this genre. The prophetic books are a well-trodden battleground. To overcome these difficulties, we need to gain a better understanding of this genre: how it functions and, perhaps more importantly, how it doesn't function. Let us begin with a basic general understanding of genre.

Longman provides a simple definition of literary genre: "A group of texts that bear one or more traits in common with each other."[1] These common traits are a series of rules and conventions that an author employs to convey meaning to the reader. Writers are guiding their readers toward understanding by following a set of conventions. As soon as we begin to read a text, we make a conscious or unconscious genre identification. This genre identification not only triggers our expectations about what we are reading but also establishes the framework within which the words are being used and therefore how they should be understood. Sounds complicated? Most of us do this effortlessly and intuitively every time we pick up a newspaper. We read differently if our eyes fall on a news report, editorial, obituary, political cartoon, or advertisement. Genre, therefore, is clearly not just a matter of the words that are used but *how* the words are used to convey meaning. In general terms literary genre can be understood as a class (or kind[2]) of writings that share rules, conventions, or traits.

The inspired authors of Scripture wrote in a variety of genres. Yet, what we do effortlessly and intuitively when we pick up a newspaper we seem to struggle to do when we read Scripture. We tend to flatten the literary variety in Scripture and default to a one-size-fits-all reading

---

1. Longman, "Literary Approaches to Biblical Interpretation," 141.
2. Genre is a French word that means "kind."

strategy that is inadequate for most biblical genres. Since genre discloses the meaning of the text, it is unimaginable to gain an accurate understanding of the content of the text without paying adequate attention to its form. We can't (or at least we shouldn't) read the Psalms in the same way we read the Epistles, we can't read Wisdom Literature in the same way we read the law, we can't read Old Testament narratives the same way we read Revelation, and we can't read the Prophets the same way we read the Gospels. Different genres require a different approach to reading. Just as in singing, we must follow the instructions of the composer by beginning with the right note in order to be in tune, so in interpretation we must follow the instructions of the author by paying attention to genre in order to be in tune with the meaning of the text.

Genre choice also provides clues to the intention or intentions of the author. The biblical writers wrote to persuade readers of truth. A key element of this persuasion is the genre that the author employed. Even a cursory comparison between the primary means of persuasion of biblical genres reveals that an author's intention is entwined with his genre choice. Narrative persuades the reader implicitly by creating identification with the characters in the story and by showing truth through plot development. Poetry persuades the reader by provoking emotions. The Epistles persuade the reader by presenting a well-articulated, logical argumentation. Proverbs persuade readers by simplifying matters in a memorable and convincing manner. Each genre leans on its own techniques to persuade the reader. It follows that to understand the intention of the author, which is a fundamental rule of hermeneutics, we need to comprehend the specific genre techniques the author has used.

## A Word, or Two, of Caution

Preachers must avoid a simplistic understanding of genre. Biblical genres are not fixed and immutable forms. A certain fluidity must be acknowledged. Genres evolve and develop over the course of time. In addition, an author may mix genres or perhaps even choose to rebel against a particular genre feature to accomplish his purpose. Although this rebellion may not be as common in Scripture as it is in modern literature, nonetheless we must be alert to how genre can morph. Longman reports that genre theorists speak of genre as an institution similar to a state, university, or church. "An individual joins an institution, follows its rules and regulations in the main, but may opt to fight for change in either a subtle or radical manner. Moreover, an author may choose to play with the usual elements of genre simply for satiric or other affects."[3] From this angle, we should not see genre as a straitjacket that a priori restricts and dictates the meaning of the text.[4]

However, it is also true that only the reader who is familiar with the characteristic features of any biblical genre will recognize when these features are intentionally being teased. This, in turn, may lead the reader to further investigation that may provide crucial insights that will shed light on the text. Consequently, whether the author is submitting to, or rebelling against, the typical features of a biblical genre, it is evident that genre plays a crucial role in interpretation.

We must also note that the prophetic genre is perhaps the most difficult of the biblical genres to define and dissect. The prophets communicated in varied and creative ways. Gentry goes as far as stating: "In one sense, prophecy is not a particular genre or type of literature, since the prophets use every possible genre and literary type to communicate their messages."[5] The prophets used a variety of genres and subgenres: narratives, parables, biographies, dialogues, sermons, letters, prayers, oracles, and visions. However, this doesn't exclude the identification of a broader prophetic genre.[6] Furthermore, this inclusion of diverse genres and subgenres is in and of itself a characteristic of the prophetic genre. The prophetic books are collections primarily, but not exclusively, of oracles and visions. As such we can identify the primary traits of prophetic genre that inevitably impinge on our interpretation and preaching of this important part of the word of God.

---

3. Longman, "Literary Approaches to Biblical Interpretation," 142.

4. The relationship between biblical writings and parallel writings of the ancient Middle East merits careful reflection. These writings have provided, and can provide, significant help in interpreting the biblical text. However, there is also the risk of emphasizing the similarities to the detriment of the differences. We need to be cautious about any interpretation that uncritically applies conventional elements of noncanonical literature to its counterpart in Scripture.

5. Gentry, *How to Read & Understand*, 13.

6. After all, even other genres, such as Epistles, also make internal use of other subgenres: prayers, hymns, confessions, autobiographical data, etc.

## THE PROPHETIC GENRE

We therefore need to create a profile for the prophetic genre to understand the message of the prophets. What are the key features and functions of the prophetic genre?

### Divinely Inspired Anthologies

The first characteristic to bear in mind is that the prophetic books come to us as divinely inspired collections of oracles and visions. Hays is not alone in helpfully categorizing the prophetic books as *anthologies*. "The prophetic books are not essays organized around propositional statements and logical argumentation. Neither are they stories driven by sequential time, action, and plot. While they are organized and logical, and while they do reflect plot (in the broadest sense), most of the prophetic books can probably best be categorized as *anthologies*."[7] Viewing the prophetic books as anthologies will help us preachers make sense of some of the elements that often baffle us: the apparently redundant repetitiveness, the juxtaposition between oracles of judgment and oracles of hope, and the weird assortment of material (narratives, parables, oracles, visions, etc.). Our confusion will be mitigated when we realize the prophetic books, like anthologies, have a compositional strategy. They tend to be organized thematically more than chronologically (review table 2 in chapter 2). This explains, for example, the apparent repetitiveness which is not evidence of a poor writing style, but rather is an intentional choice with an important rhetorical function. Gentry illustrates the purpose of revisiting the same themes in sequence:

> The normal pattern of Hebrew literature is to consider topics in a *recursive* manner, which means that topic is progressively repeated. Such an approach seems monotonous to those who do not know and understand how these texts communicate. Using the recursive approach, a Hebrew author begins a discourse on a particular topic, develops it from a particular perspective, and then concludes his conversation. Then he begins another conversation, taking up *the same topic again* from a different point of view. When these two conversations or discourses on

---

7. Hays, *Message of the Prophets*, 46 (italics original).

the same topic are heard in succession, they are like the left and the right speakers of a stereo.[8]

This recursive approach is thus enriching our listening experience. Furthermore, the effect of accumulating oracles of judgment and salvation not only enhances our understanding of the prophetic message, it also increases its force. The prophetic anthologies amplify the voices of the prophets and the themes they addressed.

We see a clear example of this recursive approach in the five successive visions in the book of Amos (chs. 7–9). The prophet first sees a vision of the judgment of God coming as a ravaging locust invasion. Amos responds to the vision by pleading with the Lord to forgive, and the Lord relents from the threatened judgment (7:1–3). The second vision is a devastating fire throughout the land. Again, the prophet intercedes for the people, and the Lord relents from sending his judgment (7:4–6). The third vision increases the volume of the impending judgment. The prophet sees a plumb line held against a wall. A plumb line is a string with a weight fastened to it. The purpose of placing a plumb line against a wall is to check if a wall is perfectly vertical or not. A tilted wall, if not fixed, will eventually collapse. The message of the vision is clear. The fall of the people of Israel, although it has been delayed by the intercession of the prophet after the first two visions, is inevitable because the people are tilted away from the Lord and his ways (7:7–9). After the brief interruption of the clash between Amos and the idolatrous priest (7:10–17),[9] the prophet has a fourth vision. The Lord shows him a basket of summer fruit. The summer fruit is the sign that the harvest season has now come to an end. Time is up! The window of opportunity to repent is now closed (cf. Jer 8:20) and the Lord's judgment is inevitable. The people are like ripe fruit ready to be consumed by the Lord's judgment (8:1–14). The final vision is the culmination of the previous visions. Amos, this time, does not dialogue with the Lord but is simply a spectator, watching what the Lord will do. Furthermore, this time the prophet doesn't see a symbol (locust, fire, plumb line, or summer fruit) but he sees the Lord himself standing by the altar and ready to launch into his severe and inescapable judgment (9:1–10). The day of judgment has arrived, and it is dreadful.

8. Gentry, *How to Read & Understand*, 17 (italics original).

9. Even this narrative, however, is not just a mere interruption but is strategically placed to reinforce the message of the visions. The plumb line test is being applied to Amaziah. He fails the test, and therefore his fall is inevitable. The tragic story of this individual illustrates what will happen to the whole nation if they don't repent.

The volume is raised to the max. We started with the Lord threatening, and then immediately relenting from judgment in the first two visions (7:1–6). Then the Lord announced, with the vision of the plumb line, that his judgment was inevitable. It was just a matter of time (7:7–9). The fourth vision of the basket of summer fruit signaled that the time was now ripe for judgment. In this final vision we see the Lord standing to deliver his judgment. Through the recursive, cumulative, and crescendo effect of these visions, the book of Amos is turning up the volume of the Lord's warnings of impending judgment.

Interpreting the prophetic books, therefore, requires us to give serious thought to the intentional compositional strategies employed by the authors. In practice this means endeavoring to understand the purpose, themes, and structures of the prophetic *anthologies,* and allowing these to influence our interpretation of single oracles. A high view of Scripture demands we take seriously the literary context of a passage.

Determining the literary context of a single oracle is especially important because, as Tucker explains, there can be a potential difference between the original function of an oracle compared to its function in a prophetic book. "When the speeches which had been delivered over the years on various and sundry occasions were collected and then written down, they were given a new and different life. . . . A speech which originally served one purpose may serve a different one in the context of the book."[10] Greidanus agrees: "the new literary context may change the thrust of a passage."[11] Imagine, for example, the first occasions in which Jeremiah proclaimed to the people of Judah that their exile in Babylon would last seventy years. Undoubtedly this would have been received as extremely bad and discouraging news considering that the false prophets were much more optimistic (and wrong) about the duration of the exile—a mere two years (Jer 28:1–4). However, the purpose of this detail about the seventy years within the structure of the prophetic book is to encourage and reassure the readers (Jer 29:10–11; cf. Dan 9:1–2). We must therefore be aware that in some cases the function of a prophetic speech, in transitioning from oral form to written form, may have changed. Not all cases have a sharp contrast like this example from Jeremiah, but this does exemplify the reason why we need to take seriously the literary context of single oracles within the prophetic anthologies.

---

10. Tucker, *Form Criticism of the Old Testament,* 70–71.

11. Greidanus, *Modern Preacher and the Ancient Text,* 259.

## Oracles

However, even though the prophetic message comes to us in a written form, the prophetic message was first delivered in an *oral form*. The prophets stood in great cities like Jerusalem and Samaria and proclaimed a message from the Lord to the people of Israel and Judah. This original oral quality should affect our understanding and interpretation of the genre. The prophetic books are primarily a collection of speeches called *oracles*. Westermann simply defined prophetic speeches as "the words of God delivered by a messenger of God."[12] This ties in with the basic prophetic task. In Hebrew there are three words for "prophet." The most frequently used word is *nabi*. Although there is some debate among scholars, the majority agree it relates to the calling the prophets received from God. However, it is likely this term morphed over the centuries to not only include the passive connotation of being "called by God" but also the active connotation to "call on behalf of God."[13] Thus, the prophet is called by God to call others to God. Delivering God's oracles was the job. The prophets always made it clear they were speaking on behalf of God. They introduced the oracles with the formula "thus says the Lord," and then they delivered a message in which the Lord spoke in the first person.

The gravity of this task influenced their choice of language. What language should be used to speak on behalf of the Lord? The prophets chose poetry. Alter offers this insightful explanation: "Since poetry is our best human model of intricately rich communication, not only solemn, weighty, and forceful but also densely woven with complex internal connections, meanings, and implications, it makes sense that divine speech should be represented as poetry."[14] So, "thus said the Lord" was followed by oracles of passionate poetry.

## Poetical Language

Thus, another dominant feature of the prophetic genre is *poetical language*. Poetry provokes intense experiences and emotions. The prophets chose poetry because they were keen to channel this intensity of emotions to persuade their audiences. The beauty of Hebrew poetry, which is

---

12. Westermann, *Basic Forms of Prophetic Speech*, 90.

13. See Greidanus, *Modern Preacher and the Ancient Text*, 229.

14. Alter, *Art of Biblical Poetry*, 176.

rich in imagery and passion, made it the ideal language for the prophets to use to deliver the words of the Lord. As preachers it may be difficult for us to become experts of Hebrew poetry. Nonetheless a rudimentary understanding of the forms and features of Hebrew poetry will reap its rewards in assisting our interpretation of the message of the prophets for the church. We need to become familiar with the language of the prophets.

Their language of choice was poetry. However, the prophets were not against using prose. Indeed, several sections of the prophetic books are in prose. Moreover, the line between prosaic and poetical language in Hebrew Scriptures in general, and the prophetic books in particular, can be blurry. It is not unusual to find both typical elements of prose and poetry in the same oracles. Nonetheless if we consider a spectrum of language from prosaic to poetic, we can collocate the genre of prophetic literature on the poetic side of the spectrum. The prophets preferred using poetry to deliver the message that they had received from the Lord to his people. The prophets were poets. However, we do well to remember that the prophets were also, and perhaps primarily, preachers. Indeed, this is probably what prevented them from using exclusively poetry. The prophets wanted to be direct. They wanted to make sure their message arrived unambiguously to their audience. Therefore, if using prose or elements of prose facilitated the clarity and directness of their message then they were willing to compromise their poetry. Alter suggests this "powerfully vocative character" is what differentiates prophetic poetry from other kinds of biblical poetry. "Prophetic poetry . . . is devised as a form of direct address to a historically real audience."[15] Despite this peculiarity of directness, the main characteristics of Hebrew poetry are found in the prophetic genre. We have already touched on some of these elements in the previous chapter when we analyzed the rhetoric of the prophets. Nevertheless, it is worth considering some of them again this time from the perspective of how these devices of Hebrew poetry impinge upon our interpretation of the prophetic message.

## Think Parallelism

When we think of poetry, we think rhymes. When the Hebrew poets thought of poetry, they thought parallelism. The basic feature of parallelism is that two or more lines are grouped together to form one thought.

---

15. Alter, *Art of Biblical Poetry*, 174–75.

The interplay between the lines reveals the meaning. Although the relationship between the lines can vary,[16] we need to learn to read the lines of a parallel structure together to understand the substance of what is being communicated. This requires a different approach to reading. We are used to reading sentences and paragraphs. In the prophetic literature we need to become familiar with reading lines and parallel constructions. The layout of our Bibles can sometimes help us by strategically breaking off the poetic lines. Learning to read parallelism involves slowing down to ponder the interaction between lines. This is the key that will help us understand the meaning of the text, as well as feeling the intensification of the idea that is being expressed. Berlin explains it superbly: "Parallelism focuses the message on itself but its vision is binocular. Like human vision it superimposes two slightly different views of the same object and from their convergence it produces a sense of depth."[17] Grasping the advancement of meaning and intensification in parallelism will greatly aid our interpretation, and therefore our preaching, of the prophetic genre. Ponder, for example, how the interplay between lines in these examples reveals, clarifies, and intensifies meaning:

> Ah, sinful nation,
> a people laden with iniquity,
> offspring of evildoers,
> children who deal corruptly! (Isa 1:4)

> But do not gloat over the day of your brother in the day of his misfortune;
> do not rejoice over the people of Judah in the day of their ruin; (Obad 1:12)

In the first example, the guilt of the people of God is increased not just by the use of various words for sin ("laden with iniquity," "evildoers," and "deal corruptly") but especially by highlighting the special relationship that they had with the Lord. They were not just a nation or a people, but they were the Lord's offspring and children, and therefore their rebellion is even more grave. In the Obadiah example, the interplay between the two lines brings greater clarity. The broader terms of the first line ("gloat over," "brother," and "misfortune") are explained with more specific terms in the second line ("rejoice," "people of Judah," and "ruin").

16. See Appendix A for an introductory and, to some extent, simplified table of different types of parallelism.

17. Berlin, *Dynamics of Biblical Parallelism*, 99.

The prophets used intensification to persuade their listeners. Therefore, use of parallelism was not driven by merely aesthetic reasons or even simply to increase memorability. They chose a parallel structure because, as Alter observes, it lends itself well to the intensification effect that the prophets wanted to create. "One frequently encounters, especially in the Prophets and Job, a structure of intensification, a sort of crescendo development, in which certain images and ideas introduced in the first parallel versets are stepped up from line to line and brought to a certain climax."[18] The choice of parallelism, therefore, is geared to help the listeners and readers feel this crescendo and, in the case of the prophets, start to *feel* the heat of judgment or the refreshment of salvation. As Alter explains, this crescendo effect is a key reason why the prophets chose to deliver their urgent message using poetry. "This poetic vehicle of parallelistic verse offered a particularly effective way of imaginatively realizing inevitability, of making powerfully manifest to listeners the idea that consequences they might choose not to contemplate could happen, would happen, would happen without fail."[19] Simply put, packaging an oracle of impending judgment in a parallel structure helped the people not just understand the reality of looming judgment but also to feel it. We can see then how becoming familiar with the prophetic genre, with its frequent use of parallelism, helps us understand the *meaning* and the *purpose* of the prophetic message.

### Figurative Language

Another feature of prophetic literature is the abundance of figurative language. The prophets painted with words. The prophetic literature is saturated with images. The prophets drew these images from their immediate context: lions, horses, chariots, sheep, shepherds, rivers, clay pots, potters, water, cisterns, arrows, hunters, walls, cities, palaces, trees, vineyards, locusts, morning dew, etc. The prophets showed great skill in using simple and mundane elements to express profound truths. Figures of speech (metaphor, simile, personification, hyperbole, irony, world play, etc.) were the paintbrushes that the prophets used to paint memorable pictures on the canvas of people's hearts. By its very definition figurative language is not meant to be taken literally. It would be a great and grave

18. Alter, *Art of Biblical Poetry*, 31.
19. Alter, *Art of Biblical Poetry*, 92.

heresy to understand literally that the Lord is like a moth and like dry rot (Hos 5:12). The prophets are revealing great truths, but they are doing so through figures of speech, and this ought to influence our reading, understanding, and preaching.

As mentioned in the previous chapter, the prophets particularly loved using metaphors. Metaphors are not designed to be dissected; rather they are meant to be imagined and contemplated. The purpose of metaphors was to make an impression in the people's hearts and help them feel the emotional force of the prophetic message. We must allow the prophets to guide us in understanding these metaphors. Arthurs suggests that "Metaphor is a dance both parties must dance. When metaphor fails because the receiver doesn't understand the image or thinks the sender is speaking literally, then the dance becomes a wrestling match. But when a metaphor works, it really works!"[20] I hope you managed to dance with Arthurs and grasp his metaphor about metaphors. Isaiah, Jeremiah, Ezekiel, and company are all excellent dance partners, it is up to us to follow their lead.

Consider, for example, how inadequate our understanding of Jeremiah 2 would be without knowing how to handle metaphors. The message of the prophet in this chapter is packaged in the following metaphors: Israel was a young, faithful bride (2:2) that chased after false gods (2:5–13) and thus became a wild donkey in heat (2:24); the Lord is the fountain of living waters, yet Israel went after the false gods that are broken cisterns that can't hold water (2:13); Israel was more inclined to drink the water from the Nile (trusting in the Egyptians) and the Euphrates (trusting in the Assyrians) rather than trusting the Lord, the fountain of living waters (2:18). These primary metaphors of this chapter are then supported by a plethora of minor metaphors that include lions, camels, prey, firstfruits, harvest, trees, stones, vines, seeds, wasteland, darkness, slaves, yoke, swords, thieves, whores, virgins, soap, stains, ornaments, and skirts. These are all drawn from just one chapter. Metaphor city! This shows how important it is for preachers to grapple with metaphors and with all the figurative language in order to feel the emotions the prophets are conveying and grasp the realities they are representing. Even if we feel more at ease with propositional statements we need to learn to explore and perhaps even enjoy this image-laden language. We need to read slowly and think deeply. We need to ponder the vivid imagery and let the

20. Arthurs, *Preaching with Variety*, 47.

images brew in our minds. To be competent interpreters of the prophets, as Chalmers says, we need to become good contemplatives:

> The picture of the interpreter as a laboratory scientist needs to be balanced by the recognition that good interpreters are also contemplatives—people who spend time ruminating over the text, who enter the experience of the text and allow the text to capture their imagination. Unless both emphases (analysis and contemplative engagement) are at work, it is unlikely that the interpreter will fully grasp the prophets' message for their original audience, and by extension, their audience today.[21]

Moreover, we must not miss another important function of poetical and figurative language. Figurative language is not just a clever way of saying something that could be said in a more straightforward fashion, but it is also a technique to influence our perception of reality. The prophets were keen to give us a different way of imagining the world. Figurative language forces us to consider ideas from a different angle. This introduces us to another important dynamic of the prophetic genre that we should consider before drawing out some important interpretive guidelines to follow.

## Visionary Literature

The prophetic books can also be roughly classified as visionary literature.[22] This is another key trait of prophetic genre that affects our interpretation. The prophets were not just speakers that called the people back to the Lord, they were also visionaries who depicted an alternate reality. I consider this to be broadly true of the prophetic corpus as a whole, and not just of the apocalyptic sections[23] or the so-called "vision reports."[24] The prophets were visionaries. The Torah explains that having visions is a

21. Chalmers, *Interpreting the Prophets*, 118–19.

22. Ryken, *How to Read the Bible as Literature*, 165–75.

23. Undoubtedly this visionary component is even more apparent in the apocalyptic genre. However, the apocalyptic genre is often, and rightfully in my view, considered a subcategory of prophetic literature. Therefore, the visionary component peaks in the apocalyptic sections of the prophetic books (e.g., Dan 7–12; Zechariah), but, as I will argue, it is a trait of the prophetic genre in general. For a discussion of how the apocalyptic grows out of prophecy, see Chalmers, *Interpreting the Prophets*, 120–43.

24. Vision reports are a type of oracle. We will consider the vision reports when exploring the various types of oracles in chapter 7.

hallmark of being a prophet: "When a prophet of the Lord is among you, I reveal myself to him in visions" (Num 12:6). The same idea is echoed in prophetic books: "I spoke to the prophets; it was I who multiplied visions, and through the prophets gave parables" (Hos 12:10). As we mentioned earlier, the Old Testament uses three different terms for "prophet," and the two terms that we have yet to consider—*Hozeh* and *Roeh*—are related to the activity of seeing or being a seer. Prophets see clearly. They see things as they really are. They see the past, the present and, at times, the future. They have the right perspective on reality. For this reason, it is not surprising that all of Isaiah's prophecy (and not just Isaiah 6) is described as "the *vision* . . . that Isaiah *saw*" (Isa 1:1). The book of Nahum is introduced as "the book of the *vision* of Nahum" (Nah 1:1). Habakkuk's oracle is "the oracle that Habbakuk the prophet *saw*" (Hab 1:1). The point is that many of the oracles, and not just the visions, reveal a different perspective on the world by introducing us to, or reminding us of, a greater reality that goes beyond what we see in the present. Therefore, whilst the prophets communicate with a strong dose of realism and directness, a key feature of prophetic literature is this visionary dimension.

The prophets offered a vision of a reality that was dramatically different from the situation the people were in. The prophets' purpose of casting a vision, positive or negative, of the future was to cause an immediate response. Raising eyes to see what tomorrow holds is a great way to get anyone to embark on a new direction in the present. The prophets often presented the future reality as the reversal of the present reality. Judgment was described as the stripping away of all the blessings the people were enjoying at the time in which the prophets delivered their message (Isa 3:16–26). Salvation instead was presented as experiencing the opposite of what the people experienced during times of judgment (Isa 9:1–7). On other occasions the prophets offered a vision of a reality that transcended the visible reality of this world. However, even in this case these visions were geared toward impacting the world in which the prophets and their listeners lived in. Consider, for example, the impact of the vision Isaiah (6:1–5) had of the Lord sitting on the throne, or the vision Ezekiel had of the divine chariot (Ezek 1). Both visions allowed the prophets to see a reality behind the visible world and thus enabled them to live in this world with a greater conviction in the sovereignty of God. Ryken considers this intentional change of perspective a key function of this type of literature: "Visionary literature assaults a purely mundane mindset; in fact, this is one of its main purposes."[25] The prophets take us on a tour beyond the world as we know and experience it. They show us that things are not always as they appear. They allow us to peek behind the curtain and set the "here and now in cosmic perspectives."[26] They enable us to see ourselves and the world around us as part of the ultimate story. This story is unfolding in the present and in the future, in this world and in the world to come, on earth and in heaven. It is a bigger story than we can imagine or fathom, yet we are part of it. We are not alone in this story but are joined by: celestial beings; nations; saints and sinners past, present, and future; inanimate elements of creation (mountains, sea, branches, rivers, stars, etc.); and, of course, the ultimate protagonist, the Lord. The prophets are challenging us to imagine a reality that is difficult for us to grasp because it is beyond the normal dynamics of what we see. They transport us "from the immediate context to a horizon of ultimate possibility."[27] From these ultimate realities the prophets invite us to look back (or look down) and see this world from a different vantage point. They invite us to see the temporal in view of the eternal. In doing so, the prophets are not primarily interested in enabling us to *understand* all that is or that will take place, but want us to *sense* and be *transformed* by this distinct way of seeing reality.

This explains, at least in part, the reason why the prophetic books and oracles do not always follow a linear or logical structure. These structures are ideal in the transfer of precise and coherent information. The goal of the prophets, and therefore of the prophetic genre, however, is not primarily to *inform* but to *transform*. To achieve this, they employed a dream-like structure. The prophetic books and oracles, like dreams, do not tend to be primarily logical; rather they tend to be series of apparently disjointed elements (images, symbols, thoughts, people, places, etc.) that, grouped together, provide a vivid, yet at times confusing, experience. This does not mean they are devoid of any sequence. Dreams are often frenetic and intense, yet even our most bizarre dreams have a sequence or a vaguely discernible plot. The same can be said of the prophetic oracles. Typically, there is a progression, a palpable intensification, as we noted in the previous chapter. However, we must keep in mind that the primary function of the prophetic genre is not to enable us to connect all the dots

25. Ryken, *How to Read the Bible as Literature*, 167.

26. Alter, *Art of Biblical Poetry*, 183.

27. Alter, *Art of Biblical Poetry*, 189.

of the prophetic message, but rather to be jolted by seeing our lives from the correct vantage point. This change of perspective, as Ryken explains, is a shock to the system:

> Visionary literature, with its arresting strangeness, breaks through our normal way of thinking and shocks us into seeing that things are not as they appear. Visionary writing attacks our ingrained patterns of deep-level thought in an effort to convince us of such things as that the world will not always continue as it now is, that there is something drastically wrong with the status quo, or that reality cannot be confined to the physical world that we perceive with our senses. Visionary literature is not cozy fireside reading. It gives us the shock treatment.[28]

We have completed our profiling of this genre. As mentioned at the beginning, defining and describing the prophetic genre is a tough task. Nevertheless, we have identified the main traits of this kind of literature. Here is my effort to bring some of the key elements we have seen together: The prophetic books are anthologies of vigorous oracles and persuasive visions delivered by the prophets to the people of Israel in beautiful, yet functional, poetical language designed to align our view of reality with God's view and thus transform our lives. With this understanding we have now become somewhat familiar with the environment we are in. We have found our bearings and our footing. We are now ready to explore this world of oracles and visions.

## GUIDELINES FOR INTERPRETATION

In order not to get lost in this exploration, let me offer a decalogue of interpretive guidelines that should keep us on track. These are broad guidelines that can be applied across the prophetic books, and not just to the narrow category of prophecies regarding the future.[29] In a sense we are simply making explicit some of the implications that inevitably emerge from our considerations of the main traits of the prophetic genre.

---

28. Ryken, *How to Read the Bible as Literature*, 169–70.

29. The discussion of the interpretation of prophetic literature often focuses narrowly on how to interpret the predictive elements of prophecy, rather than providing interpretative guidelines for the prophetic literature in general. This focus only equips the interpreter's understanding of a limited section of the prophetic genre. It is for this reason that I first offer general guidelines in this chapter before tackling how to handle future prophecies in the next one.

## Decalogue

1. *Grasp the compositional strategy of the book.* The prophetic books do have an internal logic and unity. We can begin to discover a prophetic book's macro structure by reading it multiple times and asking the right questions. What are the primary themes that dominate the book? How do these themes develop as the book unfolds? Are there any obvious demarcations of literary units? Good commentaries also help us find answers to these questions. Once we recognize the structure and purpose of a prophetic book, we are better placed to understand both its overall message as well as the content and function of specific oracles contained within it.

2. *Think oracles.*[30] Since oracles are the main characteristic of the prophetic genre, rightly interpreting the prophets will depend largely on our ability to identify the logic, sections, and subsections of the oracles.[31]

3. *Anchor the message to its historical context.* We need to listen to the message of the prophets through the ears of the original hearers. The more we investigate the prophets' historical, theological, political, social, and moral contexts the better we will understand their message for us today.[32]

4. *Identify the prophet's intent.* "The prophets . . . were preeminently poets with a 'message.'"[33] They proclaimed the oracles of God to the people of God in a specific historical context. These speeches were not just entertainment but were powerful divine speeches aimed at bringing about transformation. The prophets spoke with a goal in mind. Often, they denounced the horror of people's sin and warned them of judgment in order to call the people to repentance. On other occasions, particularly in times of difficulty, the prophets proclaimed the power and the promises of God to instill faith in their listeners. They preached to elicit a change. Identifying

---

30. Fee and Stuart, *How to Read the Bible*, 193.

31. In chapter 7 we will take a closer look at the various forms of prophetic oracles.

32. In chapter 6 we will travel to the world of the prophets to consider the importance of historical research in determining the meaning of the prophetic message.

33. Alter, *Art of Biblical Poetry*, 203.

the intent of the prophet's sermon can be a beacon that can help you work through the details of an oracle.

5. *Develop literary sensitivity to the poetic language and imagery.* To interpret prophetic literature we need to spot, enjoy, contemplate, and understand the typical parallel structures and the wide-ranging arsenal of figures of speech the prophets employed: hyperbole, metaphor, simile, wordplay, sarcasm, personification, etc.

6. *Listen with your heart, not just your head.*[34] Because the language of the prophets is designed to *transform* more than *inform*, we need to follow Sandy's advice and listen with our heart: "We need a hermeneutic of the heart; in most cases, prophecy is emotional as much as it is cerebral."[35] The prophetic books are breathtaking for the beauty of their form and the depth of their content. The prophets were keen to move and, at times, even shock their listeners. They employed poetry to convey staggering truths in stunning ways. Interpreting poetry cannot be achieved by distant and detached dissection. Poetry demands emotive engagement. Therefore, to grasp the prophetic message, we must approach their poetry with both an active mind and an open heart. We must be prepared to read slowly, think deeply, and *feel* intensely.

7. *Use your imagination.* The prophets often want us to gain a new perspective on our reality by placing this world, including our lives, within the context of ultimate realities. Picturing this new perspective requires imagination. It is not an uncontrolled imagination since we are on a guided tour.

8. *Proceed with caution when approaching future prophecies.* The genre choice is prompting us (or perhaps shouting at us) to recognize that the intention of the authors and the Author of the prophetic books was not to give us a blueprint for the future but to help us feel the reality that the Lord is sovereign.[36]

9. *Focus on the full picture rather than on the pieces of the puzzle.* The oracles typically have a main point that is super clear. This main point is reinforced with many details that may prove to be much

---

34. Sandy, *Plowshares and Pruning Hooks*, 198.

35. Sandy, *Plowshares and Pruning Hooks*, 198.

36. In the next chapter we will put on our safety equipment and discuss the challenges of interpreting the predictive elements.

harder to understand. The best strategy to understand the details is to step back and look at the bigger picture.

10. *Stay humble.* The prophetic literature is powerful, fascinating, and complex. When interpreting the prophets, we should lean on the side of caution rather than dogmatism, humility rather than arrogance. Humility is a key virtue of the best interpreters of the prophetic books.

## QUIRKS AND PERKS

"Do your best to present yourself to God as one approved, a worker who has no need to be ashamed, rightly handling the word of truth" (2 Tim 2:15). As preachers we are exhorted to rightly handle the word of God. This includes rightly handling the prophetic books. The prophetic genre certainly has its quirks and perks. It is our job, as interpreters and preachers, to get to know these quirks and know how to fully benefit from the perks. The Lord inspired a significant portion of his word in this particular genre. This was not an error or a poor choice. It was the best possible choice to convey this part of the Lord's revelation to us and to achieve in us what he wants to achieve. The Lord is inviting us to travel through the world of the prophets for this part of the journey of Scripture. Understanding and enjoying the key features of the environment of the prophetic world is the best way to progress in our journey. Complaining or mistreating this environment will not only prevent us from making any progress but may also cause us to go off track. The above guidelines will not only keep us on track but will enable us to enjoy the scenery of this part of God's special revelation.

# Chapter 5

# COME BACK FROM THE FUTURE

> "I am God, and there is none like me, declaring the end
> from the beginning and from ancient times things not yet
> done, saying, 'My counsel shall stand, and I will accomplish
> all my purpose.'"
>
> —ISA 46:9B-10

PROCEED WITH CAUTION WHEN approaching future prophecies. This command from our decalogue merits further probing. We are intrigued by the future. A surprising amount of people are willing to pay good money to know today what will take place tomorrow. This inquisitiveness leads many Bible readers to rush to the prophetic sections of Scripture to look for quick answers. Haste, however, is a poor counselor, and can lead to many interpretive errors (and horrors). We must proceed with caution, and not rush to unwarranted and simplistic answers, when interpreting prophetic literature. Notably, some of the greatest differences among evangelical scholars emerge in the sections of the prophetic books that reveal the future. Furthermore, not only do scholars disagree on how to interpret them, they also disagree about which sections of the prophetic books should be considered future prophecies. This should be a warning sign for us. If we ignore this warning sign we are likely to end up off the road. And if we are pastors or preachers, then we are not just driving ourselves, but a busload of people, off the road. In this chapter we want to slow down to consider how to interpret and preach future prophecies. I will resist the temptation of presenting and defending my own eschatological view.[1] Rather than offering quick answers, I am much more interested in helping us ask the right questions. After all, the brightest students are not the ones that know all the right answers but the ones that ask the right questions. The same is true of students of prophecy. In this chapter we pose three key questions that will help us accurately understand and faithfully preach future prophecies. Before we do this, however, we must ascertain if the prophets did indeed speak about the future.

## FORETELLERS AND FORTHTELLERS

The prevailing *popular* opinion is that the prophets were primarily predictors of the future. The prophets are commonly imagined as eccentric messengers with the God-given ability to see and announce the future ahead of time. The prophets are thus considered divinely sanctioned *foretellers* who, without the aid of a crystal ball, were able to provide information about the future. Fee and Stuart dissent from this wave of public opinion and provide striking statistics to support their argument. "Less than 2 percent of Old Testament prophecy is messianic. Less than 5 percent specifically describes the new-covenant age. Less than 1 percent concerns events yet to come in our time."[2] Although these statistics are hard to evaluate without knowing the criteria used, it seems obvious that it is inaccurate to consider predicting the future the main function of the prophets. The prophets were much more than mere foretellers.

In view of this, the prevailing *scholarly* opinion is to primarily consider the prophets as God's forthtellers (i.e., speaking forth the word of God) rather than foretellers. The emphasis is on placing the prophets within their historical context. The prophets declared the word of God to the people of Israel in their day. Therefore, we must travel back to the world of the prophets to understand the message they proclaimed, rather than speculating about possible and fanciful future fulfillments. When you catapult the prophetic *word* out of the prophetic *world* you reduce

1. Eschatology is the technical term that refers to the study of what Scripture teaches about the end times. A good place to start to compare the primary eschatological viewpoints is the Counterpoint series (See Gundry and Block, *Three Views on the Millennium and Beyond*; Gundry and Pate, *Four Views on the Book of Revelation*; Gundry and Hultberg, *Three Views on the Rapture*).

2. Fee and Stuart, *How to Read the Bible*, 182.

the prophets to little more than journalists who reported on what would take place several millennia later. In doing so, the prophetic message becomes largely irrelevant to their original audience. Most scholars are thus highly suspicious of any interpretation that does not take into serious consideration the historical context in which the prophetic message was originally delivered.[3]

Whilst this cautious approach has merit, we risk overstating the case. As often happens in theology, the pendulum swings rapidly from one extreme to the other, spending far too little time in the center. The prophets did speak about the future. The prophets were visionaries. They offered a God-given vision of the past, present, and the *future*. Their books are full of forward-looking warnings of judgment and promises of salvation. Often the prophets predicted the immediate future. Sometimes they looked beyond and announced the distant future. In both cases they lifted the eyes of the people to glance at their collective tomorrow. So, were the prophets foretellers or forthtellers? Both. They were God's forthtellers who foretold the future to bring about change in the present.

## THE PROPHETS AND THE FUTURE

So then, the issue is not *if* they spoke about the future but *how* they spoke about the future. This is where it gets tricky. The prophets did not lay out the future in a neat and tidy timeline. Nor did they provide a prophetic compendium in which they explained the fulfillment of each prophecy in clear and precise language. Instead they used language and images from their context to paint a picture of the future that far exceeded their experiences and imaginations. To begin to see this picture clearly, we must avoid the myopia of uncritically superimposing our own eschatological system on the prophetic message; rather, we must attentively and patiently linger until the picture that the prophets painted comes into the right focus. Here are three questions to ponder that will help us linger when contemplating specific prophecies.[4]

3. See Chalmers, *Interpreting the Prophets*, 34–37; Fee and Stuart, *How to Read the Bible*, 187–211; Wright, *Sweeter than Honey*, 179.

4. I have drawn and benefited from D. Brent Sandy's insights on the language of biblical prophecy. Sandy lists a longer list of seven questions, which he calls "problems," that contribute to making interpreting the prophets a challenge. I have limited the number of questions to bring greater focus. Nevertheless, when tackling these three questions I also deal with some of the other problems Sandy highlights (Sandy, *Plowshares and Pruning Hooks*, 33–57).

## To what degree, if any, is the prophecy clothed in figurative language?

"I shot myself in the foot." The meaning of this sentence changes drastically depending on its context. If I am desperately shouting it down the phone to an ambulance operator, it has one meaning. If I am casually using this phrase to lament to my spouse that the job I volunteered to do will take much more effort than I expected, then the connotation will be much different. The same sentence has different meanings depending if it is used (and taken) literally or figuratively. The wording, tone, and context offer clues to discern the way in which I am using this phrase. You do not have to be a linguist to grasp that the meaning of words changes drastically when someone is speaking literally or figuratively.

The Old Testament prophets spoke both literally and figuratively. Many of us tend toward a default literal reading of all of Scripture, including the prophets. We choose this approach in order to lean on the safe side. The problem is that this literal reading of Scripture easily slips into a literalistic reading of Scripture. What I mean by a literalistic reading is focusing exclusively on the meaning of single words rather than on how the words are being used and linked together to convey meaning (grammar, syntax, genre, etc.). Even the Reformers, who championed focusing on the plain sense of Scripture, did not intend that all of Scripture should be read the same way. Rather they advocated for reading in accordance with the conventions and norms of the specific types of literature. Applying this principle to the prophetic genre, which leans heavily toward poetry, means our default literal reading may not be the best approach. I would equally caution against a default figurative reading of the prophetic genre because not all the prophetic message is expressed in poetry. The prophets use a wide range of language that goes from literal to figurative. Indeed, at times the prophets blended the two, forming a hybrid. What this means for us is that a key to understanding the prophetic message is determining when we should employ a literal reading, when we should employ a figurative reading, and when we should employ a middle-of-the-road reading.

Consider, as an example, the description of peace that the prophet Isaiah offers when describing surprising animal behavior (11:6–9): wolves dwelling with lambs, leopards lying with goats, lions lounging with calves, bears grazing with cows, and a child playing with snakes. What is the prophet describing? A time when kids will literally play with snakes, and wolves and lambs will be best chums? Or is he using this description of animals to announce the reversal of the effect of the fall on all of creation? Or is he using the animals, as often happened in the ancient world (cf. Jer 5:6), as representatives of nations, thus describing the end of wars among nations? Or is he simply painting a utopian picture of peace in concrete language so that we long for that day, but without necessarily offering us details of how the actual dynamics will be experienced? Note that in none of the possible interpretations has the prophecy been deprived of a real historical fulfillment. All interpretations point to a real historical time in the future when peace will prevail. The issue, therefore, is not historical versus figurative; rather, the issue concerns with what degree of literalness (or, if you prefer, with what degree of figurativeness) the future historical event is described. This nuance is important because the push toward an exclusively literal reading of Scripture is driven by a desire to defend the historicity of Scripture. We must, however, realize that in no way does a less literal reading of Scripture necessarily preclude a strong stance in favor of its historical accuracy. Furthermore, a true desire to honor Scripture includes not only the commendable desire to defend its historicity but also a firm commitment to reading (interpreting and preaching) Scripture according to the linguistic properties that the authors employed and the Author inspired.

So, how do we determine if the prophet is speaking literally or figuratively? I am afraid I know of no shortcuts. We linger. We look carefully. We scrutinize the text. We assess the choice of wording. We look for figures of speech. We note if the language employed is poetic, prosaic, or a hybrid. We widen our lens and consider the context. We allow this context to influence our evaluation of the literalness of the language used. Consider, for example, how the context sheds light on Isaiah's description of the desolate country (1:7): "Your country lies desolate; your cities are burned with fire; in your very presence foreigners devour your land; it is desolate, as overthrown by foreigners." Our first instinct may be to take the description of the desolate country (1:7) in a literal sense. Isaiah's words seem to be a fitting representation of what occurred as a result of the foreign invasions that took place during the prophetic period. However, doubts emerge when you look at the immediate context in which Isaiah is using various images, varying from sickness (1:6) to a booth in a vineyard (1:8), to describe the dreadful spiritual condition of the people of Israel. Based on both the literary and historical contexts it seems best to consider Isaiah's language as a figurative description of the spiritual state of Israel that, during his lifetime, became an apt description of the desolation of the country.

How are we to then read prophetic literature? A default literal reading is simply naïve. Similarly, a default figurative reading is incautious. Let us patiently linger to consider if the language is literal or figurative to avoid shooting ourselves in the foot.

## To what degree, if any, is the prophecy subject to conditions?

"It is not *what* you said, it is *how* you said it!" I have heard this sentence once or twice in my lifetime. I need to hear it from time to time to be reminded that in communication meaning is not just conveyed by content but also by tone and context. These elements cannot be separated. We grasp this intuitively from a young age. For example, I recently thundered the following words to my kids during an exasperatingly long (and warm!) drive to the beach: "I will turn the car around and we will head home!" My children had spent most of the journey arguing with each other and I had reached my limit. What these words reveal (apart from my faulty parenting) is how content, tone, and context intermingle to convey meaning. This is especially true when emotions run high. At first glance it may appear that I was making a flat *unconditional* announcement. The beach was no longer our destination. However, your understanding of my words changes when you discover that an "if-clause" prefixed the above statement. "*If* I hear one more word from either of you, *then* I will turn the car around and we will head home!" The wider context clarifies that for the beach to remain our destination, certain *conditions* needed to be met. My tone also contributed to clarifying the meaning and the conditions of the threat. The precise wording that I used, "*one more* word from either of you," was hyperbolic. As you might imagine, my goal was not to completely silence my kids for the rest of the journey. I wanted them to stop arguing, not for them to stop speaking altogether. Guess what? It worked. After a time of silence to soak up my reprimand, they chatted away for the rest of the journey excited about the prospect of a day at the beach. When we then reached the beach, the kids did not accuse me of being a liar for not following through with my threat of going home after one more word. They had understood by the context and tone the true purpose and meaning of my words. This illustrates that even young kids can grasp that strong, emotive language can often sacrifice precision for the sake of persuasion.

These are all factors that we must keep in mind when seeking to determine the meaning of the prophets' persuasive oracles. The prophets made striking statements, both promises and threats, about the future. The task that we have as interpreters is to consider the content, context, and tone of their words.[5] It is up to us now to ascertain which of these bold statements are flat predictions of the future that will take place no matter what, and which have a conditional component to them. We should not assume that all that the prophets said about the future is set in stone; instead we should be on the lookout for the "if-clause." The Lord illustrates this dynamic, and its relationship with his sovereignty, to the prophet Jeremiah by sending him on a field trip to a potter's house (Jer 18:1–5). Seeing a potter at work enables the prophet to understand how *the Potter* works (Jer 18:6–10):

> O house of Israel, can I not do with you as this potter has done? declares the Lord. Behold, like the clay in the potter's hand, so are you in my hand, O house of Israel. If at any time I declare concerning a nation or a kingdom, that I will pluck up and break down and destroy it, and if that nation, concerning which I have spoken, turns from its evil, I will relent of the disaster that I intended to do to it. And if at any time I declare concerning a nation or a kingdom that I will build and plant it, and if it does evil in my sight, not listening to my voice, then I will relent of the good that I had intended to do to it.

The message is clear. What the Lord declares concerning the future of a nation, for good or for bad, is dependent on the people's response to his word. This conditional component in no way negates that the Lord is sovereign; rather, it is how the Lord exercises his sovereignty in history. After all, regardless of how much the Potter is willing to concede to the clay, the controlling factor always lies within his hands.

---

5. Out of these three elements, identifying the tone is the most challenging. Whilst tone can easily be grasped in oral communication, determining an author's tone in literature is much harder. Here are initial steps to take to determine the prophetic tone: 1) consider the word choice; 2) ponder the imagery; 3) read the oracles out loud; 4) get to know the author; 5) associate the passage to a color or a melody; 6) think about the content; 7) familiarize yourself with the different prophetic forms and oracles; 8) trust your gut. We will return to this matter in chapter 7, when we will consider how to replicate some of the prophets' rhetorical techniques.

The task of spotting the conditional component is straightforward when the *protasis* (the if-clause that expresses a condition) is explicit. However, we need to be aware that on some occasions it may be implicit. The best-known example is Jonah's brief prophecy to Nineveh: "Forty more days and Nineveh will be destroyed" (Jonah 3:4). These words appear to be unequivocal and irrevocable. Yet, as we know by the continuation of the narrative, they contained an implicit conditional clause, to the relief of the Ninevites (3:9–19), and to the frustration of the prophet (4:1). Moreover, by the prophet's reaction we learn that this implied conditional clause was no surprise to him because it is rooted in God's character (4:2). This episode in Nineveh exemplifies that the if-clause dynamic may be at work even when not overtly stated.

Two additional considerations from the book of Jeremiah complicate things further. The first is that the if-clause can have an expiry date. The window of opportunity for the people to turn back to God will not stay open forever. The Lord is slow to anger, he is willing to patiently wait for the people to repent, but he will not wait forever. The Lord warns his people of this by sending Jeremiah a second time to the potter's house (19:1). This time the prophet is invited to buy a flask (i.e., hardened clay). The Lord then instructs the prophet to go and smash the flask in the valley of the Son of Hinnom[6] (19:2) to illustrate the Lord's judgment on the city of Jerusalem (19:10–13). If the people did not change their ways, then they would soon become a hardened vessel that would be broken "so that it can never be mended" (19:11b). The if-clause had an expiry date. After such a date, even the intercession of men like Moses and Samuel would not reverse the inevitable (Jer 15:1).

The second consideration from Jeremiah is that a conditional element may be at work even in the promises of blessings, and not just in the threats of judgment. We tend to assume that embedded in the threats of judgments lies an implied opportunity for repentance, yet we fail to see that the promises of blessings can also be tied to a response of faith and obedience. We simplistically consider the threats of judgment to be conditional and the promises of restoration to be unconditional. This optimistic conclusion is not entirely off track. By the grace of God, we can cling to many unconditional promises in his word. However, we must

---

6. A valley in the south side of Jerusalem where Jeremiah's contemporaries practiced child sacrifice (7:31). It became a burning dump outside the city. *Gehenna* (cf. Matt 5:22, 29–30; 10:28; etc.), which is a transliteration of the Hebrew term *Gehinnom* (the valley of Hinnom), and became a reference to the unquenchable fires of hell.

also be alert to the fact that at times conditions are linked to the promises of God. Throughout his ministry Jeremiah clashed with false prophets. Jeremiah was claiming to speak on behalf of the Lord, warning the people of judgment in the form of the enemy's sword, famine, and removal from the land (14:1–12). On the other side you had a more conspicuous group of so-called prophets who were also claiming to speak on behalf of the Lord and were reassuring the people with these words: "You shall not see sword, nor shall you have famine, but I will give you assured peace in this place" (14:13). Without a doubt this second message was more attractive. Jeremiah had a hard (and long) time competing against this group of prophets. He ended up accused of being a traitor, an ally of the Babylonians. The success of the larger group was not simply because their message was more alluring but also because their message seemed to echo blessings that the Lord had promised: "I will give peace in the land, and you shall lie down, and none shall make you afraid. And I will remove harmful beasts from the land, and the sword shall not go through your land" (Lev 26:6). In view of these promised blessings, how do we then explain the exile? Were the more conspicuous group of prophets right? The context of the promises of peace, protection, and prosperity within the Mosaic covenant (Lev 26) makes it explicit that these promises were contingent upon obedience to the word of God. The if-clause with which the paragraph begins makes the conditional component crystal clear: "if you walk in my statutes and observe my commandments . . . " (Lev 26:3).

The prophets lived in a dramatic time and used dramatic language. The people of God were drifting along the river of indifference, not realizing that around the bend awaited a deadly waterfall. The people, however, were blind and deaf to all the warning signs. Their hearts were cold, indifferent, or even hardened. The prophets stood at the edge, desperately pleading with the people to change direction. Desperate times called for desperate measures. It was not the time to calmly work through all the fine print or to detail all the conditions of the threats and promises. It was a time to shock the people with bold language. It is now our responsibility to explore the prophetic word by engaging in some hard thinking: Is the prophecy conditional or unconditional? Do all the prophecies of judgment include an implied opportunity for repentance? Is there an expiry date on the if-clause? What about the prophecies of restoration? Are they conditional or unconditional? If they are conditional, what are the conditions? These are weighty questions without simplistic answers. To begin to find the answers we must give careful thought not just to *what* they said but also to *how* they said it. We have one more multifaceted question to consider before establishing some guidelines that will give us concrete help when preaching future prophecies.

## To what degree, if any, has the prophecy been fulfilled?

"The hike was tough, but the view sure is breathtaking." This has been my cliched observation the handful of times I have made it to the summit of a mountain. For a city boy, leaving streets and traffic jams to venture to the mountains can be a challenging experience. Mountaineering is not my forte. I seem to easily lose my bearings as I struggle up uneven paths, wearing the wrong type of shoes. The difficulty is exacerbated by the constant illusion of being able to see the summit within a stone's throw, only to then discover it was a mere optical illusion—the so-called false peaks. Nevertheless, once I do manage to reach the summit, I recognize the breathtaking view is well worth the effort of the climb. Interpreting future prophecies can be like mountaineering: easy to lose your bearings, often you feel ill-equipped, and optical illusions are a constant dynamic; and yet if you persevere you will be rewarded with stunning views. The feeling of disorientation is strong when you are trying to determine which period the prophet is speaking about, or when you are trying to pinpoint the precise fulfillment of a specific prophecy. Part of the difficulty is that prophecies can be fulfilled in at least five different, yet at times overlapping, ways. Let us explore these various ways together by taking a trip to the mountains.

### Immediate Fulfillment

This is the most common type of fulfillment. The prophets were speaking primarily to the people of Israel and Judah in their historical context. Many of the prophecies were short-range prophecies that were fulfilled during, or shortly after, the lifetime of the prophet who made the prediction. The prophet Micah, for example, lived from the reign of Jotham (750–735 BC) to the reign of Hezekiah (715–687 BC). His first oracle (1:1–7) was an announcement of judgment upon Samaria. The Lord announced through the prophet that he would make Samaria like a "heap in the open country" (1:6). Not long after (722 BC) the pronouncement of these words, the brutal Assyrian army captured Samaria and scattered the people of Israel across their empire (2 Kgs 17:6). The fulfillment of this sobering prophecy took place in Micah's lifetime. Micah also prophesied that Jerusalem would become "a heap of ruins" (3:12). This took place over a century later (587–586 BC), yet still within the context of Old Testament history. Jeremiah was an eyewitness to this tragic event (39:1–10). Indeed, Jeremiah had the bittersweet (I suspect primarily bitter) experience of seeing the fulfillment of what he had predicted. These examples illustrate that the most obvious place to find the fulfillment of a specific prophecy is in the immediate context. This is true not only for the many prophecies of destruction of Samaria and Jerusalem, but also for the judgment on the surroundings nations and for the prophecies of physical restoration following the exile. If you trace the prophet's obvious line of sight, you will have a good chance of finding the mountain he is describing.

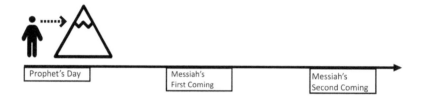

**Immediate Fulfillment:** The fulfillment of the prophecy takes place in the immediate historical context of the prophet.

## Distant Fulfillment

In some instances, having considered the immediate historical context, it becomes obvious the prophets were prophesying about an event that did not take place in their lifetime, but rather many centuries later. The prophets demonstrated remarkable precision with both short-range and long-range prophecies. The time lapse between the prophecy being announced and its fulfillment can be long centuries and, on some occasions, even millennia (cf. Isa 65:17–25). Nevertheless, because this time lapse was not always evident to the prophets and their hearers, the prophecy continued to have a significant impact upon them. Furthermore, even when the time lapse was evident, the prophecy was nonetheless relevant to the original hearers because its purpose was to widen their horizon and offer a new perspective.

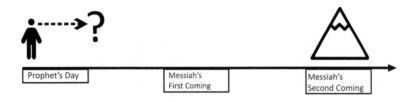

| Prophet's Day | Messiah's First Coming | Messiah's Second Coming |

**Distant Fulfillment:** Long-range prophecies that point to an event that will take place many centuries after they were spoken. The prophet is often unaware of the time distance.

Consider, for example, the impact of the prophecy of Isaiah 9:2 on the original audience. "The people who walked in darkness have seen a great light; those who dwelt in a land of deep darkness, on them has light shone." These words would have been of great comfort to a people who would soon "be thrust into thick darkness" (8:22). The immediate context (8:1–22) reveals that the thick darkness was caused by the dark shadow of the imminent invasion of the Assyrians. The first territories that would be overcome by the gloom of the Assyrian invasion were the northern lands, such as Zebulun and Naphtali, the so-called Galilee of the gentiles (9:1). Yet these are the very places Isaiah singles out to announce that their darkness will not last forever. Into a dramatic circumstance, where all the people could see was distress and darkness, the prophet lifts their eyes to show them that a great light is coming that will dispel all darkness. What hope and comfort for the people of Israel in the day of Isaiah! Yet we know the fulfillment of this prophecy took place over 600 years later when Jesus began his public ministry in Galilee, in the territory of Zebulun and Naphtali (Matt 4:12–17).

The question then becomes: Did the prophet and his audience know it was a long-range prophecy? Did he know the mountain he was describing was many miles away? The first impression you get by reading Isaiah is that he expected it to happen in his day or, at the very least, in the immediate future. The prophet ties the unfolding of these events ultimately to the birth of a remarkable child: Wonderful Counselor, Mighty God, Everlasting Father, and Prince of Peace (9:6–7). Note the words the prophet uses to describe the arrival of this child: "For *to us* a child is born, *to us* a son is given." The prophet seems to indicate all these events would happen *to them,* yet no child in Isaiah's day could even come close to the above description. Furthermore, from our vantage point we clearly see the prophecy is pointing forward to Jesus, the only One who can legitimately hold these titles. In view of this we may be tempted to conclude that Isaiah misread the timing of the fulfillment of this prophecy. However, that would be unfair. The prophet Isaiah, like the rest of the prophets, was interested in placing the spotlight on the certainty and impact of the prophetic event rather than on the time of fulfillment.[7] This was a long-range prophecy with an immediate impact.

As we journey through the prophetic writings, we will encounter long-range prophecies. The Lord enabled the prophets to predict the future in order to accredit the prophets (Deut 18:22), and also to demonstrate his superiority compared to other gods (Isa 46:8–11). This was, and continues to be, one of the main functions of long-range prophecies. Seeing how the prophetic words are fulfilled centuries after they were first uttered testifies to the power and veracity of the word of God.

Furthermore, the purpose of the long-range Old Testament prophecies was to lift the eyes of the people to look to a future age. What age were they looking to? To narrow the question: Did the new age that the prophets announced portray the first coming or the second coming of Christ? The New Testament writers disclose that this new age involves the first and the second coming of Christ. This new age was inaugurated with the incarnation of the Divine Child Isaiah spoke about. With the Messiah's arrival, the kingdom of God decisively and permanently broke into human history (Luke 17:20–21). Yet the ultimate consummation of this new age will take place at the second coming of the Messiah. This tension is frequently and helpfully captured with the expression "the kingdom of God is already and not yet." Today we are living in an overlapping age where the kingdom of God has already been inaugurated, and yet its full manifestation lies in the future. Oscar Cullman famously illustrated this dynamic by likening it to the period between D-Day and VE-Day at the end of the Second World War. D-Day was the decisive moment the Allies landed on the Normandy beaches. This was the game-changer that

7. Isaiah's lack of interest in timing is also evident when you look at the tenses of the verbs that Isaiah used throughout this prophecy. The prophet used past-tense verbs ("the people who have walked in darkness have seen a great light"), present-tense verbs ("for to us a child is born, to us a son is given"), and future-tense verbs ("his name shall be called") to describe a series of events that were in the future compared to his vantage point. Timing was simply not his main concern. Moreover, describing future events with past-tense and present-tense verbs conveyed the certainty that the Lord would fulfill what he had promised.

determined the victory of the Allies in France and across Western Europe. VE-Day was the day, nearly a year later, when Nazi Germany surrendered, and the Allies declared victory. We live between God's D-Day and God's VE-Day. We live with a solid hope, knowing the decisive day, the game-changer, has already taken place. "The hope of the final victory is so much the more vivid because of the unshakably firm conviction that the battle that decides the victory has already taken place."[8]

With this understanding we are better positioned to consider how and when the long-range prophecies have been, and will be, fulfilled. The Old Testament prophets pointed forward to this age to come. Some of their long-range prophecies have already found their fulfillment in the first coming of the Messiah (D-Day), some are in the process of being fulfilled, and some await fulfillment in the second coming of the Messiah (VE-Day). With regards to the prophecies that still await fulfillment in the future, it is worth taking a leaf out of the Old Testament prophets' book and focusing on the certainty and impact of the future prophecy, rather than speculating about the timing or the detail. We will come back to this.

### Progressive Fulfillment

A third type of fulfillment is the progressive fulfillment. At times, the prophets grouped prophecies together that pointed both to an immediate and to a distant fulfillment. We have already seen a hint of this in the last example in Isaiah, where the prophet transitioned rapidly from the immediate context of the imminent Assyrian invasions (Isa 8) to the distance fulfillment of the arrival of the Messiah (9:1–9). This type of transition is not uncommon in the prophetic writings and can be even more sudden than the above example. This is where the analogy of the mountains really comes into its own. Progressive fulfillment is commonly and helpfully illustrated with the analogy of a mountain range. When you see a mountain range in the distance it appears that all the mountains are approximately in the same location and attached to each other. When you travel closer to the mountain range you discover it was an optical illusion, as the mountains actually have great valleys separating them. However, from your original standpoint these great distances could not be detected. Similarly, when the prophets spoke about the future, they seemed to

8. Cullman, *Christ and Time*, 87.

have had two-dimensional sight. They presented events, separated from one another by a considerable time lapse, as taking place simultaneously. However, as we travel through time and get closer to the events, we realize that century-long valleys separate one event from the other.

The prophet's "frontal" perspective.

Sideview perspective emphasizing the time distance between the events.

**Progressive Fulfillment:** Prophecies related to events that are separated from one another by considerable time gaps but described as simultaneous by the prophet.

The best-known example of this is found in Isaiah 61:1–2: "The Spirit of the Lord God is upon me, because the Lord has anointed me, to bring good news to the poor; he has sent me to bind up the brokenhearted, to proclaim liberty to the captives, and the opening of the prison to those who are bound; to proclaim the year of the Lord's favor, and the day of vengeance of our God." Jesus read from this passage in the synagogue in Nazareth (Luke 4:16–22) and masterfully helps us notice the time lapse between aspects of this prophecy. He achieved this by interrupting the reading of the passage mid-sentence. Jesus omitted "the day of vengeance of our God." Before he reached these words, he rolled up the scroll and took his seat, attracting the gazes of all who were present. Having captured their attention, he then proclaimed: "Today this Scripture has been fulfilled in your hearing." Why did he not include the section about the vengeance of God? The prevailing explanation is that Jesus omitted it because the display of wrath will take place at Christ's second coming. From the standpoint of Isaiah, the year of the Lord's favor and the day of vengeance seemed simultaneous, yet from our standpoint we see a great temporal valley between the fulfillment of these two aspects of the same prophecy.

Since the prophets skip over time valleys, we should take into consideration that a single oracle may contain aspects that have been fulfilled in the past, aspects which are in the process of being fulfilled in the present, and aspects which await fulfillment in the future. Past, present, and future history all come into play.

## Typological Fulfillment

A close relation to the progressive fulfillment is the typological fulfillment. Typology can be understood as a person, institution, or event in the Old Testament that represents (or foreshadows) a similar yet greater person, institution, or event in the New Testament. We learn this interpretive approach directly from the authors of Scripture.[9] It is therefore not surprising to find typology also in prophetic fulfillments. On occasions, the prophets predicted an event would soon take place in their immediate context, that typologically foreshadowed a similar, yet greater, event in the more distant future. This is distinguishable from the progressive fulfillment in that in this instance the prophet is describing a single event, and not the unfolding over time of several events clustered together. However, this single event reflects an even greater event in the future. Sometimes this type of fulfillment is referred to as dual fulfillment, in which the immediate event is the partial fulfillment and the ultimate event is the full and final fulfillment.

A famous, and to some extent mysterious, example is Isaiah's remarkable prophecy that "the virgin shall conceive and bear a son, and shall call his name Immanuel" (7:14). As New Testament believers we immediately, and correctly, see this prophecy as being a staggering prediction of the virgin birth of Christ (Matt 1:21–23). What we often neglect to consider however is the way in which this prophecy found its fulfillment in Isaiah's day. These words were given by the prophet Isaiah to Ahaz, king of Judah. In response to the threat of the Syro-Ephraimitic coalition, king Ahaz places his faith in the king of Assyria (2 Kgs 16:1–9) rather than placing his faith in the Lord (7:9). To redirect the king's faith away from the

---

9. The New Testament writers often referred to the Old Testament using this interpretive paradigm. Paul, for example, tells us that Adam was a type of Christ (Rom 5:14), the Passover lamb foreshadowed the sacrifice of Christ (1 Cor 5:17), and the rock in the wilderness prefigured Christ (1 Cor 10:4).

Assyrians and to himself, the Lord, via the prophet Isaiah, invites the king to ask for a sign (7:10–11). Ahaz foolishly and hypocritically turns down the offer to see a sign (7:12). The Lord therefore decides to take matters into his own hands and announces he will nonetheless give a sign: "the virgin shall conceive and bear a son, and shall call his name Immanuel" (7:14). The prophet immediately applies this sign to his own day with the imminent crisis of the attack of the Syro-Ephraimitic coalition (7:16–17). Inevitably this raises the questions of who is the foreannounced son and, perhaps more intriguingly, who is the virgin that will give birth? Remaining within the immediate context of Isaiah, the sign-child appears to be Isaiah's son. Although his name was not Immanuel (God is with us), but the more awkward to pronounce *Maher-shalal-hash-baz*,[10] his birth was the sign (8:18) that the Lord would be Immanuel. He would *be with his people* (8:8, 10) and deliver them. This deliverance takes place before the boy was able to cry mother or father (8:3–4). Inevitably this means the most likely candidate to be the virgin was Isaiah's wife, the prophetess. In what sense was the prophetess a virgin? Do we have another virgin birth story in the Bible? The Hebrew word translated "virgin" is *almah*. This Hebrew term refers generally to a "young woman." Therefore, the sign given to Ahaz that the Lord was going to deliver his people was that a young woman would bear a son. By the context we can identify the woman as Isaiah's wife. This was the immediate fulfillment of this prophecy. In no way does this immediate fulfillment impoverish the ultimate and miraculous fulfillment we read about in the Gospels. Several centuries after Isaiah, and yet two centuries prior to the birth of Christ, the Septuagint[11] translators translated the Hebrew *almah* with the Greek *parthenos*. This Greek term has a much narrower meaning than the original Hebrew term. The term *parthenos* is the specific term "virgin." This translation is appropriate since young women in Israel were usually assumed virgins (cf. Gen 24:43; Exod 2:8). Yet this translation narrowed the range of meaning significantly from *almah*. When Matthew applied this prophecy to the birth of Jesus it was intentionally in reference to the more specific term *parthenos* that was established by the Septuagint. Thus, the sign the Lord gave that he would be with his people (Immanuel) escalated significantly from the days of Isaiah to the birth of Jesus. The pregnancy of the young prophetess foreshadowed the truly remarkable pregnancy of

10. *Maher-shalal-hash-baz* means "quick to the plunder, swift to the spoil."

11. The Greek Translation of the Old Testament frequently used and quoted by the New Testament authors.

the young virgin from Nazareth. The birth of Isaiah's son was the partial fulfillment that pointed forward to the birth of the Son of God, the full and final fulfillment. The presence of God with his people in the days of Isaiah was the appetizer, the incarnation of Immanuel the entrée.

How much did Isaiah understand of the typological and escalating dimension of his prophecy? Hard to know. On the one hand we are told by Peter that it was revealed to the prophets that they were not serving themselves but us (1 Pet 1:12). On the other hand we are also told the prophets searched and inquired about the grace (including the person and time) they prophesied about (1 Pet 1:10–11). Furthermore, the purpose of Peter's paragraph (1 Pet 1:10–12) is to convince us that the salvation and grace we enjoy goes way beyond the understanding the Old Testament prophets had or the angels have. Based on this it seems safe to assume that on occasion the prophets did not realize the full import, all the shades of meaning, of their divinely inspired words. The full reach of some prophecies was only known to the ultimate Author of the prophetic books and not to the human authors. Scholars use the Latin expression *sensus plenior* (fuller sense) to describe this dynamic.

Returning to our mountains may help illustrate how typological prophecies function. Imagine the prophet standing at the foot of a mountain. He describes what he sees with his God-given words. However, he does not know that behind the first mountain hides a much more impressive mountain. This second mountain shares some of the characteristics with the first mountain. Indeed, the reason why it is a much more impressive mountain is given by the fact that it has many of the same features of the first mountain, just in a greater and superior scale. In a sense the first mountain can be considered a decent miniature version of the second mountain. Therefore, in describing the first mountain the prophet is also describing the second more impressive mountain. Moreover, some of the slightly hyperbolic descriptions of the first mountain may prove to be a to-scale description of the second mountain. This, of course, does not take place by chance; it is ultimately the Lord who inspired the words of the prophets and the Lord sees both mountains.

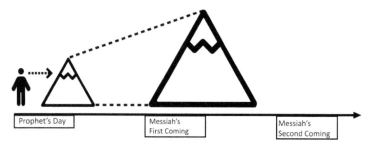

**Typological Fulfillment:** The prophet describes an event that would soon take place in his immediate context that foreshadows typologically a similar yet greater event in the more distant future.

Furthermore, in the case of typological or dual fulfillment, the relationship between the two fulfillments may not just be that the partial fulfillment (the type) typifies the ultimate fulfillment (the antitype), but that it also serves as a guarantee. The fact that the Lord partially fulfills the prophecy in the immediate context may be thought of as a down payment for the ultimate fulfillment. This way of operating can be traced back as far as Genesis and the promises to Abraham. The ease with which Abraham purchased a field in the promised land during his lifetime (Gen 23) was a partial fulfillment that served as a confirmation to Abraham that the Lord would fully fulfill his promise of giving the land to his offspring (Gen 12:7). The same dynamic appears in other dual-fulfillment prophecies.

The difficulty, of course, that we have as interpreters is to know when prophecies point to a single fulfillment and when we can expect multiple fulfillments. In the guideline section we will think about how to handle future prophecies in the pulpit even when we are uncertain of their fulfillment. But first, one last category of fulfillment to consider.

*Cyclical Fulfillment*

A final category of fulfillment, which to some extent overlaps with the previous two, is the cyclical fulfillment phenomenon. If we look across the sweep of salvation history, we will notice patterns, similar events cyclically recurring. The prophets contribute to this by clothing their future prophecies in language from past events (or past patterns). Girdlestone, over a century ago, compiled a helpful list of significant events and people from their past that the prophets used to describe the future (see table 4).[12]

| Events and People | Biblical Reference |
| --- | --- |
| Creation | Isa 65:17; 66:22; 2 Pet 3:13; Rev 21:1 |
| Paradise/Eden | Isa 51:3; Rev 22:1–2 |
| Flood | Isa 54:9; 1 Pet 3:5–7 |
| Destruction of Sodom and Gomorrah | Jer 23:14; Ezek 23:14; Matt 10:15; Rev 19:20 |
| Egyptian Bondage | Hos 8:13; 9:3 |
| Exodus | Hos 2:15; Isa 27:12–13 |
| Wilderness Life | Isa 4:5, 35 |
| Elijah | Mal 4:5; Matt 11:14; Rev 11:5 |
| David | Isa 9:7; 11:10; Amos 9:11; Jer 23:5; Hos 3:5; Ezek 37:22–25 |

*Table 4: Biblical Patterns*

Since salvation history progresses with repeated patterns, it is not surprising that some prophecies that look to the future do not refer to a single (or dual) event, but rather to these recurring patterns. They are describing the type of mountain we will meet time and time again as we journey through history. This phenomenon is related to how fulfillment language in Scripture functions. When we think of a fulfillment of a prophecy we typically think of a one-to-one correspondence between a prophetic word to a single event in the future. However, fulfillment language in Scripture has a broader meaning. The word "fulfill," both in the Hebrew *male* and in the Greek *pléroó*, is often used in Scripture with the meaning of "filling up" or "to make full" (cf. Gen 29:28; Exod 23:26; Matt 3:17; Rom 15:29; Phil 2:2). This meaning well represents how the fulfillment of some prophecies takes place. The same prophecy may have multiple fulfillments that are filling up or making full the prophecy. Therefore, a prophecy does not necessarily expire after a single fulfillment, but rather the same prophecy may have multiple fulfillments throughout history. The prophetic word is gradually and cyclically filling up throughout history until it will reach its full completion, its *sensus plenior*. We must

---

12. Girdlestone, *Grammar of Prophecy*, 40–44.

learn to expand our understanding of prophetic fulfillment to align it with the concept of fulfillment that the biblical authors had.[13]

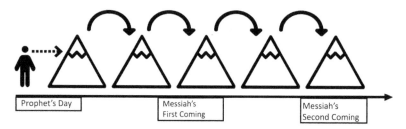

Prophet's Day    Messiah's First Coming    Messiah's Second Coming

**Cyclical Fulfillment:** Prophecies that do not refer to a single (or dual) event, rather to patterns of recurring events throughout salvation history.

This cyclical fulfillment dynamic of course takes place because prophecies reveal the way in which God typically acts in history. A clear example is Isaiah's prophetic word about the hardening of hearts (6:9–10). Isaiah's words did not just find their fulfillment during his ministry but also during Jesus' ministry (Matt 13:14–15; John 12:40), during Paul's ministry (Acts 28:26–27), and I suspect during your ministry too. This one prophecy has been filling up to its full significance over the course of millennia. After all, since God's past actions were driven by who he is, it is not surprising that they are a pattern of how God continues to act through history. Furthermore, as Alter observes, the prophet's choice of poetic language, "tends to lift the utterances to a second power of signification, aligning statements that are addressed to a concrete historical situation with an archetypical horizon."[14] Thus, the prophets were able to speak simultaneously to and about their immediate context and, through the vehicle of poetry that the Lord inspired, to and about situations far beyond their immediate context. All of the above means that even after a clear fulfillment, prophecies are not disposable because, at the very least, they continue to reveal God's purpose and pattern of behavior throughout salvation history.

---

13. This broader understanding of the biblical concept of fulfillment also helps shed light on why Matthew (2:13–15) sees the Messiah's escape from Herod to Egypt as the fulfillment of the calling of Israel out of Egypt (Hos 11:1). The words of the prophet Hosea were clearly in reference to Israel, yet their significance did not expire with Israel but found their fuller and final significance in Christ.

14. Alter, *Art of Biblical Poetry*, 182.

We have completed our tour of the prophetic mountains. Mountains can be tricky places. You do not become a mountaineer overnight. Yet, if you want to faithfully preach the prophets, keep your hiking gear nearby. The hikes can be tough, but the views sure are breathtaking.

## GIVE ME SOMETHING TO PREACH

"Give me something to preach!" I think I hear you mumbling (or perhaps screaming) these words in reading these pages. By focusing on the complexity of these questions, you may end up being afraid of preaching the prophetic books. I understand. Certainly it is good to ask these questions and to be aware of some of these challenges, but Sunday is coming. We need to stand in front of the congregation and proclaim the word of God. How can we preach with authority and clarity if our minds are flooded with questions? As Robinson said: "A mist in the pulpit can easily become a fog in the pew."[15] Our people need certainties, not doubts; answers, not questions. I agree. So, let me conclude by offering some practical advice in the form of *six things, even seven,* that we should not be afraid of doing if we want to preach the prophets with authority and clarity. In doing so I will weave examples throughout from a recent sermon I preached from Haggai 2:1–9.

*Do not be afraid to give answers.* We have focused on the importance of asking questions, so this may seem like a contradiction. It is not. We ask questions to find answers. That is the purpose of questions. If we are asking the right questions and willing to wrestle with them prayerfully and deeply, we will often find answers. To return to our previous analogy—if we attentively and patiently linger until the picture that the prophets painted comes into focus, then the picture will become clear. Prophecy will yield its meaning and will have the clarity we are looking for. We see an example of this in the passage from Haggai. Let me remind you of the context. The Lord sent the prophet to the people of Judah to exhort them to rebuild the temple after the exile. The people had set aside rebuilding the temple and concentrated on rebuilding their own homes (1:4). Furthermore, even once they had started to reconstruct the temple they were soon disheartened because the temple they were building was a far cry from Solomon's glorious temple (2:3). Haggai's second oracle addresses this issue by giving the people a new perspective of the present

---

15. Robinson, *Biblical Preaching*, 101.

(2:4), the past (2:5), and the future (2:6–9). The forward-looking aspect of the prophecy was by far the trickiest to interpret. The promises the Lord gave the people of Judah were astonishing (2:6–9):

> For thus says the Lord of hosts: 'Yet once more, in a little while, I will shake the heavens and the earth and the sea and the dry land. And I will shake all nations, so that the treasures of all nations shall come in, and I will fill this house with glory,' says the Lord of hosts. 'The silver is mine, and the gold is mine,' declares the Lord of hosts. 'The latter glory of this house shall be greater than the former,' says the Lord of hosts. 'And in this place I will give peace,' declares the Lord of hosts.

This passage is rich with promises, and if you begin digging you will uncover some of its treasures. By asking the right question you will discover that soon after this prophecy, King Darius of Persia issued a decree ordering that the cost for the reconstruction of the temple should be paid in full and without delay from the royal avenue (Ezra 6:1–12). Therefore, as Haggai had prophesied, the nations around Judah provided for the construction of the temple (Ezra 6:13–18). The prophecy had been, at least in part, immediately fulfilled. Nevertheless, some aspects of the prophecies remained unfulfilled. The temple built in Haggai's day could not compete with Solomon's Temple. Furthermore, the completion of this temple was not sanctioned with the descent of the cloud of the glory of God as took place upon completion of the tabernacle and the inauguration of Solomon's Temple (Exod 40:34–35; 1 Kgs 8:10–11). More digging required. As you continue to trace the history of the Second Temple you will then discover Herod the Great expanded and refurbished it. He transformed the temple in Jerusalem into a masterpiece. Moreover, half a century after the refurbishment the special presence of the Lord entered this temple, not in the form of a cloud, but in the form of the incarnate Son of God (John 2:13). From this vantage point, the latter glory of the house was greater than the former (Hag 2:9). The Lord had beautifully and wonderfully kept his promise. You have found a treasure. Time to show it to your people. It is not wrong to reach conclusions and give answers, but we must make sure these answers are not rushed and are not driven by superimposing our theological system onto the text. So, we are willing to travel the road of hard questions because we know this inquisitiveness is our best chance to reach answers. Once we reach a destination, we do not shy away from giving the answers we have found.

*Do not be afraid to* not *give answers.* The word of God is infallible; we are not. As preachers we often feel the pressure of being the in-house expert who should have all the answers. This can lead us to give answers we do not have or to offer a simplistic explanation to a complex matter. This is dangerous. Much better to admit not knowing an answer (or at least not a complete answer) rather than causing our people to confuse our own dubious speculations with the inerrant truth of the word of God. Our attitude to the word of God will speak louder than our speculative answers from the word of God. Sections of the prophetic books are breathtaking for the beauty of their form and the depth of their content. The prophets conveyed staggering truths in stunning ways. This should prevent us from arrogantly claiming or even thinking we have all the answers. I am skeptical of those who seem to have a perfectly neat map of the future and claim the ultimate interpretation of all past, present, and future prophecies. Typically, to have such a neat map, they have settled for simplistic answers and have subjected the prophetic books to their preconceived theological systems. As preachers we need to proclaim, not domesticate, the prophetic literature.

Moreover, we must also recognize Scripture is infallible, but not omniscient. Scripture does not contain the answers to all our questions, even if our questions are legitimate. Everything the Bible says is true, but the Bible does not say everything about everything. Indeed, Scripture itself teaches us that the Lord our God intentionally did not give us all the answers because the secret things belong to him (Deut 29:29). The purpose, then, of God's Revelation is not to satisfy our curiosity but to transform our reality. In Scripture, we thus find all we *need to know* about the past, present, and even the future to live a godly life (2 Tim 3:14–17). In view of this, at times, the best way to serve our people is not to clutch at straws but to model humility before the word of God. The pulpit is not the place for speculation. Therefore, rather than trying to prove to our people that we have mastered biblical prophecy it is much more important to them that we live a life mastered by the word of God.

In my sermon from Haggai I was cautious not to speculate about the final phrase: "In this place I will give peace" (2:9). Has this taken place yet? If yes, in what form? The original hearers would have probably understood this prophecy as a promise of physical and political peace in Jerusalem. However, a prolonged time of shalom has never quite materialized in Jerusalem following the exile. Even the temple, which had received a significant upgrade by Herod the Great, was then destroyed by the Romans in AD 70. Therefore, if a physical and political peace is in view then this prophecy still awaits fulfillment. Alternatively, just as the prophecy about the glory of this house found an unexpected fulfillment in the incarnation of the Son of God, perhaps this aspect of the prophecy also points to the One who came to preach peace, make peace, and indeed is our peace (Eph 2:14–17). Of course, in this case, the peace is spiritual more than political. Considering these possibilities, I chose not to argue the case for one or the other of these possible fulfillments. Rather than making contention a prominent feature of the sermon, I focused on the value of trusting in the only One who can and will bring about *true shalom*. I will return to this in my sixth suggestion to illustrate how I achieved this without getting lost in a forest of details.

*Do not be afraid to get help.* Although this advice is not specific to preaching the prophets, I consider it to be especially relevant for this type of literature because of the challenges we encounter. Many aspects of preaching, from preparation to delivery, are typically done alone. You spend hours in a study alone. You are behind the pulpit alone. You experience the postsermon blues alone. Preaching can be lonely. This is inevitable for some aspects of preaching, but not all. The hard work of preparation, for example, would benefit from greater teamwork. Yet this is rare. As preachers we are used to working alone. Furthermore, many of us tend to hide all our findings until the big Sunday morning reveal. We behave like a mobile phone company that prevents any leaks to the press until the big launch day of their latest model. This is unfortunate, because discussion with others breeds clarity. Especially if the others are well chosen. One of the benefits of working in a theological institute is you spend your days with Bible people. Over the years this has proven most helpful to me for sermon preparation. Many times, a conversation with a colleague or a student about my preaching passage has proven to be enlightening. Although not everyone has the privilege of being surrounded daily by others of this caliber, still we can actively seek help from fellow preachers, pastors, elders, trusted believers, or even our spouse. You will greatly benefit from their insights. You may find it uneasy at first, but I assure you the plusses significantly outweigh the minuses. Find the others in your context and include this in your sermon preparation routine.

Of course, we can get help not just from friends nearby but also ones who are further away, not only from friends of today but also friends of yesterday. Many of these friends (commentaries, lexicons, dictionaries, etc.) sit comfortably on the shelf, ready to come to our aid to shed light on the essential background, a Hebrew term, or the inner dynamics of our preaching passage. These friends allow us to gain perspective from others who have spent time contemplating the specific prophetic text. We are privileged to have access to multiple resources from which we can glean extremely helpful observations that will help us see with greater clarity and recognize areas of widespread consensus. Yet we ought not to depend solely on their conclusions without spending the time contemplating in first person the prophetic text. That would be like admiring a piece of art simply by reading its description by an art critic. Nothing can, nor should, replace direct engagement in the text. Nevertheless, the art critic may help you notice something you would have not spotted on your own. Therefore, we should consult others and get their help, but we must make sure their observations help us see what really is in the text.

When preaching from Haggai I got help from a friend I had never met before. I came across Rev. T. V. Moore's commentary on the book of Haggai.[16] Moore convincingly argues that the translators who opt for a plural translation of verse 7 ("the treasures of all nations shall come in"[17]) make a better choice than the translators who opt for a singular translation ("the desire of all nations shall come"[18]). This is important because the singular translation the "desire of all nations" is commonly understood as a reference to the Messiah and thus would have radically changed the thrust of the sermon. Moore provides the following objections to the singular translation: (1) the noun *chemdah* does not mean the thing desired, so much as the quality of making it desirable (i.e., *beauty*); (2) the verb "come" is plural and can only be properly construed with a singular noun when it is a noun of multitude; (3) Christ, in point of fact, is not the desire of all nations, but rather their aversion (cf. Isa 53:2); (4) the content of the next verse excludes that it refers to Christ and confirms that it refers to treasures; and (5) the Septuagint and other older translations know nothing of this interpretation.[19] Moore's helpful insights enabled me to see, and therefore also preach, this passage with greater clarity.

*Do not be afraid to go to the New Testament.* Of course, we hit the jackpot when our help comes from inspired authors of Scripture. As we

16. Moore, *Prophets of the Restoration.*

17. ESV translation.

18. KJV translation.

19. Moore, *Prophets of the Restoration*, 75–76.

noted in chapter 1 the New Testament writers often cite or allude to passages from the prophets. When this takes place, we have a significant advantage. The New Testament authors did not necessarily answer all our questions about the prophetic word. Indeed, on some occasions, their treatment of the prophetic passage may add questions rather than provide answers. Nonetheless, the New Testament writers provide essential clues that can guide us as we navigate the future-looking prophetic message. The author of Hebrews, for example, provided clues for interpreting another challenging part of my preaching portion in Haggai: "Yet once more, in a little while, I will shake the heavens and the earth" (Heb 12:26). Hebrews explicitly states this is a reference to the final shake when the unshakable kingdom of God will be fully manifested. When this takes place all temporary things will be removed whilst all that has an eternal value will remain (Heb 12:25–29). The author of Hebrews thus exhorts us to live in the present, with constant gratitude and reverential worship, as we look forward to this great event in the future. We therefore see how some aspects of Haggai's prophecy have been fulfilled in the past whilst other aspects are still awaiting their final fulfillment. This is another example of a prophecy that is being progressively fulfilled (or progressively filled) throughout salvation history. Revelation 21:24–26 also nudges us in this direction by alluding to these verses in Haggai. Other New Testament authors shed light on other prophetic books. Matthew, for example, provides significant help to us in interpreting Malachi by revealing that both the messenger (3:1) and Elijah (4:5) were John the Baptist (Matt 11:10–14). These New Testament references do not remove all questions, nor do they indicate if these prophecies have found their complete fulfillment (cf. Rev 11:4–6), but they do provide significant help. Therefore, we should not feel guilty of jumping ahead to the New Testament to see how the story continues, provided we then remember to jump back to our original preaching passage to trace the full story. The New Testament passage should shed light on, not replace, the Old Testament passage.

*Do not be afraid to preach to transform more than to inform.* We have seen the difficult questions we encounter when trying to establish the fulfillment of a specific prophecy. Because of these challenges we may find ourselves preaching prophecies without knowing if they are literal or figurative, if they are conditional or unconditional, and if, and how, they have been or will be fulfilled. In these instances, in addition to displaying the humility we have already spoken about, the key is to focus on the purpose of the prophecy and not its fulfillment. Limiting our interest in the prophets to our desire to find prophecies that were fulfilled in the first coming of Christ or to speculate about prophecies that remain unfilled is at best a partial, and at worst an improper, use of biblical prophecy. Remember, the purpose of prophecy is to transform more than to inform. Thus, in preaching prophecies, rather than falling into an eschatological trap and hypothesizing about possible fulfillments, it is much better to highlight their purpose. This is where we encounter a surprising simplicity. Wright helps us observe that often the prophetic message fits into two basic categories. "Either: giving an individual or all the people a *warning or threat* of judgment to come—and then calling them to repent and change (messages of judgment). Or: Giving an individual or all the people a *promise* of salvation and blessing to come—and then calling them to hope and trust in God (messages of hope)."[20] Because of this simplicity we are able to identify the purpose of the prophetic oracle even when we are unsure about the fulfillment. When the prophets were warning the people of judgment, they were calling them to genuine repentance. When they were anticipating the future salvation, they were fostering faith, hope, and obedience. Because most prophecies fall into one of these two trajectories, we can easily know the general direction our sermon should take. This does not mean all sermons from the prophets will be the same, because each prophetic oracle has its own nuances. Nevertheless, it allows us to know we are headed in the right direction, even when we are unsure about the specific fulfillment. We can therefore call the people to respond appropriately to the word of God.

As we have seen, Haggai's prophecy is fraught with plenty of fascinating avenues to pursue. The focus of the sermon could easily become getting our teeth sunk into the various layers of fulfillments. I suspect many (some?) would find this interesting, but would it be helpful? The goal of preaching is not primarily to download information into the minds of our listeners. We aim higher. The goal is to bring about transformation in their hearts and lives. This was Haggai's goal too. He painted a picture of the future to energize the people of Judah in the present. The people were stuck in the past, remembering Solomon's Temple (2:3). Nostalgia of the good old days demoralized them. The temple they were building was worth nothing in their eyes. Into this gloomy atmosphere Haggai boldly asserted the best was yet to come—the latter glory of this house would be greater than the former (2:9). He announced the Lord

20. Wright, *Sweeter than Honey*, 179 (italics original).

of hosts would once again decisively intervene in their story. The Lord would even cause the surrounding nations to provide the necessary funds and thus ensure the glory of this temple would surpass Solomon's great temple. What a prospect for the disheartened postexilic community! The prophet had rekindled hope. It was now time for the people of Judah to dry their eyes, roll up their sleeves, be strong, and get back to work (2:4–5). They needed to be reminded that, despite their limited resources, their stammering efforts were part of God's grand design. We also need to be reminded of this. When we are discouraged by the lack of resources, we need to look to the One who has access to unlimited resources. When we are deflated by the lack of results, we need to remember we serve the One who can bring unparalleled glory out of debris. When we are ready to quit, we need to know that, whilst the "work in progress" sign is still up, the Grand Architect already sees and guarantees the beauty of the final product. Therefore, rather than going down the rabbit hole of speculative fulfillments, we follow Haggai's lead and preach to transform. We revive hope, foster faith, and inspire obedience by lifting the eyes of our people out of the rubble to see that they are part of God's unshakable kingdom.

*Do not be afraid to lean back on the big story.* When we think about what the Bible reveals about the future, we are often concerned with the details rather than captivated by its significance. The focus of the biblical writers is the opposite. They are less concerned with giving us the details and more concerned with wanting us to feel the implications of knowing the Lord is sovereign over history. They tell us to live our lives, knowing the ship of history will soon reach its final port. This forward-looking dimension is part of the DNA of the Christian faith. The prophets contributed massively to creating this view of the future. They placed the immediate in the context of the ultimate. They continuously encouraged us to live the present in view of the future, to see our lives as part of the great metanarrative.

This prophetic goal explains why the prophets went back and forth from their present to the future, from the details of their story to the generalities of the big story. The implication for us is that whilst we may struggle to grasp all the time-specific details we will continuously be reminded of the big story. Even when the outworking of the specific judgments may elude us, the reality of the ultimate judgment can still challenge us. Even when the timing and dimensions of the promises of salvation may confuse us, the reality of the ultimate salvation can still comfort us. Thus, as preachers, even when the details are blurry to us, we can continue to call our people to live their story as part of God's story (and not vice versa). Whilst this should never become an excuse to neglect careful investigation into the details, it is a legitimate card to play.

I played this card in my Haggai sermon. I mentioned early that I was undecided about the fulfillment of the promise of peace. I struggled to determine how the promise about the temple and the promise about a time of peace intermingled. This, however, did not leave me without anything to say about this portion of the passage. The trajectory of the temple and the trajectory of true shalom can be traced from Genesis to Revelation. Haggai's prophecy is thus part of the journey from Eden to the new Jerusalem. Therefore, at the very least, we can say Haggai's prophecy is ultimately pointing forward to the new Jerusalem. In Revelation we read the new Jerusalem is a city filled with the presence of the Lord that will have no temple, "for its temple is the Lord God the Almighty and the Lamb" (Rev 21:22). We also discover it is a city where there will be no night, no death, no mourning, no crying, and no suffering. A place where the Lord will give peace (Hag 2:9). By pointing forward to the end of the story I am not excluding that Haggai's prophecy may also be referring to another time of peace, whether political or spiritual, I am simply choosing to lean on the big story and invest my precious sermon minutes on what is certain.

*Do not be afraid to rely on the Holy Spirit.* The seventh suggestion is not distinct from, but should permeate and steer, the previous six. Paul underscores the importance of this by quoting the prophet Isaiah: "What no eye has seen, nor ear heard, nor the heart of man imagined, what God has prepared for those who love him" (1 Cor 2:9). Paul groups together the parts of our body that gather information (eyes, ears, and heart[21]) to highlight that we will never be able to discover what God has prepared for those who love him by relying only on our own abilities. We need to rely on the Holy Spirit. Indeed, one of the main roles of the Holy Spirit is to illuminate us. Paul goes on to show the Holy Spirit is fully qualified to carry out this role for two reasons. Firstly, because the Holy Spirit has done his research. He searches the depths of God and therefore is qualified to reveal the mysteries of God to us (1 Cor 2:10). Secondly, in the same way the thoughts of a person are only known by his spirit, so the thoughts of God are only known by the Spirit of God (1 Cor 2:11).

---

21. "Heart" in the Bible does not just refer to the locus of our emotions. Heart is understood as the center of our entire being, including our intellectual and moral spheres.

Paul then goes on to express how the Holy Spirit not only enables the reception, but also the teaching, of these spiritual truths (1 Cor 2:12–13). Undoubtedly this was especially true of Paul and the apostles (cf. John 14:26), but it ought to be true of us too. Indeed, there is no indication in the passage that Paul is speaking only about himself and the apostles. We can therefore trust that the One who inspired Paul and the other biblical writers enables us to understand and preach the same inspired word. We exegete meticulously, we think deeply, we read extensively, we listen carefully, we research abundantly, we pray fervently, and we prepare thoroughly, but ultimately we believe that through all of this the Holy Spirit will give us something to preach.

I preached this sermon from Haggai at my home church in Rome in March 2020, just as Italy was hit hard by the Coronavirus. For a couple of weeks Italy was the epicenter of the virus. As a church and a nation, we faced unprecedented times. From health to finances, the immediate future looked bleak. Uncertainty and discouragement lurked around every corner. In those unsettling days the word of God, through the prophet Haggai, encouraged us by reminding us of his presence in the present (2:4), his protection in the past (2:5), and his provision in the future (2:6-9). In particular, the Lord's promises about the future sunk deep into our hearts that Sunday. In the section of the passage that speaks about the future we read of no instruction from the Lord to his people. Rather, we simply have a series of pledges that the Lord commits to for the benefit of his people. The message was clear to the people of Judah and to us. The Lord calls us to worry about being faithful in the present and to let him worry about the future. The *Lord of hosts*, a title repeated five times in this section, has sovereign authority over all circumstances and all viruses. The Holy Spirit had given me something to preach.

# Chapter 6

## COME BACK FROM THE PAST

> "Blessed be the name of God forever and ever, to whom
> belong wisdom and might. He changes times and seasons;
> he removes kings and sets up kings; he gives wisdom to the
> wise and knowledge to those who have understanding."
>
> —DAN 2:20-21

THE TITLE OF THIS chapter, and the previous one, allude to the famous trilogy *Back to the Future*.[1] The science fiction movies follow the adventures of Marty McFly and the eccentric scientist Doc Brown as they travel through time in the legendary DeLorean time machine. Watching this trilogy is both entertaining and demanding. Entertaining because of the thrilling storyline. Demanding because of the challenge of keeping track of where and when the protagonists are and how this relates to the overall story. Yet, the better you follow the unlikely duo as they bounce between past, present, and future, the better you grasp the full story. A similar dynamic takes place when you study the prophets. To preach the prophets you need to travel through time. As we have seen, the prophets, at times, take us to the future to show us our present from a new point of

---

1. I am not the only one who has associated biblical prophecy to these time-travel movies. For example, Kaiser alludes to it in the title of his book on biblical prophecy (Kaiser, *Back Toward the Future*) and Köstenberger and Patterson use it as the title of their chapter on biblical prophecy in *Invitation to Biblical Interpretation* ("Back to the Future: Prophecy," 319–64).

view. However, if we want to engage seriously with the prophets, before we even dream of traveling to the future, we need to travel back to the past. The prophets come to us from a distant world. The better we understand the world of the prophets the better we are positioned to proclaim their message to our world. In this chapter we will join the prophets in their own backyard.

The prophets ministered over a time span of three frantic centuries (750–450 BC). Broadly speaking it is useful to divide the prophetic age into three periods: the divided kingdom (750–722 BC), the Kingdom of Judah (722–586 BC), and the postexilic community (586–450 BC). To comprehend each period, we need to explore both what was taking place within the territory of Israel and Judah as well as the wider geopolitical scenario. This journey back will serve as an introduction, or perhaps a refresher, that will prepare us to preach the prophets. However, since our journey requires more effort than simply dialing the desired date into the DeLorean time machine, we will begin by underscoring the importance of embarking on this quest.

## ESSENTIAL TRAVEL

It is a basic hermeneutical rule that we must always read a passage of Scripture in its own historical context before asking how it speaks to us today. But why is this so important? Here are three reasons we can illustrate from Obadiah, the shortest prophetic book.

1. *Knowledge of the historical context unlocks the message of the prophets.* This is the fundamental reason why we pay attention to the historical context. The Lord chose to reveal his eternal word, relevant to every person in every setting, to specific people in specific settings. He chose not to speak above cultures but into and through specific cultures, wrapping his timeless message in time-bound garments. As Duvall and Hays point out, this understanding of divine inspiration ought to steer our interpretation of Scripture:

> We believe that the way we approach the Bible (i.e., the way we listen to God) should match how God gave us the Bible (i.e., the way God chose to speak). Otherwise, we will likely misunderstand what God is trying to say to us. Since God spoke his message in specific, historical situations (i.e., to people living in particular places, speaking particular languages, adopting

a particular way of life), we should take the ancient historical-cultural situations seriously.[2]

In our case, this involves investigating the historical-cultural context that shaped the prophets, their audiences, and their oracles. The historical-cultural context, also known as "the world behind the text," includes many spheres: historical, cultural, geographical, political, social, religious, and economic. All these spheres influenced the prophetic message.

Consider how background knowledge sheds light on parts of Obadiah's message. This prophecy[3] is directed to the nation of Edom, and it is bad news for them. The Lord announced that, although the Edomites arrogantly considered themselves to be big, the Lord would make them small (v. 2). A key part of their pride was predicated on their confidence that they lived in a secure and inaccessible location. The Edomites lived in a mountainous region to the southeast of Judah. Their elevated location (up to 5,000 feet above sea level) lead to an elevated ego. Living up in the hills gave the Edomites a false sense of security. The Lord condemned and mocked their feeling of invincibility by using geographical language to announce their downfall (vv. 3–4). "The pride of your heart has deceived you, you who live in the clefts of the rock, in your lofty dwelling, who say in your heart, 'Who will bring me down to the ground?' Though you soar aloft like the eagle, though your nest is set among the stars, from there I will bring you down, declares the Lord." The meaning of Obadiah's initial words of judgment can be fully understood only against the backdrop of the topography of the region.

This is just one example of what we encounter throughout the prophetic books. The historical context frames the prophetic message. Each prophet spoke God's word into a specific historical occasion. This particular context influenced how the prophets communicated. As we have seen, they were brilliant communicators. As such, they knew their

2. Duvall and Hays, *Grasping God's Word*, 116–17.

3. The book of Obadiah has no superscription and therefore we cannot be sure of the exact dating. Nevertheless, the content of the book, the wider biblical information, and some historical evidence offer significant clues. The widespread consensus is that this prophecy was given in the window of time between Jerusalem's fall (586 BC) and Edom's fall (mid-sixth century). The primary reasons that lead to this dating: the book presents the fall of Jerusalem as a past event (11), the fall of Edom as a future event (15–16), the severity of the description of the fall of Jerusalem best fits with the event in 586 BC and not the other alternatives that are sometimes put forth, and the similarity with the prophecies of Jeremiah and Ezekiel suggest that they were describing the same event.

audiences well (worldview, convictions, feelings, behavior, economic status, etc.). They kept their finger on the pulse. They were well-versed in history and kept up to date with currents affairs. Like any good communicator they leaned on all this knowledge to speak effectively to their audience. They knew when to be explicit and when to be subtle. They used loaded words, cleverly relying on the presumed knowledge of their listeners. In brief, they knew how to best communicate the message of the Lord to the world of their listeners because they lived in the same world. The world behind the text was their world. We, however, belong to a different world. Therefore, we need to travel back and listen to the prophets conveying God's word to their listeners to hear what the prophets are saying to us today.

Furthermore, traveling back to the world of the prophets reminds us that Scripture is not fiction but history. We know this on paper, and yet we lose sight of it. The claim of historicity is a central tenet of Scripture and of the Christian faith. God's self-revelation took place in the arena of history. Although the primary goal of Scripture is not to narrate history but to reveal God, history plays a crucial role. The Bible is more than merely an historical account, but it is not less. This is part of the power of Scripture. Just as the potency of a film is increased when you know it is based on a real story, so is the potency of the Bible when you know it is a true story. The Bible is real-life drama!

2. *Knowledge of the historical context enables us to spot immediate fulfillments of prophecies.* We discovered in the previous chapter that the immediate context is the first and best place to look for fulfillment of prophecies. Yet we will only be able to spot these fulfillments if we have sufficient knowledge of the key events of the prophetic era.

Obadiah predicted the Lord's severe judgment upon Edom. The heart of the judgment is, "As you have done, it shall be done to you; your deeds shall return on your own head" (v. 15). Edom's vile conduct turned out to be a boomerang that returned to knock them out. The details of the judgment are frightening. Edom will be consumed by foreign nations (v. 16), burnt up like rubble that catches fire, and will have no survivors (v. 18). This took place shortly after the prophecy was given in the mid-sixth century. The Babylonians conquered their natural fortress and defeated the Edomites. Their fate was such that the prophet Malachi (450 BC) described the territory the Edomites were so proud of as a devastated hill country and a desert for jackals (Mal 1:3). History reveals that because of their tainted history, the Edomites lost their place in history.

This example shows how researching people, places, nations, events, and dates enables us to recognize fulfilled prophecies. In these instances, doing our historical homework is well worth it, as it will increase our precision and confidence when preaching the prophetic text. This confidence will exude in our preaching and will impact our people.

3. *Knowledge of the historical context adds color to our preaching.* Many preachers consider researching the background information as necessary but tedious. They know the importance of it, but they do it begrudgingly. This attitude comes across in how they share historical information in the pulpit. It is not uncommon to have preachers apologize in advance before conveying the history bit. They attempt to do it as quickly and as painlessly as possible, much like pulling out a tooth. This is not ideal because it fails to honor the mode of divine inspiration and also because it transfers to our listeners a negative bias toward the historical information. Moreover, I think in having this negative attitude toward the history bit preachers are missing a trick. A well-researched and engagingly presented backstory can prepare hearts for receiving the word of God. I have heard preachers effectively plant their listeners *into* the world of the Bible, preparing the way for the Bible to be planted *into* the lives of their listeners: circumstances, pressures, fears, and worldviews narrated with such vivid language that you cannot help but read yourself into the story. Let me show you what I mean with a potential introduction to the book of Obadiah:

> Sometimes the closer you are to someone the more competitive you are. This is true of siblings, football teams, and even nations. It was true of Judah and Edom. They were next-door neighbors, and they were rivals; they hated each other. Believe it or not, they were blood relatives, but it was bad blood that ran between them. Their animosity can be traced back to their founding fathers. These two nations came from twins (Jacob and Esau). Their mother says they even fought in the womb. The two nations followed suit. Backstabbing was the norm. Their hatred bubbled for centuries and erupted in 586 BC when another great nation, Babylonia, devastated Judah. It was brutal. The Babylonians demolished the temple and burnt houses. They tore the population to shreds. The few survivors were so starved that their own children looked appetizing (Lam 4:10). The Edomites, Judah's next-door neighbor, had a front-row seat to this catastrophe. They were located in the mountains just southeast of Judah. They laughed. They cheered like football fans celebrating

the winning goal against their historic rivals. Some of them even ventured down, not to offer a helping hand, but to steal anything worth stealing. Some of the Judean survivors managed to escape from the Babylonians by heading south and crossing the border into Edom. With their backs to Jerusalem and tears in their eyes these homeless Judean refugees struggled up the hills. They hoped to find something approximating compassion from the Edomites. After all, they were brothers. Imagine how they felt when they saw the Edomites cheering on the Babylonians and toasting the destruction of Jerusalem. On their part, the Edomites could not believe their luck when they saw this group of refugees. They captured them, mocked them, beat them, and then handed them back over to the Babylonians. I can imagine some of the questions the survivors had as they were being dragged to a foreign land, owning nothing but the blood-stained and smoke-infused clothes on their backs: How could God let this happen? Why did he let the Edomites get away with it? Why does God close his eyes to the evil in this world?

Weighty questions. Have you ever asked these questions? I have. When you see the suffering, despair, and hopelessness in us and around us it is hard not to. When your house is on fire I think you are allowed to ask these questions. The world is full of voiceless victims screaming: "Why does God close his eyes to the evil in this world?"

Obadiah tackles this dilemma. He confirms the Lord's eyes are wide open. The Lord sees the evil across the world and one day soon he will do justice. The "Edomites" will not have the last laugh. Let us turn to Obadiah . . .

With this approach the historical context is not an awkward barrier to overcome at the beginning of your sermon but your entrance hall, welcoming people in. The historical context does not deserve to be presented as tedious and irrelevant information but as a vivid story with key insights that heighten the intensity and the relevancy of Scripture. Good storytelling makes the Bible come alive, enabling us to hear and feel the message of the word of God like never before. To do this well requires in-depth knowledge coupled with a good imagination that can only be obtained by thorough research. You also need to give careful thought to your choice of words. Think through your wording meticulously and become a good storyteller. Your people will be blessed by it.

These three reasons are the fuel in our time machine that help us to travel back. While we're in the past, let us now zip through the three major prophetic periods. Note that this accelerated tour will help you spot the key landmarks, but each prophetic book requires its own more detailed visit. Also, note that whilst most of the prophetic books reveal their historical setting, other books do not give us the precise dating. However, even in these instances we are not left entirely in the dark because we are often enlightened by internal and external clues. I will note the books that have some uncertainty regarding their dating and add a footnote justifying their placement. Time to jump into our time machines (i.e., Bible commentaries, surveys, dictionaries, and atlases) and start our whistle-stop tour.

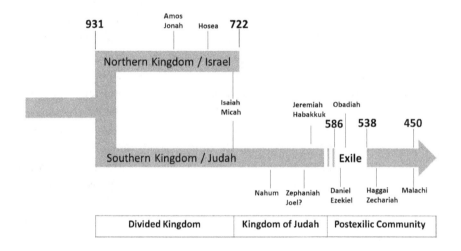

## THE DIVIDED KINGDOM (750–722 BC)

The year was 931 BC when, following the reign of Solomon, the Kingdom of Israel split in two: the Northern Kingdom identified as Israel (or Ephraim[4]), under the leadership of Jeroboam with the capital city of Samaria; and the Southern Kingdom identified as Judah, under the leadership of Rehoboam (Solomon's son), with the capital being Jerusalem. The reasons for this tragic event were both spiritual and political. On the spiritual front Solomon's idolatry was the cause of the split (1 Kgs

4. Ephraim was the name of the largest tribe of the Northern Kingdom of Israel that was often used as a synecdoche (a figure of speech where a part is taken to represent the whole) for the Northern Kingdom.

11:33–36). On the political side it was Rehoboam's foolishness in following the wrong advice (1 Kgs 12:1–24). Let us take a closer look at what was taking place inside and around these kingdoms.

## Inside: Days of Decline

The best place to read about much of the history of the prophetic period is 2 Kings. However, I must warn you, it is not a pleasant read. The camera goes back and forth between the two kingdoms, reporting on the various kings. Sadly, the frequent refrain is the kings "did what was evil in the sight of the Lord." Although this verdict was common for the kings of both kingdoms, it was 100 percent true of the kings of Israel. The Northern Kingdom had a rapid succession of kings from different dynasties with an average reign of only ten years. Most reigns came to an abrupt, murderous ending, and *all* did what was evil in the sight of the Lord. The Kingdom of Judah faired a little better. They had a slower succession rate and only the one dynasty, the lineage of David, sat on the throne in Jerusalem. Despite this greater political stability, they too were on a downward trajectory. From time to time we find the pleasant surprise of a king who followed in the footsteps of David (i.e., Azariah, Jehoash, Jotham, etc.) and did what was right in the eyes of the Lord. Nevertheless, the overall decline across both kingdoms was palpable.

The literary prophets[5] entered the stage with the goal of reversing the trend. Since most of the kings had turned their backs on the Lord and the priests were corrupt, the Lord commissioned the prophets to call the people back to himself. During this period, we read of several prophets in action in both kingdoms.

The first literary prophet to enter the stage ironically was not a professional prophet. *Amos*[6] was a country boy from the south who was sent to the affluent Northern Kingdom to expose their sins of idolatry and social injustice. *Hosea*[7] was soon to follow. He also forcefully confronted the

---

5. This expression aims at differentiating the prophets that authored an inspired book (i.e., Isaiah, Jeremiah, Ezekiel, etc.) from other prophets we read about in Scripture, who had a prophetic ministry but did not author a divinely inspired book (i.e., Elijah, Elisha, Micaiah, etc.). These oral prophets ministered approximately a century before the literary prophets.

6. Amos (1:1) carried out his ministry in the days of King Uzziah (767–40 BC) of Judah and King Jeroboam (781–53 BC) of Israel.

7. Hosea (1:1) prophesied during the reigns of the following kings of Judah: Uzziah

people of their sins, particularly their idolatry, by embodying the tragedy of the people's unfaithfulness to the Lord by his own personal story with an adulterous woman. The prophets *Micah*[8] and *Isaiah*[9] were the next prophets to enter the scene in what would prove to be the twilight years of the Northern Kingdom. They reinforced the same basic message to the people of Israel and Judah: repent or you will face judgment. Regrettably, the people did not stop this downward spiral, and this had imminent tragic consequences for the Northern Kingdom that we will soon spot by looking outside of Israel's borders.

## Outside: Assyrian Mix-and-Match Strategy

In line with the Mosaic covenant (Deut 28), spiritual decline led to material and political decline. Although the elite in the Northern Kingdom were affluent within the context of Israel's economically stratified society, the overall picture was that the glory days of King David and Solomon, with the extended territory and wealth, were gradually fading away. Israel and Judah were not the key players on the geopolitical scene. The nation of Assyria was the courtyard bully of the day. The Assyrians rose to power and made their presence known across the Middle East. They were known for brutality. Nobody wanted anything to do with the awful Assyrians, including *Jonah*.[10] Nineveh was the capital of the Assyrian Empire, and therefore you can understand his reluctance to go anywhere near the place. Yet, after some supernatural convincing and some *deep* thinking, he entered the enemy's territory and delivered the message to the Ninevites. Unlike, and to the shame of, the people of Israel and Judah, the people of Niniveh repented.

However, this repentance proved to be short-lived, and under the leadership of Tiglath-Pileser III (745–727 BC) the Assyrian aggression escalated. Tiglath-Pileser III's reign was characterized by military success. The Assyrians used their cruel and violent reputation to harass surrounding nations. Smaller nations formed coalitions to try to resist but to

---

(767–40 BC), Jotham (750–35 BC), Ahaz (735–15 BC), and Hezekiah (715–687 BC).

8. Micah (1:1) prophesied during the reigns of the following kings of Judah: Jotham (750–35 BC), Ahaz (735–15 BC), and Hezekiah (715–687 BC).

9. Isaiah (1:1; 6:1) prophesied under the same kings as Micah as he began his ministry the year in which King Uzziah died (740 BC).

10. We know from 2 Kings 14:23–28 that Jonah prophesied during the reign of King Jeroboam (781–53 BC) of Israel.

no avail. The Northern Kingdom went down this road by forming a coalition with the Syrians (known as the Syro-ephramitic coalition) but this road proved to be a dead end. The prophets warned that the only solution was to turn to and trust the Lord. This warning fell on deaf ears, so the Assyrians conquered the nation of Israel. In 722 BC, after a lengthy siege, the Assyrians destroyed Samaria, deported the nation, and dispersed the people. Deportations were a pivotal part of the Assyrian strategy to dominate vast territories. They mixed the various populations to blur their identities and weaken any attempt to organize resistance. Thus, the northern tribes of Israel were relocated across the Assyrian Empire.[11]

Soon after, the Assyrians turned their attention to the Kingdom of Judah. Another Assyrian, King Sennacherib (705–681 BC), reached and surrounded Jerusalem. The outcome of the battle seemed obvious. This was the superpower of the day against the small nation of Judah. This was David against Goliath at a national level. Thankfully, the people of Judah were led by one of the few good kings. Hezekiah listened to the prophets, specifically to *Isaiah*, and did not go down the road of intrigue and alliances. Rather he trusted in the Lord. The Lord miraculously delivered Jerusalem by sending an angel to strike down 185,000 Assyrian soldiers (2 Kgs 18:18–18; 19:32–36; Isa 37:36). It really was another David-against-Goliath story. Sennacherib's own account of this event makes interesting reading. "As to Hezekiah, the Jew, he did not submit to my yoke, I laid siege to 46 of his strong cities, walled forts and to the countless small villages in their vicinity . . . himself I made a prisoner in Jerusalem, his royal residence, like a bird in a cage. I surrounded him with earthwork in order to molest those who were leaving his city's gate."[12] His testimony confirms they did not conquer Jerusalem, although, as is typical of ancient documents, he puts a positive propagandistic spin on it.

The miraculous deliverance of the Southern Kingdom proved the ultimate reason for the deportation of the Northern Kingdom was not the strength of the Assyrians but rather Israel's sinfulness. The Lord had judged the people of Israel using the Assyrians as the rod of his anger (Isa 10:5). The prophet Isaiah went on to announce (Isa 10:6–15) that although the Assyrians were an instrument of God to bring judgment, this did not

---

11. This mixing strategy caused the descendants of the northern tribes to intermarry with gentiles and assimilate elements of Mesopotamian culture. This explains why the Samaritans were then despised and considered half-breeds in the New Testament period.

12. Pritchard, *Ancient Near East*, 270–71.

make them exempt from being on the wrong side of God's judgment. The Assyrians continued to dominate the Middle Eastern landscape for close to another century but eventually the Lord intervened to judge Nineveh, the epicenter of this brutal nation. The announcement of this judgment comes from the mouth of the prophet *Nahum*.[13] The book of Nahum can be viewed as a sequel and counterbalance to Jonah. The purpose of the book is to comfort (the name Nahum means "comfort") the people of God by revealing that the Lord will judge Nineveh. The reason for the judgment is unmistakably the Assyrian brutality: bloodshed, massacres, deportations, and torture. Nahum called Nineveh the "bloody city" (3:1) famous for its "unceasing evil" (3:19). Various Assyrian kings admitted, indeed boasted about, the extent of their evil and violence. Ashurnasibal II (883–859 BC) chronicles his brutality in one of his campaigns: "With the masses of my troops and by my furious battle onset I stormed, I captured the city; 600 of their warriors I put to the sword; 3,000 captives I burned with fire; I did not leave a single one among them alive to serve as a hostage . . . Hulai, their governor, I flayed, his skin I spread upon the wall of the city of Damdamusa."[14] Sennacherib (705–681 BC) also boasted of his violence to his enemies: "I cut their throats like lambs. I cut off their precious lives [as one cuts] a string. Like the many waters of a storm, I made [the contents of] their gullets and entrails run down upon the wide earth . . . Their hands I cut off."[15] Ashurbanipal (669–626) also took pleasure in torturing his enemies: "I pierced his chin with my keen hand dagger. Through his jaw I passed a rope, put a dog chain upon him and made him occupy a kennel."[16] These snapshots confirm the prolonged and systemic cruelty that characterized the Assyrians over many centuries. No wonder the Lord judged the Assyrians. In 612 BC, Nineveh was destroyed by the Babylonians. The impressive city reduced to ruins.

---

13. The book of Nahum does not have a superscription. Nevertheless, the prophet gives some clues that enable us to place the book with a good degree of certainty. The prophecy took place before the destruction of Nineveh in 612 BC. Since the prophet refers to the fall of Thebe, capital of Cush (modern-day Ethiopia), as an event in the past (3:8–10) we know that it was written after 663 BC. Furthermore, the reference to Thebe only makes sense if poised when Thebe lay in a state of desolation. This limits the time range since Thebe was rebuilt in 654 BC. Thus, we can place Nahum's prophecy in a narrow window (663–54 BC).

14. Luckenbill, *Ancient Records of Assyria and Babylonia*, 1:146.

15. Luckenbill, *Ancient Records of Assyria and Babylonia*, 2:127.

16. Luckenbill, *Ancient Records of Assyria and Babylonia*, 2:319.

This marked the end of the Assyrians, the brutal empire that had deported Israel.

## THE KINGDOM OF JUDAH (722–586 BC)

With the nation of Israel out of the picture, the spotlight was on Judah. Some of the prophets, like Isaiah and Micah, who had blown the horn for the Northern Kingdom continued to do the same for Southern Kingdom. The prophetic voice was even louder because it was amplified by the catastrophic end of the Northern Kingdom. Did the people of Judah listen? Did they escape judgment? We will answer these questions by again sketching the history of what was taking place inside and outside of Judah's border.

### Inside: Days of Disillusionment

Sadly, throughout the seventh century, the people of Judah continued to ignore all warning calls. They continued in this downward spiral of rebellion. This rebellion was epitomized by Hezekiah's son Manasseh (687–642 BC). Although Manasseh enjoyed a long tenure characterized by a measure of political and economic success, the biblical writers were exclusively interested in highlighting the catastrophic spiritual dimension of his reign. Manasseh did evil in the eyes of the Lord (2 Kgs 21:2), leading the people into deeper and deeper levels of idolatry. So much so that following his reign, Judah's fate seemed sealed (2 Kgs 23:26–27). From this moment onward, even when good kings like Josiah (640–609 BC) brought reform, this reform quickly faded away. The people of Judah were charging down the path of disobedience and were ignoring all warning calls. They believed themselves to be exempt from judgment because they had the temple and a king from David's lineage. The prophets dared to disagree with this ill-founded belief and continued to call the people to repent. *Jeremiah*[17] and *Ezekiel*[18] both used the analogy of two sisters to drive home their message (Jer 3:7; Ezek 16:46): the Kingdom of

---

17. Jeremiah (1:1–3) prophesied under various kings of Judah, from the reign of Josiah (640–09 BC) until after the fall of Jerusalem (586 BC).

18. Ezekiel carried out his ministry in Babylon from 593 BC, the fifth year from the deportation of King Jehoiachin (Ezek 1:1–3) until 571 BC, the last dated oracle (Ezek 40:1).

Israel as the elder sister and the Kingdom of Judah as the younger sister. Despite the prophets' best efforts this turned out to be another case where the younger sibling followed the older sibling down a path of destruction. The prophet *Zephaniah*[19] made a last-ditch attempt by unequivocally announcing the dreadful day of judgment would fall upon the people of Judah. We have good reasons to believe the prophets *Joel*[20] and *Habakkuk*[21] also joined the substantial choir of prophetic voices. Joel used the vivid description of a devastating locust invasion to warn of an even greater invasion in the land of a foreign nation. The Lord announced in the book of Habakkuk that the unthinkable was about to take place. The Babylonians (also known as the Chaldeans) would soon be used by the Lord to judge the people of Judah. Just as the Lord used the Assyrians to judge the Northern Kingdom now, he would use the Babylonians to judge Judah. The Babylonians were the new Assyrians.

## Outside: Babylonians' Cherry-Picking Strategy

The first prophet to introduce us to the Babylonians was the prophet Isaiah. The first part of Isaiah's book (1–39) finishes with a poignant narrative. Following Jerusalem's miraculous delivery from the Assyrians in 701 BC, King Hezekiah fell ill. It seemed his days were over. Indeed, the prophet Isaiah told Hezekiah to put his affairs in order because his time was up (38:1). Hezekiah, however, fervently called upon the Lord and the Lord answered his prayer (38:2–22). News of Hezekiah's remarkable recovery reached neighboring kings, including Merodach-baladan king of Babylon. He sent envoys with letters and a gift (39:1). Hezekiah gladly welcomed the Babylonians and offered them a grand tour of his treasure house and his kingdom (39:2). When Isaiah discovered the identity of

19. Zephaniah (1:1) prophesied during the reign of Josiah, the last good king of Judah (640–09 BC).

20. The prophecy of Joel does not have a superscription or many historical clues. It is perhaps the hardest book to place, as evidenced by the wide range of theories that go from before the Assyrian invasion (722 BC) to after the Babylonian invasion (586 BC). I place Joel just before the Babylonian exile for the following reason: the various references to the temple indicate that the temple had not yet been destroyed, the prophecy is an announcement of a future judgment, and the linguistic and thematic parallels between Joel and other prophets of this period (Jeremiah and Ezekiel).

21. The main indicator for the dating of Habakkuk is the prediction of the imminent Babylonian invasion (1:6) thus we can place this prophecy toward the end of the 7th century BC.

the delegation, he broke the news to King Hezekiah that one day all that he had boastfully showed them would one day be taken away to Babylon (39:3–8). Thus, the historical interval in the book of Isaiah ends with the Lord closing the doors of Jerusalem to the Assyrians but with Hezekiah opening the doors to the Babylonians. Trouble was brewing.

Over the following decades the Babylonians increased in strength. They eclipsed the Assyrians as the regional superpower in 612 BC when they destroyed Nineveh. With the Assyrians annihilated, the only real threat for the Babylonians were the Egyptians. The Babylonians assured their supremacy by defeating the Egyptian Empire in the famous battle of Carchemish (605 BC). The Babylonian Empire was the new sheriff in town, having control over the entire Middle Eastern region. Their foreign policy for controlling this large territory was different from that of the Assyrians. They cherry-picked and deported only the high-caliber people from the various nations. Essentially, they removed all leaders and potential leaders that had the capability of successfully organizing a rebellion. Thus, in 605 BC, the Babylonian king, Nebuchadnezzar, besieged Jerusalem and dragged back to Babylon the top layer of the people of Judah. *Daniel*[22] and his three friends were part of the crème de la crème and thus were deported. They were enrolled in the Babylonian university where they were taught the Babylonian language and literature. The young men also received new names linked to the Babylonian gods.[23] The strategy was clear. The goal was to brainwash the young men and give them a new Babylonian identity. Nebuchadnezzar even stole some of the treasures from the temple in Jerusalem to dedicate them to his gods. He was doing everything in his power to get the young men to switch teams by presenting his team as the winning side. He failed! From the outset of the book of Daniel we are reminded the Babylonians besieged Jerusalem not because they were stronger but because the Lord gave Jehoiakim into Nebuchadnezzar's hands (Dan 1:2).

Despite this first deportation, Judah continued to be a hot spot and a difficult territory to control. King Nebuchadnezzar had to intervene again

22. Daniel lived in Babylonian during the exile. Indeed, his life seems to correspond approximately with the seventy years that the people of Judah were in exile. The stories narrated in this book therefore range from 605 BC (1:1) to 536 BC (10:1).

23. Daniel ("God is my judge") was renamed Belteshazzar ("Bel, protect the king"). Hananiah ("God is gracious") was renamed Shadrach ("Enlightened by Aku"). Mishael ("Who is like God?") was renamed Meshach ("Who is like Aku?"). Azariah ("the Lord is my helper") was renamed Abednego ("Servant of Nebo").

in 598–97 BC and deport a second group of Judeans. This group included the prophet *Ezekiel*. Ezekiel, however, was not taken to the headquarters in Babylon but was sent with other exiles by the Chebar Canal. Indeed, Ezekiel received his call and carried out his ministry whilst in exile.

By this stage, the prophets, particularly *Jeremiah*, announced that the window of opportunity to escape judgment was shot. The Lord unleashed the Babylonians to judge his people. The appropriate response therefore was to accept the Lord's chastisement. Jeremiah illustrated this by saying that those who go into exile were the "good figs" whilst those who continued to resist the Babylonians, and thus resist the Lord's discipline, were the "bad figs" (Jer 24). Despite the clear directives, the people of Judah, fueled by the false prophets, continued their pattern of insurgencies against the Babylonians. King Nebuchadnezzar reached his final straw and in 586 BC attacked Jerusalem once and for all. The devastation was total. The city, including Solomon's glorious temple, was burnt to the ground. Yet, the prophets that had predicted this devastation (Jer 6, Ezek 5) were once again keen to attribute the ultimate explanation of this tragic event to the Lord's hand of judgment and not to the muscles of a foreign nation. The book of Daniel eloquently draws our attention to this way of understanding these events by showing us that the same king that burnt down Jerusalem was ironically unable to burn three young Jews in his own back yard. Having Shadrach, Meshach, and Abednego walk out of the fiery furnace unharmed and without a smoky smell was proof the fire in Jerusalem was ultimately not caused by the Babylonians but by the blaze of God's wrath. The Babylonians were simply the matches.

The book of Lamentations offers an insight into the aftermath of the fall of Jerusalem. Although it cannot be said this dark day was a surprise, nevertheless the anguish was real. Through Moses the Lord had clearly laid out many centuries earlier what the consequences of their disobedience would be (Deut 28). The Lord had also sent the prophets to echo the same warnings. Because the people of Judah shelved Moses and snubbed the prophets, they were now left wailing and lamenting because of the inevitable consequence of their sinfulness. Although the wounds were self-inflicted, they were also deep and painful. And during this time, as we discovered from the prophet Obadiah,[24] the Edomites did their best to rub salt in their wounds. The Edomites, however, did not have the last laugh. The special treatment given to Jehoiachin, the king of Judah, whilst

24. See previous discussion on the dating of Obadiah.

in Babylon (2 Kgs 25:27–30), hints that even in exile the Lord is still look-ing out for his people.[25] The story of the people of Judah is not over yet.

| Judgment | Covenant Curses | Prophetic Warnings | Lament |
|---|---|---|---|
| Sons and daughters in captivity | Deut 28:41 | Amos 7:17; Isa 39: | Lam 1:4–6 |
| City destroyed | Deut 28:52 | Micah 3:12 | Lam 2:7 |
| Cannibalism | Deut 28:53 | Jer 19:19 | Lam 2:20 |
| Despised by other nations | Deut 28:37 | Jer 25:9 | Lam 3:45 |

*Table 5: Curses Prophesied and Lamented*

## THE POSTEXILIC COMMUNITY (586–450 BC)

The prophet Jeremiah (25:11) had prophesied that the Babylonian exile would last seventy years, approximately a lifetime. Daniel (9:2), in exile, knew this. He longed for Jerusalem and prayed with the window open toward his home city. Daniel prayed the Lord would keep his promise and allow the people of Judah to return to Jerusalem. This prayer was not just in line with Jeremiah but with most of the prophets. A key element of the prophetic message was that after the time of judgment the Lord would restore the people to the promised land with a new and greater exodus. Let us see how it unfolded. This time we will start with what was taking place around the land of Judah before zooming in.

## Outside: Persian Live-and-Let-Live Strategy

The prophet Isaiah was one of the prophets who anticipated this period of return and blessing. Curiously, just as he was the prophet who introduced us to the Babylonians, he was also the prophet who introduced us to the next superpower, the Persians. Indeed, this time he actually mentioned by name King Cyrus of Persia, even before the king's birth. Remember, Isaiah is long gone by this stage and yet he saw, ahead of time, that Cyrus would have a pivotal role in the return of the people of Judah after the

---

25. This special treatment was also documented on Babylonian cuneiform tablets (See Pritchard, *Ancient Near East*, 274–75).

exile. Indeed, Isaiah (45:1) called him the Lord's anointed. Clearly, this change at the top from the Babylonians to the Persians was written on the wall. Literally! Daniel (5:1–30) had the task of reading and interpreting the writing on the wall which announced to the Babylonian king, Belshazzer, that his kingdom would be given to the Persians, which is exactly what happened in 539 BC.

When the Persians did take over, they applied a different strategy again compared to the Assyrians and Babylonians. Their basic policy was essentially live and let live. They exerted their dominance over a large territory by allowing the many nations under their control to return to their respective homelands. Furthermore, they also allowed them, and on some occasions sponsored them, to rebuild their places of worship. Cyrus reveals his thinking behind this strategy:

> I returned to (these) sacred cities on the other side of the Tigris, the sanctuaries of which have been ruins for a long time, the images which (used) to live therein and established for them permanent sanctuaries. I (also) gathered all their (former) inhabitants and returned (to them) their habitations. Furthermore, I resettled upon the command of Marduk, the great lord, all the gods of Sumer and Akkad whom Nabonidus has brought into Babylon to the anger of the lord of the gods, unharmed, in their (former) chapels, the places which make them happy. May all the gods whom I have resettled in their sacred cities ask daily Bel and Nebo for a long time for me and may they recommend me.[26]

The Persians therefore were not magnanimous. They were keen to earn the favor of the gods, and to a certain extent the people, because they saw it as the best tactic to maintain control of their kingdom. The people of Judah were beneficiaries of this policy. In fact, the Bible writers insist on revealing that beyond and behind these decrees the invisible sovereign hand of God was directing history. The book of Esther, for example, shows us the Lord is at work behind the scenes for the good of his people, even in the Persian headquarters of Susa.

## Inside: Days of Small Things

The books of Ezra and Nehemiah also chronicle how what was taking place in the wider Persian Empire impacted the life of the postexilic

---

26. Pritchard, *Ancient Near East*, 284.

community in Judah. Following Cyrus's decree, Judeans returned in small waves to Judah. The first group of Judeans trickled back under the leadership of Zorobabel (538 BC). The highway in the desert (Isa 35) turned out to be a small trail. When the people reached Jerusalem, no doubt they were distraught to see the city had been bulldozed. It was time to roll up their sleeves and get rebuilding. There was plenty of work to do between rebuilding their houses and rebuilding the temple, the Lord's house. The people got to work and got off to a good start. However, because of external opposition and internal division, the good start was short lived (Ezra 4). The people soon neglected rebuilding the temple in favor of rebuilding their own homes. The people had lost sight of their priorities. The Lord therefore sent the prophet *Haggai* [27] to expose the absurdity of the people's actions. The prophet called the people to recalibrate their priorities and get back to work (1:1–15). Although the people responded positively to Haggai's call to rebuild the temple, they did so in a gloomy work environment. It was evident to all of them that the temple they were rebuilding could not stand in comparison to Solomon's glorious temple (2:1–9). The exuberant predictions the prophets had given clashed with the disappointing reality. Hope began to wane. Times had changed and now everything was on a smaller scale, days of small things. The Lord, however, exhorts the people through Haggai, and his contemporary *Zechariah*,[28] to not despise the days of small things (Zech 4:10). Both prophets not only guaranteed the completion of the temple but also reinforced the promise of a glorious future. Despite this exciting future perspective, the current circumstances of the people of Judah remained flat.

The flatness the people experienced mirrored the flatness of the people's commitment to the Lord. Although the people had returned to the land, the postexilic prophets exposed that the people had not fully returned to the Lord. The people of Judah did manage to complete the temple, but their worship was half-hearted. The prophet *Malachi*[29] in-

27. Haggai gives the specific dates of his oracles (1:1, 15; 2:1, 10, 20). All his oracles take place within the space of a few months in the second half of 520 BC.

28. Zachariah was a contemporary of Haggai. Zechariah began his ministry in 520 BC (1:1, 7).

29. The book of Malachi does not have a superscription. Nevertheless, there is widespread consensus among scholars in considering Malachi a contemporary of Ezra and Nehemiah in the mid-fifth century BC. Here are the primary motivations for this dating: the temple had already been rebuilt (1:10), the presence of a governor corresponds with the Persian period, and the many parallels between the sins exposed in Malachi and the sins described in Ezra and Nehemiah.

dicted the people for shamelessly bringing second-rate animals to the Lord instead of offering their absolute best (1:6—2:9). This is even more reprehensible when contrasted with the Lord's first-class commitment to the people. According to Malachi, their survival as a nation, contrasted to the disappearance of the Edomites, is the assurance of the Lord's love for them (1:2–5). Therefore, although the return was lower key compared to their expectations, their very existence was both proof of the Lord's love and a guarantee for the future. Following Malachi an interval began in which the people of Judah were to remember Moses and wait for Elijah[30] (4:4–6), but the story was not over yet.

Here ends our whistle-stop tour of the historical context of the prophets. This summary is a good starting point to begin to see the big picture and find your bearings. In preparation for preaching any prophetic book you will want to go on multiple tours to the specific time period to walk the streets the prophets walked. Remember, the more you know the history the better placed you are to preach the text. This should be enough to motivate any preacher worthy of this title to delve into rigorous historical research. We travel through history because eternity is at stake.

## PITFALLS TO AVOID

All we have said so far will prevent us from falling into the trap of neglecting history. Before drawing this chapter to a close I must also warn you not to overreact and end up in the opposite trap. Believe it or not, it is possible to give too much weight to the historical context in the preparation and in the preaching of a sermon.

We give too much weight to history in the preparation of the sermon when we consider the historical context to be the dominating factor in our interpretation. Historical research is an important factor in the interpretation of any biblical text, but it is not the controlling factor. It rightfully has a seat at the table but should not be seated at the head of the table. The biblical text itself is our chairperson. The purpose of the historical research is to better understand the biblical text not to add to it or alter it. The text overrides historical reconstruction, not vice versa, because the locus of inspiration is the biblical text and not the history

---

30. The gospel writers identify John the Baptist as the who fulfills Malachi's prophecy of a coming "Elijah" (Matt 11:10–14; 17:10–13).

behind the text. Therefore, the study of the world behind the text is useful insofar as it sheds light on the text itself. After all, it is the meaning of the text we are after and not the perfect historical reconstruction.

Moreover, the very concept of the perfect historical reconstruction is a chimera. When we are engaging in historical research, we are never just considering naked facts but we are looking at these events through the eyes of historians. Long explains this dynamic by comparing historians to painters. "Just as the physical world does not present itself in such a way that no creative choices are required of artists who would depict some aspect of it, so the past does not present itself in such a way that historians need make no creative choices in the construction of a historical account of some aspect of it."[31] The ideas, biases, negative connotations, and even speculations of each historian shape how they interpret and report history.

Furthermore, historical-cultural research is a complex discipline because cultures are complex. As Chalmers explains:

> Cultures are incredibly complex phenomena. They embody and are shaped by a variety of social, economic, political and religious factors, to name a few. While we may be aware of the various influences and dynamics that are at play in our own native culture, it is more difficult to see the depth of complexities that are present in others, especially those which are separated from us by a vast historical and social gap. As a result, we will tend to oversimplify realities and fail to recognize the presence of diversity.[32]

We can therefore conclude that even after much research our own reading and understanding of history will remain subjective and sketchy. This does not negate the importance of historical research in our interpretation of Scripture; it simply cautions us against having an inflated and naïve view of history.

We give too much weight to history in the pulpit when we reduce our sermon to a mere history lesson. Kaiser spots this danger: "One can pay so much attention to the historical and social contexts that the message of the text itself, along with its import for later generations, is never heard in all its own right."[33] The more hours we invest in studying the

---

31. Long, "Art of Biblical History," 327.
32. Chalmers, *Interpreting the Prophets*, 65.
33. Kaiser, *Preaching and Teaching from the Old Testament*, 104.

historical context the stronger the temptation will be to display the fruit of our hard work. However, this is ill-advised. Our responsibility is not to give a lesson in biblical backgrounds but to preach the word of God. As preachers, therefore, we must carefully consider how much historical information should be included in the sermon. Although the amount of information will vary based on the knowledge of the congregation, the series length, the sermon length, and the specific prophetic book, the basic rule is to give only the historical information that is necessary to communicate the main idea of the text.

We must also decide when and how to include the necessary information. Within the context of a sermon series it may be appropriate to include a significant proportion of the background material in the first introductory sermon to set the scene. Another possibility is to give a handout detailing the historical information in advance of a new series on a prophetic book. Within the context of a single sermon we also have options. I made the case earlier, from the book of Obadiah, that it is possible to include and employ the historical setting to introduce the sermon. When this is done well it is extremely effective. However, when this is not done well it is extremely detrimental. We must remember that the majority of our listeners may consider the prophetic books important because they are part of Scripture but fail to see how they are relevant for their lives. If we begin with an avalanche of historical information, we will bury the little attention our listeners may have had. Inversely, we will gain their attention if we begin with an effective introduction.

What constitutes a good introduction? The most effective way of engaging the listener is not simply by tickling their curiosity but by uncovering a need that the biblical text will meet. Robinson explains:

> Sermons catch fire when flint strikes steel. When the flint of a person's problem strikes the steel of the word of God, a spark ignites that burns in the mind. Directing our preaching at people's needs is not merely a persuasive technique; it is the task of ministry. Therefore, we must, raise a question, probe a problem, identify a need, open up a vital issue to which the passage speaks. Contrary to the traditional approach to homiletics, which holds the application until the conclusion, application starts in the introduction.[34]

34. Robinson, *Biblical Preaching,* 123–24.

If we immediately preview how the prophetic message will touch their deep needs then the listeners will gladly journey back in history to then be able to experience God's touch in their lives.

## THE BOTTOM LINE

Anyone who has attempted to preach the prophets has realized the necessity of having a good grasp on the historical setting. Knowledge of the historical background is an indispensable ingredient in reading, understanding, and preaching any part of the word of God, but this is particularly true of the prophets due to their circumstantial nature. Therefore, our responsibility is to research the historical background of the biblical text rigorously and thoroughly. Our responsibility is also to learn to include the necessary historical background in our sermons judiciously and creatively. As we have seen, the formulas can vary. We have options, as long as we remember that bypassing the historical information altogether is not an option. Time traveling is a necessity for the preacher of prophecy. However, if we commit the fatal time-traveling mistake of getting stuck in the past, we will be of no use to the people of God we are serving in the present. The bottom line is we must master the history but preach the text because our goal is to transform more than inform.

# Chapter 7

## PREACH THE PROPHETS LIKE THE PROPHETS

> "Long ago, at many times and in many ways, God spoke to
> our fathers by the prophets."
>
> —HEB 1:1

THE THRUST OF THIS chapter is to encourage you to preach someone else's sermons. Let me be clear: I am not for one moment supporting the sad practice of downloading your sermon from the web. I agree with Piper when he says: "It seems, frankly, utterly unthinkable to me that authentic preaching would be the echo of another person's encounter with God's word rather than a trumpet blast of my own encounter with God's word."[1] The situation however is altogether different when it pertains to divinely inspired sermons recorded in Scripture. In these instances, plagiarism is not only legitimate but recommended. Applying this to the prophetic books, which are collections of prophetic sermons, I will begin by advocating that we should steal all we can from them. I will do this by highlighting an aspect that is often neglected in the discussion on expository preaching. Springboarding from this theology of plagiarism, I will then overview the broad range of rhetorical forms and features the prophets employed, offering some tips and nudges along the way for how to preach them with literary and rhetorical sensitivity.

1. Piper, "My Pastor Uses Pre-Made Sermons," lines 8–12.

## THE MISSING DIMENSION OF EXPOSITORY PREACHING

Expository preaching expresses the commitment to faithfully communicate the *content* of a passage of Scripture to the modern audience. This is not easy. It takes hours of prayer-saturated study and careful exegetical work. Yet we put in the hard work because we believe it is vital for God's people to hear God's voice. Conversely, it is fatal to preach our own ideas from the pulpit and clothe them with divine authority. We are expository preachers only if the content of our sermons exposits and expounds the content of the preaching text. This is the standard understanding of expository preaching. Whilst I embrace this understanding (and I hope you do to), I think it is incomplete. I would like to expand our understanding of "expository preaching" to include faithfulness not only to the content of the passage—*what* the prophets said—but also the form of the passage—*how* they said it.

In communication, *what* you say is heavily impacted by *how* you say it. Content and form go hand in hand and cannot be severed. This is also true of Scripture. The same truth presented in different forms has different impacts. Paul logically argues the Lord is sovereign over every nation and every detail of our lives (cf. Rom 8:28; Col 1:16–17) Paul uses direct propositional statements. The book of Esther also teaches that the Lord is sovereign over every nation and every detail of our lives but does this in a story form. The book of Esther communicates this vision of the world indirectly, without even using the word "God." The same truth is taught but in different ways, and this greatly alters the way we receive it. Paul's rigorous logic and clarity will help us to understand it cognitively. The book of Esther will help us to feel this truth and visualize what it looks like in practice. Proverbs also teaches a similar notion: "The lot is cast into the lap, but its every decision is from the Lord" (16:33). With its proverbial succinctness, this proverb crystallizes the truth for us. The result is that the brief, memorable saying becomes a portable reminder of God's sovereignty. These examples illustrate the indissoluble unity between content and form.

It therefore follows that preaching which endeavors to faithfully communicate the content of Scripture inevitably must consider how to replicate the dynamics of the form in which the content is enveloped. A high view of Scripture, and of preaching, demands this. Whether a truth is expressed in poetry or proposition, apocalyptic or narrative, law or proverb, is not incidental. To be fair, most preachers do respect this variety when *interpreting* the text. We interpret a psalm differently from an epistle, a proverb differently from the law, and the Prophets differently from the Gospels. However, appreciation of these differences vanishes in our *preaching*. We have been taught a standard sermon form that we then apply without distinction across all biblical genres. The result is all the genres of Scripture get compressed into a one-size-fits-all, cookie-cutter-shaped sermon. Even if our standard sermon form is less rigid than a three-pointer all starting with the letter P, it still may be an inadequate method of recommunicating the variety we find in Scripture.

Practically this means that we need to intentionally consider how to mirror the form and reproduce the literary and rhetorical features of the biblical text in our sermons. With this approach our sermon will no longer be a straitjacket that limits the biblical text but a tailor-made outfit that perfectly suits it. When we do this well, we increase both the explanatory effectiveness of our preaching and also our persuasive power. This preaching approach leverages the significant rhetorical devices already embedded in the biblical text that are designed to persuade the readers of truth and move them to respond. Narrative persuades the reader implicitly by creating identification with the characters in the story and by showing the truth through plot development. Poetry persuades the reader by provoking emotions. The Epistles persuade the reader by presenting a well-articulated logical argument. Proverbs persuade readers by simplifying matters in a memorable and convincing manner. Genre-sensitive preaching channels these techniques to persuade listeners.

I will admit that adding this dimension to our preaching can initially be a challenge. It is challenging not just because this aspect is not typically part of our homiletical training but also because moving from a written form to an oral form of communication is tricky. This process will inevitably involve reflection, adaptation, and creativity. I am convinced, however, that this is part of our bridge-building duty as expository preachers. As Arthurs puts it: "As preachers, we want to say what the text says and do what the text does."[2] I am also convinced it is a delightful duty that will benefit your people, renew your appreciation of the richness of the Bible, and reinvigorate your passion for preaching.

2. Arthurs, *Preaching with Variety*, 28.

## PROPHETIC STRUCTURES

When preaching the prophetic books, therefore, we need to pay attention not only to *what* the prophets said but *how* they said it. We will explore together the rhetorical forms (or structures) and techniques the prophets used. The purpose of this exploration is not just to understand the prophetic rhetoric but to ponder how to replicate it today when preaching from a prophetic text. You will be glad to hear that applying this missing dimension of expository preaching to the prophetic literature has an advantage compared to preaching from other parts of Scripture. The prophetic oracles that come to us in written form were originally delivered in oral form and therefore have many features that lend themselves well to oral communication. Let us therefore look at the primary prophetic forms to gain hermeneutical accuracy and homiletical efficiency.

### Messenger Speech: Thus Says the Lord

When we begin to analyze the rhetorical strategy of the prophets, we will soon notice the prophets did not choose a one-size-fits-all approach. As Hebrews 1:1 says, the prophets really did speak in many ways. They had an impressive toolbelt packed with many oracle forms. Depending on the task at hand they selected the most appropriate tool. Nevertheless, just as most handymen have their go-to tool, so the prophets had their go-to prophetic form: the messenger speech. This prophetic form was the purest way for the prophets to fulfill their role as God's spokesmen (Heb. *nabi)* and deliver both judgment speeches and salvation speeches.

Smith suggests these judgment speeches may have developed from the cultural contexts of kings sending messengers with a threatening decree or judges who were handing down punishments.[3] Thus, these are messages given by someone in authority, delivered through a messenger. The prophets employed this form to convey threatening messages or staggering promises from the ultimate King and Judge. The judgment speeches typically included a list of the accusations (i.e., the people's transgressions) with an announcement of the upcoming judgment. The judgments ranged from crop failure to expulsion from the land in accordance with the covenant curses Moses had outlined in Deuteronomy 28. The prophets made it explicit that they were the only bona fide

---

3. Smith, *Interpreting the Prophetic Books*, 29.

messengers and that the message came from the Lord. The simplicity and the clarity of this approach removed all excuses. The accusations were clearly outlined, the divine origin of the message was explicitly stated, and the sanctions were thoroughly announced. In some instances, the oracle included an overt call to repentance (Joel 2:12–14), whilst in other cases the need to repent was hinted at (Amos 4:1–13), and in others still it was simply implied (Amos 3:1–15).

| Judgment Speech (Amos 3:1–15) | |
|---|---|
| List of Accusations | Amos 3:2 |
| Announcement of Judgment | Amos 3:3–15 |
| Divine Origin Made Explicit | Amos 3:1, 10, 11, 12, 13, 15 |

*Table 6: Judgment Speech*

| Salvation Speech (Joel 2:18–32) | |
|---|---|
| Reason for Blessing: God's Character | Joel 2:18 |
| List of Blessings: Curses Reversed | Joel 2:19–32 |
| Divine Origin Made Explicit | Joel 2:19 |

*Table 7: Salvation Speech*

The greatest difference between the two messenger speeches is the time of blessing is not presented because of the people's behavior, but rather it is anchored in God's gracious character (i.e., Joel 2:18–32). Other than that, the salvation speeches mirrored the same emphasis on the divine origin and contained the same clarity as the judgment speeches. Indeed, in some cases salvation speeches are intentionally shaped as the reversal of previous judgment speeches. Through these salvation speeches the Lord announced he would swap famine with abundance, exile with a new exodus, and grief with joy. These contrasts create a trampoline effect. You descend into the oracles of judgment to then rise high in the oracles of salvation. Down with sin and up with forgiveness. Down with destruction and up with restoration. Down with threats and up with promises. In our sermons, we should maximize this contrast.

I recently tried to replicate this trampoline effect in a sermon on Amos's final oracle (9:11–15). The book of Amos is saturated with announcements of judgment. Yet the final word is a stunning salvation speech in which the Lord promises to overturn the judgments. Here is a section from the sermon which aimed at helping the people see and *feel* this contrast:

> The Lord who said, "the great house shall be struck down into fragments, and the little house into bits" (6:11) now says [pause], "I will raise up the booth of David that is fallen and repair its breaches, and raise up its ruins and rebuild it as in the days of old" (9:11).
>
> The Lord who said, "They shall call the farmers to mourning and to wailing those who are skilled in lamentation, and in all the vineyards there shall be wailing" (5:16–17a), now says [pause], "Behold, the days are coming when the plowman shall overtake the reaper and the treader of grapes his who sows the seed" (9:13a).
>
> The Lord who said, "Assemble yourselves on the mountains of Samaria, and see the great tumults within her, and the oppressed in their midst" (3:9b) now says [pause], "The mountains shall drip with sweet wine, and all the hills shall flow with it" (9:13b).
>
> The Lord who said, "An adversary shall surround the land and bring down your defenses from you, and your stronghold shall be plundered" (3:11) now says [pause], "I will restore the fortunes of my people Israel, and they shall rebuild the ruined cities and inhabit them" (9:14a).
>
> The Lord who said, "I will turn your feast into mourning and all your songs into lamentation" (8:10a) now says [pause], "they shall plant vineyards and drink their wine, and they shall make gardens and eat their fruit" (9:14b).
>
> The Lord who said, "Behold, the days are coming upon you, when they shall take you away with hooks, even the last of you with fishhooks. And . . . you shall be cast out" (4:2–3) now says [pause], "I will plant them on their land, and they shall never again be uprooted out of the land that I have given them" (9:15).
>
> The Lord who said, "we were by nature children of wrath" (Eph 2:3b) now says [pause], "You are my child" (John 1:12).

As you can see, I did little more than place side by side the judgments with the corresponding blessings. Yet this list of juxtapositions accentuated the contrast. The pause and the predictable rhythm also contributed to boosting this trampoline effect. The pause functioned as being equivalent to the moment in which you sink deepest into the trampoline, knowing you will soon rise to the sky.

More generally the simplicity of structure and the clarity of the message are a help to us as preachers. The straightforward forms of these messenger oracles lend themselves well to replication in our sermon outlines.

However, it is then important to recognize that although most messenger speeches follow this typical structure, they also have their unique features. For example, one of Amos's strongly worded oracles (3:1–15) has all the elements of a typical messenger speech. Yet Amos dedicated little space to exposing Israel's sins (3:2) to give more space to highlighting the inevitability (3:3–8) and severity of the judgment (3:9–15). Furthermore, the inevitability of the judgment section is masterfully delivered by a dense, unrelenting sequence of rhetorical questions (3:3–8). Therefore, the oracles that fall under the umbrella of the basic messenger speech still have their unique rhetorical strategies. As preachers we need to not only notice these particularities but also learn to take advantage of them in our preaching. A preacher, for instance, who wants to guide his listeners to their own discovery of the truth of Amos 3 should borrow the prophet's technique and include a string of rhetorical questions in his sermon to achieve this goal.

## Lawsuit Oracle: Drag Your People to Court

In chapter 2, when summarizing the prophetic message, we saw the prophets can be thought of as covenant-enforcement mediators.[4] This understanding of the prophetic task finds its ultimate expression in the lawsuit oracles. The people are brought to court to stand before the judge. The Lord is also the prosecutor (although at times this role is delegated to the prophet) who indicts his people. These oracles are saturated with legal language and include the typical elements of a lawsuit: a summon to court, witnesses, a list of charges, the evidence, and then the verdict.

We have a clear example of a lawsuit oracle in Micah 6. We immediately recognize we are being transported to a courtroom drama by the density of legal language in the opening lines of the oracle: Arise, plead your case, indictment, and contend (vv. 1–2). Once we are aware of this courtroom setting, we can spot many of the typical elements of a lawsuit. The Lord summoned the people to court (1–2). Creation (mountains, hills, and the foundations of the earth) is called in as a witness (1–2). The Lord then presents a long list of damning charges (3–12) by contrasting

4. Fee and Stuart, *How to Read the Bible*, 184.

his faithfulness (3–5) with the people's unfaithfulness (9–12). In this section the accused (the people of Israel) even get a chance to speak to present any mitigating factors (6–7). The people of Israel, however, are found guilty and therefore are sentenced (13–16). In other examples (Isa 3:13–26; Hos 4) some of these elements may be missing or harder to find; nonetheless, the same basic rhetorical strategy is exhibited.

| Lawsuit Oracle (Micah 6:1–16) | |
|---|---|
| Summon to Court | Mic 6:1–2 |
| Witnesses | Mic 6:1–2 |
| Charges and Evidence | Mic 6:3–12 |
| Verdict | Mic 6:13–16 |

*Table 8: Lawsuit Oracle*

It is not hard to imagine the effectiveness of this creative approach. The people of God were, for the most part, oblivious to their rebellion to the Lord. By dragging the people to court the prophets were able to build the case and prove that the people were indeed guilty of grievous covenant violations. Furthermore, by imaginatively placing the people in the dock, Micah prepared them to accept the verdict and the inevitable sentence. Although the prophets used this technique a long time ago, we have every reason to believe this approach would be effective today. Crimes and courtroom dramas dominate the entertainment industry: TV series, documentaries, films, and novels are filled with them. Most of our people are informed and intrigued by the courtroom setting. These lawsuit oracles are the perfect opportunity to capitalize on this interest. Drag your people to court. Set the familiar scene. Make sure they feel how uncomfortable it is to sit in the dock. Prove with compelling evidence that they are guilty. Announce the damning verdict and allow them to tremble at the rightful sentence. Even if, by the grace of God in Christ, they are acquitted they will nonetheless be transformed by their day in court.

When I preached on Micah 6, I did two simple things to recreate the prophet's courtroom setting. I immediately transported the listeners to court by displaying an image of a courtroom on the screen. I also had a chair placed next to the pulpit. I pointed to the chair and used it to introduce the two line-ups. On one side I "presented" the Lord, who was indicting his people. On the other side, sitting in the dock (represented by the chair), I introduced the accused: the people of Israel. As I began to explain the charges (idolatry, injustice, and hypocrisy) brought against the defendant, I walked over to the chair. Standing next to chair I asked: "Where do we position ourselves in this courtroom drama? Are we part of the prosecuting team? Are we part of the jury? Simply spectators? Or, considering the list of accusations and our lives, is our place in the dock with the people of Israel? I can't answer these questions for you, but as for me . . . " I then proceeded to sit on the chair. Judging by the nods, I think it is safe to say most of the people present were vicariously sitting in the dock with me.

## Disputation Oracle: Pick an Argument

Of course, not all disagreements end up in court. Disputations were an efficient way to settle matters before going to court. Disputations were logical and passionate arguments between two sides that held contrasting viewpoints. Two incompatible ideas were placed in a ring to fight it out. The prophets frequently entered the debating ring with the people of Israel. The purpose of these debates was both to demolish and to build. The prophets, as the spokesmen of the Lord's debate team, demolished the people's wrong ideas and conclusions by proving the folly of their thinking. Simultaneously, the prophets also built a case to prove the truthfulness of the Lord's conclusions and thus called the people to change their way of thinking. Just as formal debates typically have a set format, so the prophetic disputations followed a typical structure. The fallacious viewpoint was introduced, the prophets presented the case for rejecting this viewpoint (this step is known as the rebuttal), and a clear conclusion was asserted. The rebuttal is the longest and the most important section of these oracles. The prophets engagingly and convincingly built their case that then led to the inevitable conclusion. Although the use of this technique was common among many of the prophets (Isa 49:14–26; Ezek 12, 18), Malachi was undoubtedly the specialist. The entire book of Malachi is a compilation of six disputations between the Lord and the people of Judah. The first disputation provides a straightforward example. The Lord and the people have two incompatible viewpoints. The Lord boldly declares his love for the people: "I have loved you" (1:2a). The people question the Lord's love: "How have you loved us?" (1:2b). Who has the correct viewpoint? By bringing the people to consider the contrast between their current status and the Edomites' tragic fate (1:2c–4), the Lord proves both the fallacy of their thinking and the veracity of his claim. The Lord has indeed proven his love for the people and has also brought them to consider his universal sovereignty (1:5).

| Disputation Oracle (Mal 1:2–5) | |
|---|---|
| Fallacious Viewpoint | Mal 1:2 |
| Rebuttal | Mal 1:2c–4 |
| Conclusion | Mal 1:5 |

*Table 9: Disputation Oracle*

As is obvious by this example, the disputation is an imagined, yet typical, debate between the Lord and his people. We do not directly hear the people's voices, but rather their hypothetical objections are channeled through the prophet Malachi. Nonetheless this imaginary debate is effective because the prophets convincingly portray and shrewdly predict the thinking of their audiences.[5] Due to the polemic nature of prophecy, and for the purpose of persuasion, we find occasions when the prophets represent the people's ideas with a hint of caricature and satire (cf. Mal 3:13–15). The prophets did all they could to persuade the people, and so should we.

As preachers we will be fascinated when we engage with these prophetic disputations. We will discover that the wrong ideas held by the people of Israel are still around today although often wrapped in a slightly different package. There is nothing new under the sun. Demolishing false viewpoints and aligning our people's worldview with the truth of the word of God is a key part of our ministry. It is a fight we must be willing to fight because ideas matter and ideas have consequences. Fallacious ideas have deadly effects. Truthful ideas have life-giving results.

Furthermore, we will also learn from these oracles how to fight this fight. The approach the prophets took to refute these wrong ideas continues to be highly effective. The prophets show us how to tackle head-on these wrong notions by setting up an imaginary, yet realistic, debate. We can follow their lead and use this imaginary debate format as our sermon

---

5. This is not unlike the approach that we encounter in some Pauline Epistles (Romans, Corinthians). In these Epistles, Paul constructs his theological argument by predicting and answering hypothetical questions that his readers might have. This dialogical style is known as a diatribe.

structure. If we do so we will effectively replace the false and cancerous ideas wedged in our people's minds with God's ideas.

How can we be expository in *form* as well as in *content* when preaching disputation oracles? I have two suggestions. The first one is easy—involve multiple people in reading these disputations. Have one person read the direct words of the Lord recorded in the text and have someone else read the words that are attributed to the people. Scan any of Malachi's six disputations and you will immediately see why this would be effective. The second is more creative. Set up two lecterns to replicate the debate format. From one lectern present the people's viewpoint. Then move to the other to dismantle their fallacious viewpoint and convincingly argue the Lord's perspective. If done well this approach will simplify your explanation and strengthen your persuasion. However, remember the debate is asymmetrical since the rebuttal is the longest part of disputation oracles. This should be reflected in the time you spend at each lectern. We do not want to erroneously convey that both viewpoints have equal credence.

## Lament Oracle: Time to Shed a Tear

The prophets made use of laments to grieve over, and warn of, impending judgment. They gauged the spiritual temperature of the people of Israel. The results of these spiritual health checks were dire. The people's unwillingness to repent was leading them toward judgment and death. To convey the seriousness of the situation, and the need to act immediately, the prophets made use of laments. Laments were cries of distress, expressions of mourning.

Laments are common in biblical poetry. The book of Lamentations is a compilation of five laments written and recited to mourn the destruction of Jerusalem. These laments were *ex post facto*—the people lamented the terrible destruction after the event had occurred. The particularity of the prophetic use of laments is that they often were *ex ante facto*, that is, they lamented ahead of time the judgment that would take place. Jeremiah lamented the destruction of Jerusalem over a decade before it happened (8:18—9:9; 9:10–26). The prophet saw the reality of the Lord's future judgment with such clarity that it was not too early to mourn. He knew the judgment would be terrible and certain, unless the people repented, and therefore mourned over what would happen. This was a dramatic, last-ditch attempt to trigger repentance and thus avoid judgment.

The prophet Amos also uses this approach to warn the Northern Kingdom (5:1–17). He explicitly introduces this oracle as a lament (5:1). Although Israel has yet to be judged the prophet looks to the future judgment and treats it as a past event. "Fallen, no more to rise, is the virgin Israel; forsaken on her land, with none to raise her up" (5:2). The fact that the actual judgment still lies in the future, however, is noticeable because the details of what will take place were described in the future tense (5:3). Why does the prophet lament ahead of time? The reason becomes obvious in the following verses (5:4–15) which intersperse the lists of sins that merit judgment with a call to repentance to escape judgment. If the people seek the Lord they will live (5:4, 6, 14–15) and will have no reason to mourn. If they do not repent there will be an abundance of lamentations, wailing, and mourning (5:16–17). It is worth noticing the presence of the Hebrew words *qinah* ("lamentation") and *hoy* (which is here translated as "Alas," but is elsewhere translated as "Ah" or even "Woe") which can be good indicators that the prophet is employing a lament motif.

| Lament Oracle (Amos 5:1–17): | |
|---|---|
| Announcement of Lamentation | Amos 5:1–2, 16–17 |
| Future Judgment | Amos 5:3 |
| Reasons for Judgment | Amos 5:4–15 |

*Table 10: Lament Oracle*

Funerals, wailing, and mourning draw attention. They stop people in their tracks and cause people to pay attention and pay respect. Most people respond by sensitively inquiring about the cause of the mourning and by taking time to reflect on the reality of suffering. The prophets knew this and were even willing to sing a funeral dirge to grab the people's attention. The lengths to which the prophets were willing to go to grab the people's attention portrayed in part the depths of the Lord's desire to draw his people back. Most oracles, therefore, were not light-hearted but solemn.[6] They were last-chance wake-up calls. Using laments, therefore, was entirely appropriate because the prophets dealt with matters of life and death. And so do we. The message we are to proclaim today is no less

6. This is not surprising since the meaning of the word "oracle" (Heb. "*massa*") is "burden."

vital than the message of the prophets. We must convey the utmost seriousness of responding appropriately to the word of God. When preaching from Amos 5 we must stop our people in their tracks and plead with them to "seek the Lord and live" (Amos 5:6) because eternity is at stake. If the best way to do this is to make use of a death notice, then so be it. The purpose, however, should not be to create superficial sensationalism, but to replicate the goal of the text to save our people from the horror of sin and its consequences.

As well as considering creative options like bringing a death notice to the pulpit (that was a genuine suggestion), our delivery style can help convey the earnestness embedded in the lament oracles. Over the last few decades there has been a move to a more conversational delivery style in the pulpit. This has its benefits. However, when preaching a lament, we should move in the other direction toward a greater degree of solemnity. Choose a more elevated style than normal. Less chit-chat in the pulpit, and more "Thus says the Lord." This may involve slowing your pace of delivery so your people will *hear* and *feel* the weight of every word. Use less but more potent words. Leave longer pauses than usual. Give time to ponder. Resist the urge to break the tension. Allow the people to feel the solemnity of the moment. This may come across as more formal and intense than usual, but that is okay. The prophets were intense, and funerals are formal. Of course, none of this should be artificial but should come from a heart that is truly burdened by the seriousness of the subject matter. Before adopting the prophetic style, we need to make sure we have the prophetic heart. In fact, the best way to replicate the solemnity of the prophets is to feel the burden the prophets felt.

The prophets were also masters of irony. We see this in the use of ironic prophetic laments over the downfall of foreign nations. Announcements of God's judgment toward Israel's enemies were good news for Israel, and the prophets, at times, conveyed this good news by crafting their oracle as sarcastic laments. Moab seems to be the primary target of this treatment (Isa 16:6–14; Jer 48) because of its history of taunting the people of God (Zeph 2:8–11). I can imagine a gifted preacher including an ironic eulogy in his sermon to replicate the irony of these laments. This could be achieved by crafting part of the sermon as an ironic eulogy commiserating Moab-like people, those who scoff God and taunt God's people, for the condemnation that they will face (Prov 19:19). This would be both a strong warning to scoffers and a great comfort to the afflicted. "Toward the scorners he is scornful, but to the humble he gives favor"

(Prov 3:34). Wielding the irony that is present in the prophetic text is an excellent way to penetrate hard barriers.

## Oracles against the Nations: Make Sure They Overhear

This irony toward Moab brings us to consider another conspicuous group of oracles: oracles against the nations. Considering the prophetic books were written for Israel and Judah, it is notable that major sections of the prophetic literature include oracles against the nations. All three of the Major Prophets and some of the Minor Prophets include a compilation of oracles against the nations. Indeed, some of the Minor Prophets exclusively include oracles against foreign nations.

| Oracles against the Nations | | |
|---|---|---|
| Sections in Major Prophets | Sections in Minor Prophets | Whole Prophetic Books |
| Isa 13–23 | Amos 1–2 | Obadiah |
| Jer 46–51 | Hab 2:6–20 | Jonah |
| Ezek 25–32, 35, 38–39 | Zeph 2:4—3:8 | Nahum |

*Table 11: Oracles against the Nations*

What was the purpose of these oracles to the nations? Did the prophets send delegations to the foreign nation to deliver the message? We find sporadic evidence of this taking place (Jer 27:3; 51:59–64). We also have the rare instance when the Lord sends a prophet outside of Israel's borders (Jonah is the most obvious example). However, it seems unlikely all these oracles against the nations, which were typically structured as messenger speeches, were sent to the nations mentioned. And if this is the case then the primary target for these oracles was not the nations but the people of Israel. The prophets communicated indirectly with the covenant people. At times, indirect communication can be more effective than direct communication. My wife uses it to good effect. When she asks our two-year-old if he wants to have a bath, she is really nudging me to take him upstairs and bathe him. She is speaking to our son, knowing I will overhear. I am the primary target. The prophets used a similar strategy. They spoke to Israel by addressing the nations to achieve three goals.

First, by announcing the Lord's judgment upon the nations, the prophets were indirectly, yet unequivocally, conveying that the Lord was sovereign over all superpowers. The people, therefore, had every reason to trust the Lord. They could also find comfort in knowing the nations that harassed and bullied them for many years would not get away with it but would face judgment. The prophecy of Nahum has this function. It announces the Lord's judgment on the brutal Assyrians, which was a great comfort for the people of God.

Second, knowing the Lord would also judge the nations was a strong deterrent against forming alliances. This was a temptation the Northern Kingdom succumbed to with fatal consequences. This function of the oracles against the nations is evident in the book of Isaiah, which is interspersed with warnings to not form alliances with other nations (7:1—8:22; 28:14-22; 30:1-17; 31:1-3; 39:1-8). The central section of the book, which is occupied with oracles against the nations, reinforces the message: it is foolish to look to your neighboring nations for security. This explains why the longest oracles were directed toward the nations that were attractive allies (Babylon and Egypt).

A final purpose of the oracles against the nations was to entrap the people of Israel into admitting they deserved God's judgment. The prophets drew attention to the sins of the other nations to get the people to concur that these sins merited judgment. Then the prophets turned the table and showed the people of God that they too were guilty of the same sins. The accusatory finger which the people were pointing at the other nations was now pointing at them. The judgment announced to the other nations, therefore, became a mirror that revealed God's judgment to them. Furthermore, they were doubly guilty because of the aggravating factor that they had the law and were God's covenant people. In chapter 3 we saw Amos's superb use of this rhetoric of entrapment (1:1—2:6). He surrounded the people like a lion surrounds his prey. Zephaniah also employed this tactic to encircle and trap the people of Judah (2:4—3:8).

When preaching these portions of Scripture, we should consider replicating some elements of this rhetorical strategy. We would do well to recognize some of the benefits of this indirect mode of communication. We can spot them by comparing them to direct communication. The greatest benefit of direct communication is clarity. As preachers we crave clarity, and, therefore, it is not surprising that this is our default communication mode. However, direct communication also has some disadvantages, especially when the content of the message is unpleasant. As soon as listeners perceive threats, they will erect barriers. When this happens, even though the message is clear, it will have little effect because it will not penetrate. This is where indirect communication is extremely effective. Because listeners do not realize they are the true target of the message, they will keep their barriers down. This enables the message to lodge in their hearts without encountering resistance. This approach does not dilute hard truths but conveys them indirectly so they are more likely to reach their destination. The downside of indirect communication is it places a greater burden on the listeners to grasp the main point, and if the listeners are only half paying attention, then the message falls flat. Nevertheless, the prophets used indirect communication in these oracles.

We too can use indirect communication to nurture our people's faith in the sovereignty of God by announcing that all the global superpowers will one day face judgment. Furthermore, we can also use this strategy to denounce sins in society, in the workplace, and in our neighborhood before then exposing the very same sins in the church.

For example, you could begin a sermon by narrating a recent news story that illustrates the particular sin the prophetic oracle denounces. You intentionally chronicle the news story in such a way as to foster repulsion and judgment toward those guilty of vile behavior. Once you feel the disdain boiling over, you can then uncover how the same sin we loathe in others is present in our own lives in different forms. I once used this approach to uncover hypocrisy. I began by comparing commitments three Italian politicians had made during elections campaigns with what they then did once they had been elected. It was not hard to find examples and stimulate contempt. Once the contempt had simmered sufficiently, I then drew our attention to commitments that we make in song to the Lord (i.e., "Jesus, all for Jesus . . . all I am and have and ever hope to be . . . ") and then invited us to compare this with how we were living. This rhetoric of entrapment helped us realize we were guilty of the same sin we detested in others.

I also heard of a preacher who went to great lengths to deliver his whole sermon indirectly. Before the service began, he had half of the church building cordoned off. As the church members gathered, they sat in the available section. This was not a problem because on most Sundays the church was only half-full (or half-empty). The assumption was that the cordoned off half was in the process of being redecorated. When the preacher went up to the pulpit he turned and directed his entire sermon to the cordoned off side of the room. As you can imagine, those who were present were initially bewildered by this bizarre behavior. However, they soon realized the words directed to empty pews were in fact for their benefit. The sermon was an apology to the unchurched. The preacher apologized to the pews for the church's lack of zeal for reaching the lost. He apologized for their lack of love for their neighborhood. He apologized for their lack of courage in proclaiming the gospel. He admitted they had become inward rather than outward looking. My friend who was there described it as the most powerful sermon he had ever heard. Do not underestimate the power of indirect communication! If our preaching text communicates indirectly, then we should consider what we can do to reproduce a similar effect.

## Visions: A Picture Is Worth a Thousand Words

It is true that, at least at times, a picture is worth a thousand words. We should therefore not be surprised that the greatest Communicator of all time made use of pictures. On various occasions the Lord revealed his message for his people to the prophets through visions. If the messenger speeches were the purest way for the prophets to fulfill their role as God's spokesmen, the visions were the purest way for the prophets to fulfill their role as God's visionaries (Heb. *Roeh* & *Hozeh*). The task of the prophet was then to report the vision, with its explanation, to the people.

Although the basic structure of vision explanation is standard, the complexity of the vision varies. I will briefly outline the three subcategories that represent the spectrum of complexity of the visions, accompanied with some basic preaching suggestions.

| Visions: | | | |
|---|---|---|---|
| | Simple Vision | Elaborate Vision | Apocalyptic Vision |
| Vision | Amos 7:7–8a | Ezek 37:1–10 | Dan 7:1–14 |
| Explanation | Amos 7:8b–9 | Ezek 37:11–14 | Dan 7:15–28 |

*Table 12: Spectrum of Prophetic Visions*

1. *Simple visions.* The Lord communicates his message via a straightforward graphic representation that the prophet sees. We find examples of these simple visions in Amos 7. The prophet sees a plague of locusts (v. 1), a vast fire (v. 4), and a plumb line by a wall (v. 7). These simple visions, with familiar and concrete images, were warnings of imminent judgment. Considering that these prophetic messages are anchored to simple images, it makes sense to preach them by taking advantage of multimedia. I say this somewhat grudgingly as I am generally hesitant to

use multimedia in the pulpit. I am not averse to it, but I have developed a mild allergy to it due to its overuse and misuse. Most of the time I find that it adds little, and on some occasions, I even think it has a detrimental effect. Perhaps, it is just me? Despite my negative bias toward multimedia, I am willing to concede that on some occasions it can be helpful, especially when the original message was conveyed through an image. For example, showing an image of a plumb line can clarify what the prophet saw and the meaning of his message. A brief video of a swarm of locusts devouring a harvest could convey the catastrophic judgment Amos was announcing. Therefore, despite being afflicted by PowerPointphobia, I am convinced that a tactful and circumscribed use of multimedia can be an excellent means to replicate the rhetorical effect of visions.

2. *Elaborate visions.* Other prophets communicated God's message by transporting us into a world of complex visions. These visions are prolonged, detailed, and convoluted. When we enter these visions, we feel as if we have lost touch with reality, yet their very purpose is to offer the right perspective on reality. The book of Ezekiel is characterized by these extended visions. The most famous one is probably Ezekiel's vision of the valley of dry bones. The prophet first saw and experienced the graphic vision (37:1–10) and then was instructed to deliver the explanation to the people in exile (37:11–14). When handling these elaborate visions, we must recognize the purpose of the vision is not just to increase the clarity but also the potency of the message. Indeed, on some occasions, the Lord does not provide an explanation because it is implicit in the vision. Ezekiel's two temple tours are good examples. The first tour (8:1—11:25) exposes the abominable practices of the people and the subsequent judgment of God. The climax of the vision is the glory of God departing from the temple (11:22–25). The purpose of this vision, therefore, is to reveal the true spiritual condition of the people of Judah and to announce the imminent reality of judgment. The second temple tour (40:1—48:35) mirrors and overturns the first vision. The high point this time is the return of the glory of God (43:1–5). Although the plethora of details may seem excessive and redundant to us, they contribute to the depth and significance of this vision. The many details (i.e., offerings, measurements, allocations) are not just descriptions of the temple's décor, they also represent greater underlying realities (i.e., worship, God's dwelling place, God's people). Furthermore, the details added concreteness to the vision because they enabled the people to imagine what the prophet saw and described. The purpose of the vision was to direct the hopes and the

hearts of the exiled to a future time of restoration when the presence of God would once again be among his people.[7]

When preaching these visions, our temptation will be to rush to the explanation of the vision. Yet by rushing to the explanation we are impoverishing the power of the vision. These long visions are momentous. They are not just a quick illustration; they are a prolonged experience. The lengthy tour through the temple is enabling us to feel (not just understand) the horror of sin. The elaborate description of the new temple is fermenting in us the desire to experience the blessing of the Lord's presence. When preaching these elaborate visions, do not rush to the explanation. Investing over half your sermon to guide the imagination of your people to envision the scene is time well spent. Transport your listeners into the visions.

You can achieve this by using vivid language. Vivid language sparks imagination. The key to speaking vividly is to choose precise words, especially verbs and nouns, that paint a picture. Instead of "the boy sat in church," try "the teenager slouched in the back row." Instead of "the man eats his lunch," try "the builder devours his cheeseburger." As you can see from these examples the specificity of the words aids your imagination. Vague words (boy, sat, man, eats, lunch) create a foggy image. Precise words (teenager, slouch, back row, builder, devours, cheeseburger) create a crisp image. As well as the visual component (sight), search for words that will appeal to the other senses (sound, touch, smell, and taste) to describe the vision. Place yourself, and your listeners, in Ezekiel's shoes to experience the scene. Describe how it felt to trudge through the valley full of bones (Ezek 37:1–2). Describe the feeling of *touching* dry bones, the rattling *sound* of bones coming together, and the shocking *sight* of flesh and skin covering bones. Join the prophet in the middle of the valley by selecting words that evoke the senses. Vivid and dramatic language increases the power of the message. Therefore, when describing the prophetic visions, do not settle for general words but hunt for the best words.

---

7. Although the significance and the purpose of the vision is clear, interpreters differ on how this vision of the presence of the Lord among his people will be fulfilled. The primary interpretations are: 1. This vision of a new temple points to events that will take place in the future, a time of great blessing called the Millennial age. 2. The vision is an extended metaphor (allegory?) of the presence of God that new covenant people experience. 3. The vision of the temple was a visual guarantee that the people of Judah would rebuild the temple after the exile. 4. The vision points to the New Jerusalem, where the presence of God will be fully experienced.

How do we do this in practice? I find Arthurs's advice about writing a manuscript helpful:

> Try writing out a manuscript. This discipline helps slow the preparation process. It gives us time to choose vivid words. It also gives us a tangible document to edit. Caution: write a manuscript, but do not preach from it! Very few people can read conversationally. When we read, we sound like we're reading. Don't memorize the manuscript either. None of us has time for that. Just depend on the discipline of writing and editing to add some vividness to your speech. Some of the language from the manuscript will transfer to the sermon, and you'll have the best of both worlds—concrete language expressed conversationally.[8]

3. *Apocalyptic visions.* If you think the volume of details in Ezekiel's visions are excessive, then you will be overwhelmed by the intricacy of apocalyptic visions. Although full-blown apocalyptic literature developed during the intertestamental period, this genre finds its roots in the Old Testament prophetic literature. We encounter sections in the prophetic books that have several traits of apocalyptic literature (Isa 24–27; Ezek 38–39; Dan 7–12; Zech 9–14): a dualistic vision of reality (good vs. evil); a narrative framework; a stark portrayal of the evil that afflicts the world; a call to suffer and persevere in the midst of escalating suffering; a conviction of God's final victory preceded and brought about by cataclysmic events; a proliferation of familiar, yet enigmatic, symbols (objects, animals, and numbers); and celestial beings acting as interpreters and tour guides.

To fully explore how to preach the apocalyptic genre would require another book. Apocalyptic literature moves you to the core. It thrills and terrorizes you at the same time. It brings you to the brink of despair before elevating you to unimaginable heights. Apocalyptic literature is bigger than you. It makes us feel small before the ultimate showdown between good and evil. It forces us to choose a side. How can we possibly mirror these effects in our preaching? Give it your all. Once again use vivid language. Indeed use your full range of language, emotions, solemnity, and energy. The advice given for the lament oracles about infusing your language with a strong dose of solemnity and intensity is perhaps even more relevant for the apocalyptic visions. Do not hold back. Apocalyptic literature is drama, preach it dramatically.

---

8. Arthurs, *Preaching with Variety*, 51.

As well as the choice of language, to replicate the intensity of apocalyptic literature we need to also curate the content of the sermon. Of course, as expository preachers, the subject matter of our sermon will match the subject matter of the biblical text. Apocalyptic literature deals with big issues: evil, suffering, injustice, God's sovereignty, God's wrath, judgment, and final consummation. The weight of these mega topics will drive us to preach with gravitas. We must ensure our proclamation does not water them down. This includes our choice of illustrations. Calibrate your illustrations to match the serious content of the apocalyptic vision. Avoid trivial illustrations. Only include illustrations that deal with ultimate matters of life and death.

## Symbolic Acts: Show and Tell

The prophets' commitment to communicating to the people was such that they were not afraid to get their hands dirty. Literally! Ezekiel built a miniature city to show what would happen to the great city of Jerusalem (4:1–3). Ezekiel also had to lie on his left side for 390 days to represent the days of judgment toward the house of Israel and on the other side for 40 days to represent the years of judgment for the house of Judah. During this time, he was to eat meagre rations of poor-quality food baked on human dung (4:4–17). This was a visual representation of the warning of judgment the Lord was giving to his people.

Jeremiah also got his hands dirty. He purchased a linen belt and, following the Lord's instruction, placed it under a rock by a river. After some time, he returned to collect the belt and saw it was ruined. The prophet is then told the ruined belt represents the ruin the people of Judah would face (Jer 13:1–11). On another occasion, Jeremiah was told to symbolize the slavery of the people of Judah under the Babylonians by walking around with a yoke around his neck (Jer 27). Isaiah instead got his feet dirty. The Lord told him to walk around naked and barefooted like a prisoner of war to represent the Lord's judgment on Egypt and Cush (Isa 20).

Why did the Lord call the prophets to perform street theatre? Why behave so bizarrely? The goal was to grab the people's attention. A man walking with a yoke on his shoulders or a man walking around naked would no doubt turn a few heads. Similarly, the potent smell of dung or a man building a miniature version of Jerusalem would not go unnoticed. However, these dramatic actions were not only attention-grabbers but visual illustrations that conveyed the prophetic message. The pattern was that the Lord would give instructions to the prophet to do something and then would provide the fitting explanation. Therefore, the prophet would both show and tell the prophetic message. The strength of this mode of communication was that these simple acts were pregnant with profound prophetic meaning.

| Symbolic Acts: | |
|---|---|
| Instruction to Act | Isa 20:1–2 |
| Explanation | Isa 20:3–6 |

*Table 13: Symbolic Acts*

A good way to preach these portions would be to incorporate symbolic acts as part of your sermon. This does not mean we need to go as far as Isaiah or Ezekiel. Nonetheless, we can still incorporate simple actions, or use simple props, in our preaching that will achieve a similar effect of grabbing attention and illustrating the prophetic message. Even if you do not want to place a yoke on your shoulders, you could have it placed next to the pulpit or use another simple prop that represents slavery (i.e., chains). Even if you do not want to dig a hole in the wall of the church building, you can still bring a rugged bag with you to convey something of the pain of being ripped away from your home and homeland, never to return again (Ezek 12:1–16). I know in some church contexts using simple props or performing bizarre actions would be something of a shock. That is certainly a factor to consider with pastoral sensitivity. However, shock is exactly one of the rhetorical effects these actions were designed to produce. Furthermore, the goal is not simply to shock but also to illustrate the message and persuade hearts. If this second goal is achieved, then much will be forgiven. A final consideration is that, even within the prophetic books, these symbolic acts were not the standard means of communication. In a sense their efficacy was linked to their sporadic use, and the same is true today.

Nonetheless, if the prophets communicated with creativity or, to be more accurate, if the Lord communicated through the prophets with creativity, we should not be afraid to do the same. We can replicate this creativity. Our people need it, and Scripture warrants it. I still remember a sermon I heard fifteen years ago when I lived in Ireland. The preaching text was Jeremiah 18, where the Lord is portrayed as the ultimate Potter.

Next to the preacher there was a girl working a pottery wheel during the sermon. As far as I remember the preacher never once pointed to what was happening next to him, but inevitably our eyes were drawn to what this girl was doing. What we were hearing about the masterful work of the great Potter was being illustrated and enriched by seeing a potter at work before our eyes. The combination was powerful. I suspect something of this level is out of reach for most of us, but smashing a clay pot when preaching from Jeremiah 19 is within reach of most of us. All you need is the courage and creativity of a prophet.

## Mixed Genres and a Word of Caution

The prophetic tool belt also included a few other tools the prophets used more sporadically: prayers (Jer 32:16–25), letters (Jer 29), narratives (Jonah), parables (Isa 5:1–7), and hymns (Hab 3). Happily, we recognize all these genres from other parts of Scripture. The same basic methodology I have advocated so far also applies when we encounter these other genres in the prophetic corpus. We should approach them and endeavor to preach them in accordance with their literary characteristics.

Before moving on from the rhetorical structures to the rhetorical devices, I must give a word of caution. We must guard against the danger of superimposing predetermined structures on specific prophetic texts. The prophets did use standard structures; however, they did not consider them to be immutable forms. Rather they shaped and adjusted them according to their needs and purposes. There is a fine line between imposing an oversimplified understanding of prophetic forms *on* the text and thus importing external elements *into* the text, and a cultivated understanding that recognizes the prophetic forms that are *in* the text and thus allows the ideas to emerge *from* the text. We must walk this line by knowing the standard form, and yet not using it as a mold that constrains but as a template that reveals the natural shape of the specific oracle.

## PROPHETIC BUILDING MATERIALS AND FINISHING TOUCHES

Familiarity with the prophetic forms is therefore an essential ingredient to interpreting and preaching the prophets with genre sensitivity. However, if we want to recreate the dynamics of the prophetic genre, we must see more than the basic structures. We must also spot the building materials and the finishing touches the prophets used: parallelisms, metaphors, and other figures of speech. We also need to identify the prophets' tone. This is part of preaching the how in addition to the what of the text. In chapters 3 and 4, we considered the function, characteristics, and effectiveness of parallelism and metaphor. You may find it helpful to review those sections, this time with both your hermeneutical *and* homiletical caps. In other words, revisit those chapters and consider how to effectively replicate those forms in your preaching. You will be glad to discover it is not too difficult to do since parallelism and metaphors lend themselves well to oral communication. My encouragement, therefore, is simply to be intentional in incorporating these features in your sermons when preaching from a prophetic text.

## Parallelism: Restate, Rephrase, Reword

Consider the value of incorporating parallelism—the central feature of Hebrew poetry. Parallelism, unlike rhyme, does not get lost in translation. Therefore, even without being an expert in Hebrew we can appreciate parallelism and make use of it in our preaching. Remember, parallelism is more than mere repetition. Parallelism is not just saying the same thing twice; rather meaning is conveyed through the interplay of the two parallel lines. As we noted in previous chapters, this dynamic clarifies meaning, creates intensification, increases memorability, and prompts meditation. These are all effects we want to replicate in our preaching. How do we achieve this? The most obvious way is by using our own parallelism through restatement. When we restate, we express the same idea with new and different words. Restatement thus adds clarity and force to what we are expressing. Restatement is a mark of good oral communication. Most preachers use it intuitively. When preaching a portion of Scripture characterized by parallelism, we should consciously incorporate restatements, symmetry, rhythm, and intensification. We should deliberately craft our sermon with parallelism of content and form. Parallelism intended!

Jonathan Edwards made extensive use of potent parallelism in his famous sermon "Sinners in the Hands of an Angry God." Notice how Edwards used parallelism to convey the horror of hell:

"The pit is prepared, the fire is made ready, the furnace is now hot."[9]

"The old Serpent is gaping for them; hell opens its mouth to receive them."[10]

"The devil is waiting for them, hell is gaping for them, the flames gather and flash about them."[11]

The force that is generated by these parallel clauses, together with the use of vivid language, caused his listeners to shiver when confronted with the terror of God's wrath. You feel the heat. He also used parallelism to explain that sinners cannot contribute to their salvation. "And *nothing* to lay hold of to save yourself, *nothing* to keep off the flames of wrath, *nothing* of your own, *nothing* that you ever have done, *nothing* that you can do, to induce God to spare you one moment."[12] In this example parallelism adds force and clarity to his message. In most cases, effective parallel constructions are not the result of pulpit improvisation, but of careful preparation.

Furthermore, Arthurs suggests we can even go further and use parallelism to craft an entire sermon:

> Not only can we use parallelism for small units, but we can also use it to organize the entire sermon. State your point and develop it, then restate the point and develop it with more intensity, then restate it again. Sermons don't always have to march, they can also swirl in expanding arcs. If, however, you organize your message with synonymous parallelism, be careful that the arcs intensify just as the second part of a Hebrew line does. Sermons must not stall even when they state and restate themes.[13]

This approach is an excellent way to replicate another characteristic of the prophetic literature that we considered—the recursive dynamic. In the prophetic books we find themes that are revisited consecutively to explore the same topic from different perspectives. In a sense this recursive dynamic is parallelism on a bigger scale.

---

9. Edwards, "Sinners in the Hands," 7.

10. Edwards, "Sinners in the Hands," 7.

11. Edwards, "Sinners in the Hands," 11–12.

12. Edwards, "Sinners in the Hands," 16 (italics mine).

13. Arthurs, *Preaching with Variety*, 57.

I used the intensifying arcs approach to preach from Isaiah 9:1–7. Unsurprisingly it was a Christmas sermon. Gifts were being exchanged, carols sung, the sweet scent of gingerbread filled the air, and Christmas lights adorned the streets. Yet it was a difficult Christmas. Many in the church family were going through a tough time: illness, rebellious teenagers, conflicts, unemployment, and even bereavement. I remember thinking about the many empty chairs across the various Christmas dinner tables that year. Dark days! I felt the weight of this as I prepared to preach from Isaiah a few days before Christmas. Yet I was glad to be able to offer comfort from the word of God: Darkness will not last forever. The entire sermon developed and intensified this main point.

1.  *Arc 1*: Darkness will not last forever because the Lord has promised it (9:1–2). The Lord promised people living in thick darkness (cf. 8:22) that a great light will shine (cf. Matt 4:12–17). I closed this first arc by restating the main point. I then revisited the same central idea again in the next arc, enriching the motivation.

2.  *Arc 2*: Darkness will not last forever because the Lord will deliver us (9:3–5). The Lord will replace oppression with joy, slavery with freedom, and war with peace. The Lord will do this, therefore darkness will not last forever. In the third and last arc I went even deeper into the reason why darkness has an expiry date.

3.  *Arc 3*: Darkness will not last forever because unto us a child is born (9:6–7). We then spent time dwelling on the wonderful titles of our Savior that are the ultimate guarantee that darkness will not last forever.

Following the recursive pattern of the text (notice how the word "for" is repeated three times, vv. 4, 5, and 6) I was not presenting three separate reasons why darkness will end; rather, I was going through the layers to get to the ultimate reason. The parallelism of the three arcs enabled me to replicate the recursive dynamic of the text and drive the point home with gusto.

## Metaphors: Paint with Words

As well as parallelism, consider the value of metaphor. The prophets built many of their sermons using metaphors, and we can do the same. Most of us tend to prefer, or at least have been trained to prefer, logical constructions built with abstract propositional statements. This approach is well suited for sections of the Epistles but less so for the prophets. The prophets, while not requiring us to abandon logic, show us the effectiveness of metaphors. As preachers we know all too well that abstract statements can easily enter one ear and escape through the other. The vivid imagery of a good metaphor, on the other hand, forges itself in our minds. When a metaphor is implanted it is harder to remove. It lingers in our memory, it kindles our imagination, and it continues to exert its persuasive power. If we approach these metaphors simply by dissecting them and reducing them to abstract propositional statements, we end up stripping them of all their communicative force.

Speechwriter James Humes explains and illustrates the power of a metaphor by narrating how Winston Churchill changed recent history with a brilliantly crafted metaphor:

> In 1946 Churchill was a defeated man. He had lost the minister-ship a year before. Churchill worried that he could not convince Americans that Soviet troops in Central and Eastern Europe were suppressing freedom—particularly when he had lost his authority as Britain's elected leader. He knew he had to describe in graphic, vivid language what was happening to countries like Poland, Czechoslovakia, and others. Words like "Soviet imperialism," "militarism," and "tyranny" came to mind, but such words, thought Churchill, were "abstractions." To Churchill "abstractions" were shapeless words that go in one ear and out—because they don't paint a picture in the listener's mind. In his stateroom, as the train carrying the presidential entourage hurtled westward through the night of March 2, Churchill studied his map of Europe. His pen drew a black line from the Baltic Sea through Poland down through the Balkans to the Adriatic Sea. He retraced that line as he tried to think of the right picture to describe Soviet suppression of rights. Around 2:00 A.M., as the train stopped in Salem, Illinois, for refuelling, Churchill looked at the curtain dividing the sleeping part from the rest of the stateroom. Inspiration—perhaps from the ghost of Lincoln—flashed, and he wrote down on his copy of the speech a few lines in ink. The next day in the gymnasium at Westminster College he read from those notes: "From Stettin in the Baltic to Trieste in the Adriatic an iron curtain has descended across the continent." That picture phrase would galvanize America and

the free world into action; the Truman Doctrine, the Marshall Plan, and NATO followed.[14]

Few of us have the ability of Winston Churchill, but the prophets did. Indeed, the prophetic books are a treasure chest of metaphors. Most of the time all we need to do is open this treasure chest and incorporate the metaphors into our sermons. How do we do this? Sometimes the prophets used a single dominating metaphor to convey their main message, as when Ezekiel depicts Jerusalem as an unfaithful bride (Ezek 16). In the same way, we can use one dominant metaphor throughout our sermon to forge an indelible image in our listeners' minds. This was the key feature of Edwards's best-known sermon. Anyone who has come across his sermon will not forget the powerful image of sinners being held in the hands of God over the pit of hell. It is worth tracing how Edwards wielded this metaphor throughout his sermon so we can learn how to do the same. Edwards began to introduce his metaphor early on and returned to it over twenty times over the course of the sermon. He unveiled the metaphor gradually by simply introducing the image of being "on the edge of a pit."[15] Soon after he added that the only reason why sinners are not already in hell is because God "does not let loose his hand."[16] Before transitioning to the substantial application section of the sermon, Edwards brought the two parts of the metaphor together. He then continued to refer or allude to the metaphor by adding details and significance. He leveraged the metaphor to assert that your care for your life or means of preservation have no power to keep you out of the pit. "If God should withdraw his hand, they would avail no more to keep you from falling, than the thin air to hold up a person who is suspended in it."[17] Similarly, "all your righteousness, would have no more influence to uphold you, and keep you out of hell, than a spider's web would have to stop a falling rock."[18] About two-thirds of the way through the sermon he fully exploited the metaphor with a concentrated and intense description of God dangling a sinner over the pit of hell. This description added color and vividness to the metaphor, making it memorable. You do not forget the haunting image of God who "holds you over the pit of hell, much in

14. Humes, *Sir Winston Method*, 62–63.

15. Edwards, "Sinners in the Hands," 4.

16. Edwards, "Sinners in the Hands," 7.

17. Edwards, "Sinners in the Hands," 12.

18. Edwards, "Sinners in the Hands," 13.

the same way as one holds a spider, or a loathsome insect, over the fire."[19] The great theologian returned one more time to metaphor in his final appeal. "Let everyone that is yet out of Christ, and hanging over the pit of hell . . . now hearken to the loud calls of God's word."[20] Edwards's master-class shows us how to use a metaphor as the dominant sermon idea and how to weave it throughout the sermon. We can come up with our own metaphor, like Edwards, to channel the impact of a biblical metaphor, or, better still, we can harness the metaphor in the biblical text the prophets used (i.e., unfaithful bride, broken cisterns, shepherds, and flocks).

On other occasions the prophets used several metaphors to contribute to, illustrate, and support their main message. Isaiah, for example, brings together an array of metaphors in his opening oracle (1:1–9) to describe the people's wickedness. In these situations, we can use metaphors as our building blocks that substitute for traditional subpoints or, even more simply, as straightforward illustrations. When I preached from Isaiah 1:1–9, I crafted the sermon using the prophet's metaphors (and similes) to convey our sinfulness:

1.   We are rebellious children (2).

2.   We are like foolish animals (3).

3.   We are disrespectful subjects (4).

4.   We are diseased from head to toe (5–6).

## More Figures of Speech

Metaphors were not the only figures of speech the prophets used. Indeed, we find a wealth of figures of speech in the prophetic books. Figures of speech are a key element of effective communication. They infuse life into speech. They can engage and persuade the listener by providing clarity, igniting imagination, creating tension, disarming defenses, engaging emotions, and by inducing participation. Since the prophets made ample use of them, we should too. The following chart will help us become familiar with the primary figures of speech the prophets employed. Our task is to then explore, enjoy, and exploit them in our preaching.

19. Edwards, "Sinners in the Hands," 15.
20. Edwards, "Sinners in the Hands," 24.

| Figure of Speech | Explanation | Example |
|---|---|---|
| Simile | Comparison between two entities that are normally different. Characterized by the use of "as," "like." and "so." | Come now, let us reason together, says the Lord: though your sins are like scarlet, they shall be as white as snow; though they are red like crimson, they shall become like wool, (Isa 1:18) |
| Personification | Human characteristics attributed to inanimate entities. | Hear, O heavens, and give ear, O earth. (Isa 1:2) |
| Metonymy | A word or a phrase is replaced by another which is associated with it. An author may mention the "effect" to place emphasis on the "cause," or vice versa. | For every boot of the tramping warrior in battle tumult and every garment rolled in blood will be burned as fuel for the fire. (Isa 9:5) |
| Merism | Expression of the whole by indicating the two extremities. | If they dig into Sheol, from there shall my hand take them; if they climb up to heaven, from there I will bring them down. (Amos 9:2) |
| Synecdoche | Principle of representation where a part is mentioned to represent the whole. | Ephraim mixes himself with the peoples. (Hos 7:8) |
| Rhetorical Question | The author poses a question without expecting an answer because the answer is obvious. | Whom did he consult, and who made him understand? Who taught him the path of justice, and taught him knowledge, and showed him the way of understanding? (Isa 40:14) |
| Irony | The author says the exact opposite of what he really means. | Come to Bethel, and transgress; to Gilgal, and multiply transgression; bring your sacrifices every morning, your tithes every three days. (Amos 4:4) |
| Hyperbole | An intentional exaggeration to create and intensify an effect. | At the noise of horseman and archer every city takes to flight; they enter thickets; they climb among rocks; all the cities are forsaken, and no man dwells in them. (Jer 4:29) |
| Anthropomorphism | Human characteristics attributed to God. | He has stretched out his hand over the sea. (Isa 23:11) |

| Figure of Speech | Explanation | Example |
|---|---|---|
| Wordplay | The play that takes places in a use of words based on phenomena such as assonance, consonance, alliteration, and/or double meaning. | He looked for justice (Heb. *Mishpat*), but behold, bloodshed (Heb. *Mishpach*); for righteousness (Heb. *Tsedakah*), but behold, an outcry (Heb. *Tseakah*). (Isa 5:7) |

*Table 14: Figures of Speech*

The best way to make the most of the prophetic figures of speech is by intentionally crafting figurative language into our sermons. Begin by paying attention to the figures of speech in your exegetical study. I find it helpful to underline and think through all the figures of speech that are present in the specific prophetic text. I consider their function. Synecdoches invite us to see something from a different angle. Similes enrich our understanding by creating new associations. Hyperbole grabs our attention and brings emphasis. These effects happen naturally; yet, as one who is tasked to be a conduit of God's word, I discipline myself to identify their purpose so I can reproduce them. I then take time to ponder the beauty of these poetic devices. Dissection suffocates poetry whilst meditation unleashes it. Chew over the figures of speech in your text. Let them linger in your mind and touch your heart. You may find it helpful to close your eyes and let your imagination loose. Even better, go for a walk. Regardless of what you choose to do, set aside time to contemplate figurative language. The more you delight in and experience the power of the prophetic figurative language in your preparation the better you will channel it in your proclamation. Furthermore, as previously mentioned, force yourself to write a manuscript. In my experience, exploiting the prophetic figures of speech in sermons is more a matter of perspiration than inspiration. However, when we see the persuasive effect a divinely inspired metaphor can have then we will gladly put in the hard work. Let the impact Martin Luther King Jr. had by exploiting a simile from the prophet Amos inspire you: "Until justice rolls down like water and righteousness like a mighty stream" (cf. Amos 5:24).

## Tone: Get in Tune

Tune in to the tone of the prophetic oracles. The tone can vary from solemn to joyful or even satirical. Determining a speaker's tone in oral communication is usually effortless, but determining an author's tone in literature is much harder. To some extent this skill can be developed, yet it is also instinctive. When we read, what we are reading produces a reaction. We sense the author's tone. This often happens instinctively and therefore we need to trust our gut when trying to determine tone. Yet, we can aid our intuition by becoming good readers of prophetic poetry. Read carefully. Read slowly. Ponder the wording and the imagery. Read out loud. This forces you to engage with the emotions of the text and reproduce them with literal tone. I also find it helpful to associate a color or a melody that matches the tone of the oracle. Read more. Spend time getting to know the prophet by reading more of his writings. This will enable you to detect the author's personality, style, and even mood. Read again. It takes multiple visits to get in tune with the prophetic tone. The combination of our intuition and these intentional reading strategies will help us grasp the tone. Discovering the tone should not only help us understand the content of the oracle but should also set the mood for your preaching.

Consider, for example, how important it is to identify the right tone in this messenger speech. "'Come to Bethel, and transgress; to Gilgal, and multiply transgression; bring your sacrifices every morning, your tithes every three days; offer a sacrifice of thanksgiving of that which is leavened, and proclaim freewill offerings, publish them; for so you love to do, O people of Israel!' declares the Lord God" (Amos 4:4–5). If we do not note and convey the sarcastic tone of these words, we risk erroneously communicating that the Lord was exhorting the people to continue to transgress. As preachers, we have the advantage that conveying sarcasm verbally is far easier than in written form. Most of us use sarcasm regularly, so it should be easy for us to employ it in the pulpit and replicate the sarcasm of the text. You can use word choice, intonation, and body language to cue your listeners that you are employing sarcasm. The better they know you the easier it will be for them spot it. When using sarcasm in the pulpit, intentionally accentuate your cues to make it easy for your listeners to detect. Subtle sarcasm is best left for other contexts.

## STEALING FROM AN UPPER-CLASS NEIGHBORHOOD

Haddon Robinson was once asked at a Q&A what his opinion was on repreaching another person's sermon. Robinson was against this practice, but he did include a typically brilliant one-liner. "If you are going to steal, steal from an upper-class neighborhood."[21] His point was that if you must take someone else's material at least make sure you are stealing from the best. The prophetic books are full of the prophets' "greatest hits."[22] When preaching these books, we are preaching great sermons of great preachers of the past. Let us not spoil them by compressing them into our cookie-cutter sermon shape. The prophets preached highly persuasive sermons presented in various forms and impregnated with brilliant rhetorical techniques that called for unambiguous responses. Steal from their neighborhood!

21. Biola University, "Haddon Robinson," 43:20–43:30.
22. Chalmers, *Interpreting the Prophets*, 146.

# Chapter 8

## TAKE A ROAD TO CHRIST

> "And beginning with Moses and all the Prophets, he
> interpreted to them in all Scriptures the things concerning
> himself."
>
> —LUKE 24:27

OMNES VIAE ROMAN DUCUNT. "All roads lead to Rome." We can trace the origin of this expression as far back as the Roman Empire. Emperor Caesar Augustus erected a monument called the *Milliarium Aureum* ("Golden Milestone") in the central Roman Forum. It was said that all the roads across the empire led to this centerpiece. This centuries-old expression is now used figuratively to describe situations where all the elements converge to a centerpiece. Spurgeon borrowed an anglicized version of this expression from a Welsh minister to explain the relationship between Christ and Scripture:

> Don't you know young man that from every town, and every village, and every little hamlet in England, wherever it may be, there is a road to London? . . . So from every text in Scripture, there is a road to the metropolis of the Scriptures, that is Christ. . . . I have never yet found a text that had not got a road to Christ in it, and if I ever do find one that has not a road to Christ in it, I will make one; I will go over the hedge and ditch but I would get

at my Master, for the sermon cannot do any good unless there is a savor of Christ in it.[1]

Do you agree with the prince of preachers? These words that Spurgeon cites with approval are intentionally provocative. I react with both admiration and concern. On the one hand, I admire Spurgeon's commitment, and confidence, to find in every text a road that leads to Christ. On the other hand, I am concerned by his willingness to go over hedges and ditches to get to Christ.

Taking a cue from these provocative words this chapter has three complementary goals. The first goal is to crystallize the reasons why we must connect the Old Testament prophets to Christ. The second goal is to spot and circumvent ditches we may encounter in this journey. The third goal is to identify exegetically and canonically legitimate roads from the Old Testament prophets to Christ. To achieve these goals, we will join the wider conversation regarding preaching Christ from the Old Testament Scriptures and benefit from those who have thought long and hard about this topic.

## CHRIST-CENTERED PREACHING

Christ-centered preaching is widely endorsed today. Clowney and Hoekstra, Keller and Goldsworthy, and Greidanus and Chapell are all part of an impressive choir of convinced advocates of Christ-centered preaching.[2] Within this choir the terminology and nuances vary but the basic thrust is the same: preaching Scripture means preaching Christ.

Christ-centered preaching is not new. The current generation of Christ-centered preachers follows the legacy of preachers from the past who sang from the same song sheet. The difference from the past is that, whilst on some occasions in history Christ-centered voices were sparse,

1. These words that are frequently and erroneously attributed directly to Spurgeon were originally at least two steps removed from the prince of preachers. Spurgeon attributes these words to an unnamed Welsh minister, who in turn was narrating a conversation between another unnamed old preacher and a younger preacher. Nonetheless Spurgeon cites these words with approval. Furthermore, they are an accurate representation of his preaching method and ministry (Spurgeon, "Christ Precious to Believers," para. 11).

2. Langley groups together an impressive list of preachers who stress that Christ must be preached from *every* passage of the Scripture (Langley, "When Christ Replaces God," 55–56).

today we have a copious choir. At the time of this writing, preaching Christ from the Old Testament is fashionable. This does not make it right or wrong, per se. Certainly the fact that many leading evangelical voices encourage us in this direction should cause us to take notice. However, we do not simply want to follow the current craze, but rather have a deep and biblically motivated conviction. Let us therefore consider three scriptural reasons to connect the Old Testament prophets to Christ.

## To Follow Christ and the Apostles

We travel from the Old Testament prophets to Christ to follow the teaching of Christ and the apostles. It turns out Christ-centered preaching was fashionable among the apostles too. Christ-centered preaching is not a modern innovation but an apostolic convention. The apostles, in their preaching and writing, presented Christ as revealed in the Old Testament Scriptures. Johnson proves this thoroughly to the extent that he uses the term "apostolic preaching" as synonymous to Christ-centered preaching.[3]

The apostles learnt this interpretive approach from Jesus. Between his resurrection and ascension, the Lord Jesus opened the minds of the apostles to enable them to understand the Old Testament Scriptures. The key to this understanding was to discover how the three major sections of the Old Testament (Law, Prophets, and Writings) spoke about the saving work of Christ (Luke 24:44–49). This was the foundation that shaped the apostles' understanding and preaching of the Old Testament. Jesus' words ought to also convince us that connecting the prophets to Christ is not an addendum but is foundational to understanding and preaching the prophets.

Peter certainly was convinced the prophetic books reveal Christ. According to Peter, by the Spirit, the prophets spoke about the grace and salvation in Christ (1 Pet 1:10–12). Furthermore, he adds that this revelation of Christ in the Prophets was for our benefit. Paul was on the same page. Paul declared to Timothy that the sacred writings (i.e., the Old Testament) were able to make him wise for salvation through faith in Christ Jesus (1 Tim 3:15). This conviction is also evidenced by Paul's summaries of the content of his preaching ministry: "Jesus Christ and him crucified"

---

3. Johnson, *Him We Proclaim*, 1–97. Murray also argues that Jesus, Peter, Paul, and John were unanimous in teaching that the Old Testament was about Jesus (Murray, *Jesus on Every Page*, 9–42).

(1 Cor 2:2), "him we proclaim" (Col 1:28), and "the unsearchable riches of Christ" (Eph 3:8). Paul of course had been preaching from the Old Testament, the only Scriptures available, and yet the content of his preaching was Jesus Christ. The apostles, therefore, were convinced Christ was not an appendix but the climax of the Old Testament.

This may be surprising considering that the name "Jesus Christ" does not appear in the Old Testament. How can the Old Testament be about Jesus and yet not name him explicitly? It seems like a mystery. Were the apostles guilty of illegitimately reading Christ back into the Old Testament story? I do not believe so. Paul solves this mystery for us in an illuminating doxology at the end of Romans (16:25–27). Indeed, in the final lines of this epistle Paul uses the term "mystery." This a key Pauline term. Paul's understanding of the term is rich. He uses it to describe God's masterplan of salvation for all nations, which is progressively revealed and manifested (cf. Eph 3:1–5; Col 1:24–19). The center of God's masterplan is Jesus Christ. Paul reveals this masterplan was "kept secret for long ages but has now been disclosed" (Rom 16:25b–26a). At first glance this may seem to indicate the Old Testament did not reveal this Christ-centered masterplan, but rather this is something which is *now* disclosed through new revelation. However, as we continue to track Paul's argument, we discover this mystery which is now disclosed is made known "through the prophetic writings" (16:26b). You see the paradox? The same prophetic writings that previously had kept this masterplan hidden now make it known.

I once heard Tim Keller, a keen Christocentric preacher, explain this dynamic using, as an illustration, the movie *The Sixth Sense*.[4] If you have not seen the movie be prepared to have it spoiled (it is over twenty years old). This fictional movie narrates the story of a boy who has the bizarre and unwanted ability to communicate with ghosts. Understandably this is traumatic, so he starts to meet with a psychologist (played by Bruce Willis) to help him deal with this. The movie narrates the relationship between the boy and the psychologist. The movie ends with an unexpected twist. The psychologist realizes he is dead and has been dead all along. This discovery comes as a shock both to the psychologist and to the viewer. It had been kept hidden throughout the movie. However, as you can imagine, once you have this information you are no longer able to watch the movie the same way again. This knowledge radically changes

---

4. In his book, Keller attributes this illustration to Old Testament professor Tremper Longman (Keller, *Preaching*, 86–87).

all subsequent viewing experiences. Indeed, you notice aspects that were there from the beginning but which eluded you. You notice the psychologist never interacts with anyone apart from the boy. You notice that even when the psychologist thinks he is part of a conversation, no one is addressing him. You also have the correct interpretative key to understand the coldness and distance the psychologist perceives from his wife. The point is, the key information at the end of the story changes forever what you see in the first part of the movie. Furthermore, this key information enables you to see what had been hidden, yet revealed, all along.

A similar dynamic takes place in the Old Testament. Now that the centerpiece of God's masterplan has been disclosed, we cannot help but notice how the Old Testament Scriptures make known this mystery. We cannot help but notice how the Old Testament prophets reveal Christ even though the name "Jesus Christ" never appears. Indeed, we now have the correct and ultimate interpretative key that unlocks the ultimate meaning of the Old Testament. To use Pauline language, it is through Christ that the veil is taken away (2 Cor 3:14). Without Christ as our interpretative key, our reading, and therefore our preaching, of the Old Testament will always be partial and veiled.

Connecting the Old Testament prophets to Christ, therefore, is not just a trend but a biblically warranted approach. Indeed, it is not just warranted but necessary. Since the Old Testament prophets speak about Christ, we are not faithfully preaching them unless we are preaching Christ. This is not a bonus or an extra, this is intrinsic to careful exposition of the word of God.

## To Escape Moralism

We also travel from the prophets to Christ to escape moralism. The prophets called the people to turn away from their sin to escape judgment. They also called the people to obey in order to experience God's blessings. These calls can erroneously be interpreted and preached as "be good" exhortations to earn God's love and to be rewarded with his blessings. This happens when we interpret and preach a specific oracle by removing it from the broader biblical framework. Fee and Stuart invite us to approach each single episode in the Old Testament as part of God's story with Israel, which in turn is then part of the ultimate story of redemption.[5] Applying this to the prophetic books means that we are not to interpret what the prophets called the people of Israel to do in isolation but as part of these overarching stories. The Lord graciously saved Israel from slavery in Egypt. He redeemed them and made them his precious treasure. He made them the object of his love. He *then* called them to *respond* in obedience to his grace in order to experience and enjoy the fullness of his blessings. If the people rebelled, however, they would inevitably face the consequences of this rebellion. The prophets called the people to obedience as part of this larger story. They presuppose the context of the broader narrative. Therefore, we should not extract the prophetic words from the broader salvation story. Indeed, we need to intentionally place the prophets within the biblical framework. This history of salvation is the necessary context to interpret and preach the prophetic oracles. Since Christ is the epicenter of the history of salvation, he is the lens through which we interpret, preach, and live all Scripture. When we do not connect the prophetic words to Christ, we preach "be good," moralistic sermons.

What is the problem with moralistic sermons? They breed inward-looking believers who have no strength to pursue holiness. Believers who struggle forward, hauled by their own strides, much like Fred Flintstone's leg-powered car, do not get far. The power to live a life worthy of the Lord does not come from ourselves but from the engine of the gospel. The grace of God in Christ powers our sanctification. Or, to use Pauline language, it is the grace of God that trains us to renounce ungodliness and live godly lives (Titus 2:11–12). Paul introduces this concept of "training grace" as the theological basis that enables believers to live in accordance with sound doctrine (2:1–10). The Lord provides *saving* and *sanctifying* grace. Paul explains this training grace is a direct result of Christ's work of redemption. Christ "gave himself for us to redeem us from all lawlessness and to purify for himself a people for his own possession who are zealous for good works" (2:14). Therefore, it is in and through Christ that we find grace to truly pursue holiness. Preaching "be good" sermons often does little good because it indicates the right direction but does not provide the strength to walk in it. "Be good" sermons are often powerless.

---

5. Fee and Stuart introduce the concept of reading episodes in the Old Testament on multiple narrative levels in relation to the genre of Old Testament stories. Nevertheless, this is also pertinent when we interpret the prophetic oracles since they are framed by the biblical storyline (Fee and Stuart, *How to Read the Bible*, 91–92).

Chapell goes even further and suggests "the deadly be's" are not just devoid but also subvert the message of the Gospel. "Messages that strike at the heart of faith rather than support it often have an identifying theme. They exhort believers to strive to 'be' something in order to be loved by God. Whether this equation is stated or implied, inadvertent or intentional, overt or subtle, the result is the same: an undermining of biblical faith."[6] Therefore "be good" sermons are not just powerless but also poisonous.

> Simply railing at error and hammering at piety may convince people of their inadequacy or move them toward self-sufficiency, but these messages also keep true godliness remote. Thus, instruction in biblical behavior barren of redemptive truth only wounds. Though it is offered as an antidote to sin, such preaching either promotes Pharisaism or prompts despair.[7]

Chapell's diagnosis is astute. When our preaching calls our people to lean on their own strengths to respond to God's word, we will either crush our people into despair or lead them down a path of self-righteousness. When Christ is not the focus of our preaching then our people's eyes will most likely not be fixed on their Savior but on themselves, and this is fatal. Even when Scripture does encourage a measure of introspection (Ps 139:23; Lam 3:40; 2 Cor 13:5) it does so not to advocate that we look to ourselves to find strength. Rather, the purpose of introspection is to recognize our sinfulness so that we will then repent and turn to Christ. The solution is in Christ, not in ourselves.

Therefore, we connect the prophets to Christ to escape moralism and to find the strength to respond to what the prophets are calling us to do. If we want believers to be holy, the key is not to beat them with moralism but to lead them to Christ. When we travel down the road to Christ, we are filling up their tank. We are fueling the true catalyst of the Christian life and being strengthened by the gospel. We make our people like Christ when we take them to Christ, not because this is a magic formula but because it is by contemplating him that we are transformed in his likeness (2 Cor 3:18). Therefore, preaching that focuses on Christ aligns with the way in which the Spirit operates in the life of believers. Paul explains that when we behold Christ, the Spirit transforms us from one degree of glory to another. This gradual, and to some extent mysterious,

6. Chapell, *Christ-Centered Preaching*, 289.

7. Chapell, *Christ-Centered Preaching*, 294.

process of sanctification takes place when our eyes are fixed on Christ. Similarly, our obedience to Christ stems from our love for him (John 14:15). Therefore, exalting Christ in our preaching fosters loving hearts, which in turn produces obedient lives.

## To Encounter Christ

The final reason to travel from the prophets to Christ is to encounter Christ. This may be stating the obvious; however, it is too important to neglect. Eternal life is to know Christ and through him the Father (John 17:3). In line with this understanding of eternal life, the goal of preaching is not merely to describe Christ but to introduce people to Christ so they will truly know him. The knowledge we are after is not just intellectual but experiential, not just factual but personal. We want our people not just to know *of* him but to commune *with* him. The goal of preaching, therefore, is much higher than simply accurately conveying truthful information. Preaching is also more than an impassioned exhortation to holiness. Preaching is proclaiming and presenting Christ "to captivate people's hearts with his beauty."[8]

This does not mean that as preachers we should hold back from exhorting our people to obey the word of God. Indeed, as we will see in the next section, if we fail to call our people to obedience, we are not fulfilling our duty (1 Tim 4:13; 2 Tim 3:16–17). Neither does this mean that as preachers we abandon the text and abandon our duty to explain the text. As preachers our responsibility is to exposit the biblical text, and this involves diligent preparation and careful explanation. However, just as knowledge of a set of truths is not the ultimate goal of Scripture, so explanation of a biblical text is not the ultimate goal of preaching. The goal is higher. We explain Scripture to offer Christ.[9] We preach Scripture because through Scripture we encounter him, we experience him, we know him, we see him, we enjoy him, and we dine with him. This encounter with Christ, which takes place in preaching, should not just be seen as a means to an end but as a noble end in itself. Indeed, as John Stott explained: "The main objective of preaching is to expound Scripture so faithfully and relevantly that Jesus Christ is perceived in all his adequacy to meet human need . . . The preacher's purpose is more than to unveil

8. Moody and Weekes, *Burning Hearts*, 31.

9. Moody and Weekes, *Burning Hearts*, 31.

Christ; it is so to unveil him that people are drawn to come to him and to receive him."[10] A profound and intimate encounter with Christ is the best possible outcome of preaching.

## DITCHES TO AVOID

It is not enough to be convinced of the need to connect the prophets to Christ; we also need to know how (and how not) to trace these connections. Illegitimate connections are harmful even if they come from good intentions. Our honorable desire to reach Christ at all costs may lead us off track and cause us to fall into a ditch. I see three ditches to avoid.

### Hermeneutical Ditch

The greatest danger is that our drive to get to Christ causes us to bypass, or worse distort, the prophetic text. The pressure to make a christological connection can cause us to spot something in the text that is simply not there, something imported. Many prophetic texts have a clear and obvious road to Christ. However, in other texts the connection is not as obvious. When confronted with these texts, and with Sunday looming, if we believe it to be a dogma that *every* sermon must connect to Christ then we will be in trouble. We may end up sacrificing our interpretation on the altar of a christological connection.

I have heard the Christ connection described as the infamous rabbit out of the hat. As a spectator you know it is going to happen—you are not exactly sure how, but then you are delighted when it does happen. The Christ connection should not be the rabbit out of the hat. It should not be the result of something the preacher magically performs on the text. Christ should not come out of nowhere. Rather, if the connection is legitimate, the preacher will be a curator, pointing out what is objectively (not magically) in the text and helping listeners spot it too. This is important because as preachers we are not just teaching our people the specific text, but we are modeling how to read Scripture. If we make dubious interpretive moves, then we can be sure our people will follow suit and even go beyond. They will learn from us a skewed methodology where their reading of Scripture becomes the practice of skimming over a passage simply

---

10. Stott, *Between Two Worlds*, 325.

to find the magical and ill-founded connection to Christ. Our moderate exegetical leaps will become reckless exegetical somersaults.

On some occasions Spurgeon was guilty of performing magic on the text and pulling the rabbit out of the hat. This is not a surprise, considering his willingness to go over hedges and ditches to get to Christ. His sermon entitled "The Desire of all Nations," from Haggai 2:7, is an example of an inopportune exegetical leap.[11] What I find surprising is that Spurgeon reveals his awareness that the phrase "the desire of all nations" (Hag 2:7 KJV) is best understood as a reference to the treasures the foreign nations will contribute to the second temple and not as a reference to Christ. He openly states it "is the most accurate explanation of the original."[12] He even provides evidence for this conclusion: "'The desirable *things* of all nations shall come,' which is, no doubt, the meaning, because the eighth verse gives the key – 'The silver is mine, and the gold is mine, saith the LORD of hosts.'"[13] Despite this conviction, Spurgeon, in the second part of the sermon, attributes a christological meaning to the words "the desire of all nations." He does so knowing this is "a rendering scarcely to be sustained by the original."[14] Spurgeon goes on to explain various reasons why the nations have a "dark and dim"[15] desire for Christ. Using Haggai 2:7 as a springboard, Spurgeon explained why Christ is, or at least ought to be, the true desire of all nations. However, in doing so, he departed from the meaning of the preaching text.

I am convinced of the importance of connecting the Old Testament to Christ. However, I also share Davis's conviction: "I do not honor Christ by forcing him into texts where he is not."[16] We should be averse to any distortion of the biblical text. To do so, even for the noblest of all reasons—namely, to proclaim Christ—is still a falsification of the very word of God. It is the opposite of what we are all called to do as preachers. The damage we procure when we distort the passage of Scripture will be greater than the good we had hoped to achieve. The pressure of making every sermon Christ-centered nearly inevitably will cause us to fall into this ditch and, sadly, drag our people down with us.

11. Spurgeon, "Desire of all Nations."

12. Spurgeon, "Desire of all Nations," para. 3.

13. Spurgeon, "Desire of all Nations," para. 3 (italics original), from Hag 2:8 KJV.

14. Spurgeon, "Desire of all Nations," para. 10.

15. Spurgeon, "Desire of all Nations," para. 10.

16. Davis, *Word Became Fresh*, 138.

## Theological Ditch

This ditch is harder to define but present nonetheless. I will overstate it and then refine it. By making Christ the hero of all our preaching we risk dishonoring the other two persons of the Godhead. I told you I would overstate it. In a sense, because of the deep unity within the Trinity, this is absurd. The Son is the perfect representation of the Father, and therefore we admire the Father by beholding the Son (2 Cor 4:6; Col 1:15; Heb 1:3). The Spirit is also called the Spirit of Christ, and the role of the Spirit is to draw attention to Christ (Rom 8:9; John 15:26; 16:13–14). Therefore, Christ-centered preaching can certainly be described as Spirit-led and Father-honoring preaching.

Nevertheless, it is possible that our zeal to elevate Christ unintentionally lessens our perceptions of the Father, or of the Spirit, that may emerge from a passage. I will illustrate with an example. A few years ago, I heard a sermon from Hosea 11. The preacher connected the prophetic passage to Christ using Matthew's quotation (Hos 11:1 and Matt 2:15). The preacher highlighted the contrast between Israel's ungrateful disobedience to the Father and the Son's perfect obedience to the Father. The strongest part of the sermon was when the preacher emphasized that, despite this contrast, ultimately the Father poured out his righteous wrath upon his perfect Son. Glorious gospel truth! I was impacted by the sermon and moved by the ultimate sacrifice of the perfect Son. Yet, as the words of the preacher continued to echo in my heart over the following hours and days, I began to feel uneasy. Something was off, but I was struggling to put my finger on it. I returned to Hosea. As I reread the passage, I spotted the problem. Hosea 11 is an unparalleled depiction of the Father's tender and loving heart. He is the Father who loves his child (v. 1), pleads with him (v. 2), teaches him to walk (v. 3), defends him (v. 3), guides him (v. 4), lightens his burdens (v. 4), bends down to feed him (v. 4), and disciplines him (vv. 5–6). He is also the Father who is heartbroken because of his child's rebellion (v. 8), whose heart melts when he sees his child (v. 8), whose compassion abounds (v. 8), whose forgiveness is unparalleled (11:9), and whose salvation is certain (vv. 10–11). This passage displays the Father's loving heart par excellence. Yet, the lasting impression after the sermon was not the beauty of the Father's heart; rather, the emphasis was placed on Christ, who took upon himself the Father's "burning anger" and "wrath" (v. 9) that we deserved. Christ was the hero who protected us from the harsh Father. We were left with a lasting impression of the Father that clashed with the overall description of the passage.

I have no doubt you can preach Hosea 11 with a strong connection to Christ and yet faithfully portray the profile of the Father that emerges in this passage. It is the love of the Father that sends his Son. Nevertheless, I think this is representative of a risk of Christ-centered preaching. We can end up pitting the Father against the Son. Langley sees this risk too and worries that "exalting Christ as the center of gospel preaching may inadvertently diminish the Father's role and the Father's glory."[17] This may happen because Christ-centered preaching may inadvertently cause some people to "imagine a drama of salvation in which Jesus and God are on opposites sides. The Father—harsh, demanding, and wrathful—is intent in judging us. But Jesus—kind, compassionate, and merciful—comes to the rescue and offers himself as a sacrifice in our stead."[18] To steer clear of this distortion of the gospel, Langley advocates for the broader category of theocentric preaching:

> Every preacher has had plenty of experience being misunderstood, even when we're not being subtle. If there's any chance my listeners might get the wrong idea that Jesus is the hero of a story in which God plays the heavy, or that the Father created a problem that the Son had to solve . . . then I want to bend over backwards to make it clear that the gospel is the gospel of God. I'll make God the main actor. I'll make him the subject of many of the gospel sermon's sentences. His is the eternal decree, his is the love that drew salvation's plan, his is the initiative in sending the Son, his is the power that raised Christ from the dead and put all things under his feet. To him be the glory in the church and in Christ Jesus throughout all generations, for ever and ever! Amen (Eph. 3:21).[19]

I agree with Langley that careless Christ-centered preaching can diminish and distort the Father's role and glory. I disagree with Langley that the solution is to replace the default Christ-centered approach to preaching with the broader category of theocentric preaching. I disagree because Scripture stresses that the Father has chosen to reveal himself through the Son. Christ is the final word and the eternal Logos (John 1:1; Heb 1:1–2). He is the image of the invisible God (Col 1:15). Therefore, a

17. Langley, "When Christ Replaces God," 62.

18. Langley, "When Christ Replaces God," 62.

19. Langley, "When Christ Replaces God," 65.

default Christ-centered thrust in our preaching best mirrors God's revelation. As Greidanus explains: "If done well, Christ-centered preaching exposes the very heart of God."[20]

Nevertheless, whilst I do not think it is better to settle for the broader category of default theocentric preaching, I think Christ-centered preachers must be aware of the danger of diminishing or misrepresenting the Father. Similarly, we can risk sidelining the Spirit in the age of the Spirit. The Holy Spirit helps, teaches, convicts, reveals, testifies, regenerates, renews, fills, guides, gives, seals, sanctifies, and intercedes. In view of all this, is it *always* necessary to preach a Christocentric sermon from a passage that centers on the role and the work of the Spirit? Should we deem a Spirit-focused sermon less worthy than a Christ-focused sermon? I do not think so! Indeed, paradoxically, since the role of the Spirit is to reveal Christ, a Spirit-focused sermon will in the long run create Christocentric believers even if the actual sermon is not overtly Christocentric.

I repeat my conviction that Christ-centered preaching is often Spirit-led and Father-honoring. Nevertheless, I am also aware of the great peril of this theological ditch. Our risk of falling into this ditch increases exponentially if we feel constrained to make a beeline to Christ *every* Sunday from *every* text. The risk is reduced when, whilst maintaining Christ-centered preaching as our default approach, we recognize the value of sometimes opting for a broader theocentric approach.

## Pastoral Ditch

Another potential ditch of Christocentric preaching is pastoral. Our call is to feed the sheep. As I have argued, Christ is the best and key ingredient of preaching that nourishes the soul. However, preachers who saturate *every* sermon with the flavors of the redemption story risk neglecting other key ingredients and nutrients in the word of God. We risk malnourishing by serving the same or a similar meal over and over again. To ensure our preaching is providing a balanced diet for our people we need to pay attention to the balance of Scripture and the needs of our people.

In Scripture we find a balance between sections that highlight our need for the gospel, sections that expound the gospel, and sections that call us to live a life worthy of the gospel. I do not think it is necessary (or possible) to replicate this balance in *every single* sermon. Rather, our aim

20. Greidanus, "Preaching Christ," 4.

should be to mirror this balance in our preaching in general. I say this because sometimes we try to concentrate in every sermon what cannot be fully achieved in the limited sermon time. A balanced diet is not achieved by preparing every meal with all the necessary nutrients; rather, it is achieved when, across the different meals, we are giving the right amount of all the nutrients. My impression is that sometimes, in our effort to best represent Scripture, we are trying to concentrate all the nutrients in every sermon. This probably derives from viewing every sermon as an isolated event. However, our sermons will be much more digestible if we do not see them as isolated meals but as part of a broader, more balanced, diet. How do we then decide which nutrients to include in our sermon? We follow the balance we find in Scripture.

For instance, the goal of some sections of the prophetic books is to highlight our sinfulness to *then* magnify our need for God's grace that can be found, par excellence, in Christ. Most of the book of Zephaniah has this purpose. The largest section of Zephaniah's prophecy (1:1—3:8) announces judgment—the multifaceted day of the Lord's anger. This section begins and ends with announcing the Lord's judgment upon the whole earth (1:2-3; 3:8). This global judgment is articulated with specific warnings directed to the people of Judah (1:4—2:3; 3:1-7) and to its neighboring nations (2:14-15). The prophecy of Zephaniah concludes with a shorter, yet extremely potent, section (3:9-20) which announces the multifaceted day of God's salvation. In this final section God's unmerited grace toward the nations (3:9-10) and Judah (3:11-20) shines brightly against the backdrop of the previously announced judgment. What is the best way to preach Zephaniah? Should we force ourselves to jump from each passage (or each pericope) that denounces sin and announces judgment to Christ at the end of *every* sermon? Or is it better to mirror the book of Zephaniah and let the tension ferment even for a few weeks to then get to God's salvation in Christ when the need for him is maximally felt? I suggest the impact of this latter approach may be greater. If we jump from each passage to Christ, we may paradoxically weaken the experience of Christ. On the other hand, if we hold back for several weeks the tension build-up will enable us to admire and appreciate more fully the glories of Christ. Furthermore, it would match more faithfully the purpose of Zephaniah's judgment passages. Preaching Zephaniah within the context of salvation history should not override, but rather should honor, his authorial intent.

Similarly, preaching that matches the balance of Scripture will not fail to feed our people with biblical imperatives. Christocentric preaching is the antidote to the deadly disease called moralism. However, I see a risk of swinging the pendulum too far the other way and failing to preach the force of biblical imperatives. As Kuruvilla explains: "All biblical genres in the OT engage in moral and ethical instruction; they do not serve exclusively as adumbrations of the Messiah, and neither do they solely establish salvific truths . . . There are ethical demands therein as well that must be brought to bear upon the lives of God's people."[21] Lest we slip into moralism we ensure our people know how these imperatives are rooted within the broader framework of the salvation story. However, I am not convinced the best way to achieve this is to employ a simplistic and predictable methodology in which the full redemptive story needs to be proclaimed in *every* sermon. How do we then strike the balance? By considering not only the balance of Scripture but also the needs of our people.

As preachers we should have our finger on the pulse of the congregation. We should know if our people are marching to the heartbeat of grace or to the drumbeat of legalism, and this should influence how we invest our precious sermon minutes. For instance, if we are preaching Malachi 1:6–14, we must exhort our people to offer their best to the Lord and reprove them if they are dishonoring the Lord by offering their leftovers. If we are feeding them a steady diet of Christ-centered sermons, then they will have already digested that we accomplish this command by the strength the Lord provides. This is well established in their minds and hearts. They may instead need greater help to understand what offering their best today looks like. In these situations, the best way to serve your people is to unpack and apply the biblical command. We help them to see that although we are not in danger of offering a blind animal to the Lord, we are in danger of offering our leftover time (or energy, talents, finances, etc.). We may not be in danger of bringing a blemished animal to the temple, but our giving can be just as meagre and miserable. Believers who are in Christ, and who rely on the grace of God in Christ, will benefit more from thinking through the significance and feeling the force of the biblical command rather than revisiting the redemption story. On the other hand, if our congregation marches to the drumbeat of legalism then pastoral vigilance demands a quicker explanation and application of

21. Kuruvilla, *Privilege the Text*, 243–44.

Malachi's rebuke, and a stronger connection to the engine of the gospel: we give our best to God as a response to the God who gave his best to us. My point is I do not believe Malachi 1:6–15, or any passage of Scripture, has an ideal sermon. The sermon should vary depending on the pastoral necessities of our people. This does not mean we alter the word of God based on the needs of the people; rather, we proclaim the unalterable word of God in such a way that it addresses their specific needs.

The honorable commitment to preach Christ, the key and best ingredient, from every passage of Scripture may inadvertently cause us to fall into the pastoral ditch of malnourishing our people. We are called to feed our people with the entire counsel of God. This does not entail jam-packing *every* sermon with all possible nutrients; rather, it entails preaching a well-balanced diet, one which mirrors the balance of Scripture and meets the needs of our people.

## CHRIST-CENTERED SERMON SERIES

Considering these ditches, as well as the benefits of Christ-centered preaching, I have reached the pragmatic conclusion that all sermon *series* ought to be Christ-centered rather than applying this constraint to *every* single sermon. Of course, in practice, for a series to be Christ-centered it inevitably follows that *most* sermons within the series will also be Christ-centered. However, this broader approach enables you to channel all the gains of Christ-centered preaching, and reduces the risks of falling into ditches.

Returning to Zephaniah may help illustrate this approach. A six-part sermon series on Zephaniah could have the first four sermons primarily aimed at exposing the gravity of sin and the reality of judgment (1:1–6; 1:7—2:3; 2:4–15; 3:1–8), and then the final two sermons geared at intensely displaying God's grace (3:9–13; 3:14–20). The contrast between the first four sermons and the final two would greatly accentuate the need and the provision of God's salvation which is ultimately found in Christ. Even if we do not explicitly connect each (or any) of the first four sermons to Christ, a bird's-eye view reveals this sermon series is still overtly Christ-centered. This approach enables us to preach Zephaniah christocentrically without falling into the pastoral ditch.

Another example comes from a recent sermon series I preached from Haggai. I preached four sermons to mirror the four messages delivered by the prophet (1:1–15; 2:1–9; 2:10–19; 2:20–23). Using three roads that I will soon explain, I connected each of the last three sermons to Christ. I connected Haggai 2:1–9 to Christ following the *biblical trajectory* of the temple. I connected Haggai 2:10–19 to Christ by highlighting the *contrast* that when we who are unclean come to Christ we become clean. I connected Haggai 2:20–23 by zooming in on the significance of the Lord making Zerubbabel (a descendent of David) like a signet ring. The Lord was confirming he would fulfill his *promises* of the arrival of the King that would reign forever. Hence, we then find Zerubbabel in the genealogy of Jesus (Matt 1:12; Luke 3:27). Knowing the last three sermons would be Christ-centered, I had no reason to try to force a connection to Christ from the first sermon (thus avoiding the hermeneutical ditch). I also knew Haggai 1:1–15 was my longest passage in the series, with a strong exhortation to have the right priorities and obey the voice of God. I therefore wanted the thrust of my sermon to match this emphasis (thus avoiding the pastoral ditch). Moreover, the passage stresses it is the Lord of hosts who stirred the people to respond in obedience. I therefore did not want to neglect explaining the title "Lord of hosts" and expounding that it is the Lord who stirs our spirits (thus avoiding the theological ditch). For these reasons I decided it would be best not to also add a connection to Christ in this first sermon. Nevertheless, the sermon series as a whole was distinctly Christ-centered.

Furthermore, this Christ-centered sermon series approach is not only pragmatic, it also reflects what Jesus affirmed about the Old Testament's connection to him in the famous passages in Luke (24:25–27, 44–49). After the resurrection, Jesus joined two disciples on the road to Emmaus and took them on a greater journey through the Old Testament. Considering the distance and the duration of the journey[22] it is obvious they did not touch on every chapter or pericope of the Old Testament (24:25–27). Rather, Christ "interpreted to them in all the Scriptures the things concerning himself" (Luke 24:27). Similarly, when Christ then later appeared to the apostles his focus was not to exegete each Old Testament passage, but rather to show how the broad sections of the Old Testament (Law, Prophets, and Writings) speak of him (24:44). These passages prove we must connect the prophets to Christ. However, this is not the same as Spurgeon's claim that in every Old Testament passage we can find a road to Christ. Rather, a better representation of Luke 24 is to

22. Considering the distance of seven miles from Jerusalem to Emmaus (Luke 24:13) we can assume that the entire journey lasted approximately two hours.

consider every Old Testament passage as somewhere en route to Christ, just as the road to Emmaus was also en route to Rome. Christ-centered sermon series are a good way to replicate this understanding of the Old Testament.

## ROADS TO CHRIST

On the road to Emmaus, when Christ opened the Scriptures to the two disciples by showing them how the Old Testament spoke about him, their hearts were inflamed. This is the ultimate reason why it is necessary to connect the prophets to Christ. We want our people to have burning hearts by encountering Christ.

We therefore need to learn how to connect the prophetic books to Christ.[23] I will trace the five roads I find best enable us to travel to Christ without departing from our specific preaching text. I will illustrate them with examples from the prophets.

23. Various authors have helpfully outlined various roads that we can travel down: Greidanus presents seven ways of preaching Christ from the Old Testament: redemptive-historical progression, promise-fulfillment, typology, analogy, longitudinal themes, New Testament references, and contrast. Greidanus's clarity and insights in describing these ways have greatly contributed to the growth of Christ-centered preaching (Greidanus, *Preaching Christ from the Old Testament*, 227–77).

Wright similarly presents six ways of connecting an Old Testament passage with Christ: through the story, the promises, similarities, contrasts, the response the text calls for, and the gospel of grace (Wright, *Sweeter than Honey*, 45–63).

Chapell suggests the following ways to uncover the redemptive focus of a text: text disclosure (i.e., direct reference), type disclosure, and context disclosure (i.e., placing the passage within the context of God's overall redemptive plan). He further elaborates the final option, which he considers to be the most common, in the following subcategories of how a text may be related to Christ: predictive, preparatory, reflective, or resultant of the work of Christ (Chapell, *Christ-Centered Preaching*, 281–88).

Murray links the Old Testament to Christ using ten overlapping ways of discovering Jesus in the Old Testament: Creation, characters, appearances, law, history, prophets, types, covenants, proverbs, and poems (Murray, *Jesus on Every Page*, 43–205).

Keller combines much of the above and focuses on how to preach Christ from every major genre, section, theme, figure, image, and deliverance story of the Bible. Keller, however, concludes by suggesting that we may go beyond these ways and employ our instinct and intuition to connect the whole Bible to Christ (Keller, *Preaching*, 70–90).

## Promise-fulfillment

The most obvious way to connect the prophets to Christ is to trace the fulfillment in Christ of future pointing prophecies. We noted in chapter 5 that "prophecy" is not synonymous with "prediction." Most of the prophetic oracles deal with the immediate context of the prophets. Nevertheless, traveling through the prophetic books, we will find explicit prophetic words that point to the future. These include prophecies that announce an aspect of the identity or ministry of Christ. Indeed, the New Testament authors often point to the fulfillment of these predictions in Jesus as a means of demonstrating his messianic identity. We have predictions that range from his birth to his resurrection, from his life to his death. Obviously when we are preaching from these prophetic predictions we must travel down these roads to Christ. In this section I would include the promises about the new covenant that the prophets anticipate.

A famous example is Micah's prophecy that the Messiah would be born in Bethlehem (Mic 5:2; cf. Matt 2:1; Luke 2:4–6). The prophet Micah transitions from the announcement of imminent judgment (Mic 1–3) to the prospect of restoration (Mic 4–5). This restoration will come through the ruler who will be born in the unlikely town of Bethlehem (5:2) and who will shepherd his flock with the strength of the Lord (5:4). He will be the ultimate Shepherd-King, the greater David, that will bring ultimate salvation.

Isaiah's potent description of the suffering servant (Isa 52:13—53:12) is another example of a prophecy that finds its ultimate fulfillment in Christ (Luke 22:37; Acts 8:32–35; 1 Pet 2:21–25). This prophetic passage offers an unparalleled insight into the Messiah's suffering and substitution for sinners.

As you can see these predictive passages are more than roads, they are highways that lead to Christ. Remember, however, this journey to Christ should not cause you to abandon your passage. Smith's advice is helpful: "Don't forget your text! If you do go to a parallel text in the New Testament, don't stay there. Simply show them the connection and how it is fulfilled in Jesus Christ. Then, come back to your text and finish preaching and applying its message to your people."[24] For example, when I preached from Isaiah 9:1–7, we took a trip to Matthew 4:12–17 to see how this promise that the lands of Zebulun and Naphtali would see a "great light" was ultimately fulfilled when Jesus began preaching in

---

24. Smith, *Recapturing the Voice of God*, 171.

the region of Galilee. However, we did not linger too long in Matthew because I was keen to show the significance of these specific places being singled out in the day of Isaiah. This staggering promise followed the announcement of the imminent Assyrian invasion (Isa 7:17—8:22). This invasion would bring "distress and darkness, the gloom of anguish" (8:22). The Assyrians came from the north and therefore the northern lands of Zebulun and Naphtali were the territories that would first experience their fury and be "thrust into thick darkness" (8:22). This heightens the significance of the promise of a "great light." The people who most of all experienced the horror of darkness received the promise that they were first in line to see the great—the greatest—light. This is typical of our God, and our people need to hear it. The value of the prophetic message is not limited to messianic predictions. Therefore, certainly track the fulfillment of prophetic predictions, but do not rob your people of the other treasures buried within your preaching text.

## Typology

A second prominent road to Christ is typology. Typology can be defined as a person, event, or institution of the Old Testament that represents and foreshadows a similar yet greater person, event, or institution in the New Testament. The person, event, or institution in the Old Testament is therefore a type (a model, a paradigm) of the greater person, event, or institution in the New Testament (called "antitype"). We learn this hermeneutical approach from the authors of the New Testament. The entire book of Hebrews, for example, presents a series of typological comparisons as its main thesis to show the superiority of Christ. Moreover, we see evidence of this typological approach already in the Old Testament. The prophets often applied a typological hermeneutic by referring to the past to describe future events. They looked back to creation to announce the new creation (Isa 65:17–25). They recalled the bondage in Egypt to announce a future judgment (Hos 8:13; 9:3). They referred to the exodus to announce the future greater exodus (Isa 11:12–16; 43:16–21). The prophets were keen typologists.

Greidanus helpfully identifies four characteristics of legitimate typological connections which distinguish typology from its undisciplined cousin: allegory.[25] First, a genuine type is *historical*. Only historical people,

---

25. Allegorical interpretations bypass the literary, historical, and contextual

institutions, or events should be considered types. Second, a genuine type is linked to *God's activity* in and through the types. We should "look for a type not in the details but in the *central message* of the text concerning God's activity to redeem his people."[26] Third, similar to the previous one, a genuine type necessitates a *significant analogy*. The parallel is not to be a frivolous connection of marginal details but a significant correspondence of fundamental features. Fourth, there must be an *escalation* from the type to the antitype, the "greater than" factor.[27]

These characteristics give us solid criteria for identifying types of Christ. Jesus presented Jonah as a type that foreshadowed his death and resurrection (Matt 12:40–41). In chapter 6, we consider the event of a young woman bearing a child in Isaiah's day as a type of a greater event of the Savior's virgin birth. Another type is Hosea's poignant marriage. The Lord called the prophet to marry an adulterous woman (Hos 1). As the story unfolds, we discover the prophet also pursues his adulterous wife and even redeems her (Hos 3). Hosea's marriage illustrates the unfaithfulness of the people of Israel contrasted with the Lord's love for his people. Furthermore, *God's activity* through this *historical* marriage bears a genuine and *significant analogy* between the ultimate and *greater* marriage between Christ and the church (cf. Eph 5:25–27; Mark 2:19–20; Rev 19:7–9). In a broader sense all the prophets foreshadow God's ultimate prophet (Deut 18:15; John 6:14; 7:40; Acts 3:20–22). Christ is the prophet God called to reveal his ultimate message and perfectly fulfills the prophetic office.[28]

## Biblical Trajectories

The careful Scripture reader will note some trajectories run from the beginning to the end of the biblical narrative and find their center in Christ. When we trace their development in Scripture, we invariably reach Christ. The easiest way to spot these trajectories is to start at the end. In the last chapters of the Bible we find many important biblical themes that start all the way back in Genesis and run throughout Scripture. Here are some examples identifiable in Revelation 21–22: creation, cities (Jerusalem vs

---

meaning of a text to find hidden meanings and connections.

26. Greidanus, *Preaching Christ from the Old Testament*, 257 (italics original).

27. Greidanus, *Preaching Christ from the Old Testament*, 256.

28. Murray, *Jesus on Every Page*, 116–19.

Babylon), marriage, temple, the presence of God, sacrifices, covenant, glory of God, kingdom of God, light and darkness, worship, water of life, and nations. All these trajectories are present in the prophetic books and find their epicenter in Christ. This is no accident.

Consider, for example, the prophetic contribution to the theme of marriage. We have already considered its typological development in Hosea. Isaiah, Jeremiah, and Ezekiel also employ marital language to portray Israel as the bride of Yahweh. They enrich this beautiful metaphor by highlighting both the Lord's commitment to, and love for, Israel, as well as Israel's unfaithfulness to the Lord. This trajectory then continues in the New Testament, where both John and Paul use marital language to portray Christ's relationship with the church (cf. Eph 5:25–27; John 3:29; Rev 19:7–9). The penultimate chapter in Scripture places the spotlight on the presentation of the bride (Rev 21). Therefore, when we are preaching these marital passages, we have a clear path that leads to Christ. A sermon from Ezekiel 16 that does so might look like this:

> *Sermon idea*: The best Husband relentlessly loves his horrible bride!
>
> *Introduction*: In Ezekiel 16, and across Scripture, the Lord uses marriage language to describe his love and the intimacy he wants with his people—intimacy he wants with us despite our many unattractive qualities.

I. *The Lord beautifies his bride's ugliness* (16:1–14)

a. Israel's ugly, unloved, and helpless beginning (16:1–5)

b. The Lord cleanses, clothes, adorns, marries, and beautifies his bride (16:6–14)

c. Christ cleanses and beautifies us from all our stains, wrinkles, and blemishes (cf. Eph. 5:26–27)

II. *The Lord despises his bride's unfaithfulness* (16:15–58)

a. From bride to whore (16:15–34)

b. From honor to shame (16:35–43)

c. "Like mother, like daughter" and the two ugly sisters (16:44–58)

III. *The Lord atones for his bride's unworthiness* (16:59–63)

a. The loving Husband will establish an everlasting covenant and atone for his bride's horrible deeds (16:59–63)

b. Christ loves us, gave himself for us, and makes us a perfectly adorned bride (cf. Eph 5:25–27; Rev 21:2)

To trace these trajectories without engaging in "wild flights of imagination," Clowney invites us to ask the following questions: "What truth about God and his saving work is disclosed in this passage? . . . How is this particular truth carried forward in the history of revelation? How does it find fulfillment in Christ?"[29]

## Contrast

We can also connect the Old Testament to Christ by highlighting the contrast that exists between old covenant community and the new covenant community due to Christ. Many prophetic oracles apply to us in a different manner than they did for the original audience. The reason for this difference is due to Christ's intervention in history. The saving work of Christ thus becomes the filter through which the prophetic message reaches us.

Paradoxically this is a road we discover because we come to a dead end. In the prophets we will come across many passages that announce God's judgment upon his people. Hosea 5, for instance, announces the imminent judgment the people of Israel and Judah would suffer by the hand of foreign nations due to their injustice (5:2), idolatry (5:4), and arrogance (5:5). The historical distance in itself changes the way Hosea's warning applies to us. However, we must remember these historical and localized warnings of judgment also point to the great and ultimate judgment all sinners deserve. Therefore, Hosea 5 does speak to us, not only because it exposes sin we too are guilty of but also because it foreshadows the ultimate judgment we deserve. Yet, due to Christ, we are not under judgment. Therefore, in these instances we see a significant difference that is brought about by the grace of God in Christ. The dead end of judgment becomes a road to Christ.

A good way to spot these dead ends that lead to Christ is to look for what Chapell calls the "Fallen Condition Focus" of our text. "The Fallen Condition Focus (FCF) is the mutual human condition that contemporary believers share with those to or about whom the text was written that requires the grace of the passage for God's people to glorify and

29. Clowney, "Preaching Christ from Biblical Theology," 59.

enjoy him."[30] Determining what aspect of the fallenness is exposed in a passage prepares our people to travel to Christ to find God's grace and redemption. In other words, this road links the problem exposed in an Old Testament text to its solution in Christ. As Greidanus explains this was a road frequently traveled by Spurgeon and one we will frequently travel when preaching the prophets. The prophetic message "may convict us of the gravity of human sin, it may confront us with a just and holy God, and it may remind us of the Day of Judgment. These plights cry out for a solution, and the solution is found in Jesus Christ."[31]

## New Testament Guidance

This road overlaps with the previous ones. On some occasions we are only able to spot Christocentric predictions, typologies, trajectories, or contrasts because they are explicitly stated in the New Testament. Without the enlightenment and the guidance of the New Testament writers these subtle roads would be extremely hard to detect. Moreover, in these situations we have the assurance we are traveling on legitimate roads because they have the approval stamp of the New Testament authors.

The New Testament writers leaned heavily on the Old Testament prophets. As we noted in chapter 1, we have a breadth of references that range from direct quotations to subtle allusions. These references are a great help in our journey from an Old Testament text to Christ. We should look for, and gladly accept, all the help we can get from the New Testament writers.

Consider, for example, how the author of Hebrews (2:13) traces a line from Isaiah to Christ that we otherwise would not have been able to spot. The author of Hebrews is presenting Christ as the founder (captain, forerunner) of our salvation who is able to bring many sons to glory (2:10). To achieve this the author of Hebrews refers to a few verses in Isaiah 8:17b–18 where the prophet commits to trusting the Lord and leading his own children to worship God. Hebrews therefore enables us to see Isaiah's trust in the Lord in face of the impending Assyrian threat (7:18—8:22), and his commitment to the Lord points forward to Christ's greater trust and greater commitment to bring many sons to glory. The author of Hebrews delineates a path from Isaiah 8:17b–18 to Christ.

30. Chapell, *Christ-Centered Preaching*, 50.
31. Greidanus, *Preaching Christ from the Old Testament*, 272.

Other authors of the New Testament also point to another connection from the same chapter in Isaiah. Both Paul (Rom 9:33) and Peter (1 Pet 2:8) apply the words "a stone of offense and a rock of stumbling" (8:14) to Christ. "The righteous shall live by his faith" (Hab 2:4) is another example of prophetic words that are picked up in multiple places in the New Testament (Rom 1:17; Gal 3:11; Heb 10:38–39) and connected to salvation in Christ. In these instances, when the New Testament writers show us christological connections, we have every reason to follow their guidance. Remember, however, following their guidance should not lead you to abandon but enrich your original preaching text.

## THE *MILLIARIUM AUREUM* OF SCRIPTURE

Christ is the *Milliarium Aureum* of Scripture. He is the great metropolis. The progressive yet organic nature of God's revelation inevitably connects every part of this revelation to its center. Every text in the Old Testament leads forward to Christ—the pinnacle of God's revelation and the centerpiece of God's redemption. The Old Testament prophetic books are no exception to this. As preachers of God's word, we therefore need to preach the prophets christocentrically. Our preaching of the prophetic books needs to radiate the savor of Christ. Consequently, the issue is not *if* we should preach Christ from the prophets but *how* to connect the prophets to Christ. As I have argued, I do not believe the only, or the best, way to achieve this is a rigorous dogma that from *each* text and in *every* sermon we must reach Christ. I do, however, maintain it certainly is appropriate, indeed necessary, for *all* prophetic sermon series to be Christocentric. This approach allows us to travel down the legitimate roads that surface from the prophetic books to Christ without recklessly crashing into hedges or falling into ditches.

Moreover, our goal is much higher than abiding by or proving the effectiveness of a specific preaching methodology. Our goal is also higher than having a clear road map of Scripture. Our goal is to lead our people to Christ. Thus, we travel from the prophets to Christ not to provide interesting connections but true encounters, not to prove our cleverness but his greatness, not to produce nice thoughts but burning hearts.

# Chapter 9

## BUILD A BRIDGE TO THE CHURCH

> "For whatever was written in former days was written for
> our instruction, that through endurance and through the
> encouragement of the Scriptures we might have hope."
>
> —ROM 15:4

JOHN STOTT FAMOUSLY USED the metaphor of a bridge to describe preaching.[1] As preachers we stand between two worlds: the world of the Bible and our world. Our task is to build a bridge so our listeners not only understand what the word of God meant in its original context but also how it applies today. We connect our listeners to the word of God, and transport the word of God into the lives of our listeners. In this final chapter we will think through how to build this bridge from the prophets to the church. In previous chapters we traveled over to the side of the bridge we can call the "world of the prophets." However, we do not want to remain on the prophetic side of the riverbank; rather, we want to bring their message to bear in our world. Indeed, even when we explored the prophetic message, genre, language, history, and rhetoric, we did so with our feet planted in the prophetic world yet looking over into our world. The aim throughout has been to equip us to preach the prophets, to hear and echo what God says today via the prophets. The goal of this chapter is to further bolster our bridgebuilding skills by honing in on some of

---

1. Stott, *Between Two Worlds*.

the mechanics of this process.[2] First, we begin in the prophetic world and seek to understand the meaning of the prophetic text. Second, we measure the distance between the world of the prophets and our world. Third, we build the actual structure of the bridge by identifying the timeless truth.[3] The final stage is to cross the bridge and drive the truth home by applying it to the lives of our listeners.

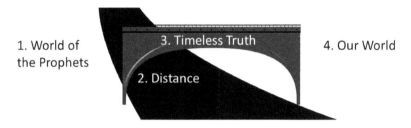

1. World of the Prophets        3. Timeless Truth        4. Our World

2. Distance

To see this process at work I will use the bookends of the prophetic literature (Isa 1:2–9 and Mal 3:13—4:3) as the primary examples throughout. For our purposes, these passages can function as an *inclusio*. These case studies are valid representatives of the wide range of the prophetic genre: imminent and eschatological, judgment and salvation, major and minor prophet, preexilic and postexilic, lawsuit and disputation oracle.

## DISCOVER THE ORIGINAL MEANING

Serious constructions usually begin with the hard work of digging. The same is true if we want to build a bridge from the prophets to the church. We need to begin by digging into the prophetic text to unearth its meaning. Until we have unearthed the meaning of a prophetic message for its original biblical audience, we should not begin to consider how it applies to us today. This is the necessary starting point. The truth we are called to bridge to our people arises from the text, and therefore we must ensure we are spending a significant amount of time in the text. The longer we spend in the world of the prophets the better we will channel their God-given message to our world today.

2. My goal is not to cover all sermon preparation steps but to consider the broader, yet overlapping, process of moving from text to application. The step-by-step process of sermon preparation has been thoroughly articulated by others (See Robinson, *Biblical Preaching,* and Sunukjian, *Invitation to Biblical Preaching*).

3. I first came across the expression "timeless truth" in Sunukjian, *Invitation to Biblical Preaching,* 42–64.

In the previous chapters we spent significant time in the prophetic world. We examined and appreciated the value of the prophetic message (chapter 2). We navigated the uncharted territory of the prophetic genre (chapter 4) and wrestled with the right questions we must ask to interpret prophetic language (chapter 5). We also traveled back in time and visited the prophets in their own backyard to pay attention to the historical context that shaped their message (chapter 6). We then analyzed and admired the various forms of prophetic speeches (chapter 7). Considering the time we have spent in the world of the prophets, and considering the tools we use to dig into the unique prophetic soil are more or less the standard exegetical tools, I will not revise them in detail in this context.[4] Rather, I will offer a checklist to ensure we are not shortcutting this vital step when preaching a prophetic passage.

1. *Read, read, and read again.* If you can read in the original, go for it. If you can't, then read a variety of accurate translations and consult an interlinear Bible.

2. *Identify the genre and the specific prophetic form.*

3. *Outline the structure of the passage.*

4. *Analyze the grammar.*

5. *Study key words.*

6. *Ponder the poetic language and imagery.* This aspect of studying the passage is perhaps less standard across all biblical genres, yet it is crucial when studying a prophetic text.

7. *Place the passage within its literary context.*

8. *Research and understand the historical context.*

Following this thorough study we will have an ocean of data on the passage. To avoid getting lost in the detail it is necessary to bring together all our discoveries in a sentence or two. The goal of this summary is to crystallize the message of your preaching text. The sentence is the *textual truth* of the passage. The *textual truth* often is long and elaborate since it tries to thoroughly capture the meaning of the text. The *textual truth* is also best written using the actual words of the passage and in the past tense since it pertains to what the passage meant to the original biblical

---

4. For an excellent introduction of the task of Old Testament exegesis in sermon preparation, see Stuart, *Old Testament Exegesis.*

audience. Remember, we have not crossed the bridge yet, we have simply ascertained what the text meant to the original audience. Digging is hard but it is how bridgebuilding begins.

*Textual Truth, Isaiah* 1:2–9: Isaiah indicted Judah for their rebellion. He portrayed them as rebellious children, foolish animals, disrespectful subjects, and infected with a pervasive disease. He announced that judgement would arrive in the form of foreign invasion and land desolation.

*Textual Truth, Malachi* 3:13—4:3: Malachi rebutted Israel's assertion that it is vain to serve the Lord: The Lord does pay attention to those who serve him, and one day he will show the distinction between those who serve him and the wicked by acting in judgment and salvation.

## MEASURE THE DISTANCE

Once we grasp the significance of the prophetic message (i.e., the *textual truth*), we need to measure the distance that separates us from the world of the prophets. Just as the width of a river may vary so the distance between a prophetic text and us can vary. In order to build a bridge, we have to gauge the distance. In some instances, the distance will seem short and therefore the journey to application will be more immediate. We may be tempted to jump or swim across the river. In other situations, the distance between the two riverbanks is such that it is even hard to see the other side, and, therefore, we question if application is even possible. In both scenarios, and in all intermediate cases, accurate awareness of the distance is crucial to building a solid bridge.

Two primary distances separate us from the prophets: historical and covenantal. We dedicated chapter 6 to measuring the historical distance,[5] so here we will focus on the covenantal distance. We assess the covenantal distance by considering both discontinuity and continuity.[6]

---

5. Which, as we saw, also includes other spheres: cultural, geographical, political, social, religious, and economic.

6. Your assessment of the level of discontinuity and continuity between the old and new covenant will depend on your theological system. In particular the relationship between Israel and the church will have a significant bearing. To begin to compare the major positions and think yourself clear, see Brand, *Perspectives on Israel and the Church*; Merkle, *Discontinuity to Continuity*.

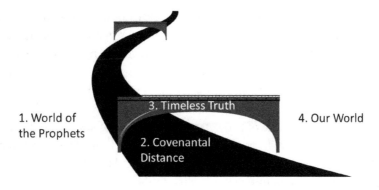

## Discontinuity

The prophets directed their message to the people of God under the old covenant. We are the new-covenant people of God. This is a significant difference. Moreover, the prophets were the enforcers of the old covenant. The old covenant, also known as the Mosaic Covenant, was established at Mount Sinai after Israel's exodus from Egypt. This covenant was a deep bond consolidated in a legal framework. The legal framework outlined not only detailed stipulations but also rewards for obedience and sanctions for disobedience. The task of the prophets was to call covenant-breakers to covenant obedience. Just as the exodus had been physical and national, as well as spiritual, so the judgments and the blessings forecasted had physical and national, as well as spiritual, connotations. The Lord announced through his spokesmen that he would judge his people: Jerusalem would be destroyed, the temple demolished, and the people expelled from the land. The future blessing was described as restoration from foreign nations, abundant produce from the land, and enjoying the presence of the Lord. The prophetic books need to be read and interpreted within this matrix.

This enables us to recognize the significant gulf that separates us from the message of the prophets. We are not under the Mosaic covenant. The threats of the Lord's judgment in the form of a foreign invasion or expulsion from the land do not readily relate to new-covenant believers. For example, Isaiah's warning that Judah will be invaded by foreign invaders that will burn cities and make desolate the land (1:7–8), does not apply directly to believers today.

Similarly, we cannot claim the material prosperity the prophets announced because these promises pertained to the Mosaic covenant. They

belonged to the people of Israel. This, however, does not mean they are irrelevant for us. Paul asserts that whatever was written in the former days
was written for our instruction (Rom 15:5). It simply means a covenantal
distance exists which must be factored in, and somehow overcome,
before we apply the prophetic oracles to New Testament (Testament =
covenant) believers.

Even some of the old covenant stipulations the law demanded and
the prophets solicited, cannot be applied directly to us. They need to be
filtered through the New Testament, and particularly through their fulfillment in Christ, before being applied to the church. DeRouchie notes
that when we follow the pattern of the New Testament authors, we see
that since "Jesus fulfills different laws in different ways, we must consider
each law on its own in light of Christ's work. The end result after doing
such work is what Paul terms the 'law of Christ' (1 Cor. 9:21; Gal. 6:2)."[7]
DeRouchie goes on to explain that when we do this, we observe than some
laws are *maintained* or even *intensified* by him (e.g., adultery, murder,
etc.). Other laws are *transformed* by him, such as the sabbath rest, which
points to the ultimate rest we find in Christ (Heb 3:7—4:11). Other laws
are *extended* when the application of specific case laws, such as not muz-
zling an ox when it treads out grain (Deut 25:4; 1 Cor 9:9; 1 Tim 5:18), are
extended to other and broader applications (i.e., "those who proclaim the
gospel should get their living by the gospel" 1 Cor 9:14). Yet other laws,
such as unclean food laws, are *annulled* by him (Mark 7:18-19). These
observations show the varying width of the river between the old and
new covenants. Therefore, if we jump over to Malachi's final and broad
exhortation, which follows his last disputation, to "remember the law of
Moses" (4:4), we will see it applies to us differently than it applied to the
postexilic community. For them it meant following all the statutes and
rules the Lord commanded for all of Israel at Sinai. For us it means following the guidance of the New Testament writers and considering how
the law applies to us in light of Christ's work and fulfillment of the law.

These are some of the observations we need to engage with to assess the covenantal distance, which can be seen in the contrasts between
the material and spiritual, national and individual, imminent and eschatological, local and global, external and internal. However, we must
recognize these articulations of the covenantal distance do not always
manifest in the same way. The river that separates the two riverbanks

7. DeRouchie, *How to Understand*, 430.

varies in width, and, therefore, these measurements need to accurately be taken from each prophetic text. Not all the promises of restorations have primarily material connotations. Not all warnings of judgment refer to imminent events. Few covenant stipulations reiterated in the Prophets refer primarily to specific and formal adherence. Therefore, to measure the distance from the prophetic text to our world it is not sufficient to determine the fundamental differences between the old and new covenants, we must also trace the varying width of the specific section of the river we are facing. The issue of continuity also affects the distance.

## Continuity

We are covenant people in a covenant relationship with the covenant Lord. The prophets addressed covenant people in a covenant relationship with the covenant Lord. These parallels alone show the significant degree of continuity that permit bridgebuilding. Thompson helpfully advises us to leverage the parallels between the two covenant *communities* to effectively apply the prophetic message to the church. The people of the old and of the new covenant both

> live under the same covenant LORD, who does not change in character or affections. They both live in the light of the past deeds for their good (whether the promises to Abraham, the Exodus, the Davidic kings, or the climactic salvation found in the death and resurrection of Christ). They both live under his demands for love and obedience as his people. And they both live in hope that God's promises of ultimate salvation and judgment will be fulfilled.[8]

Tracking these parallels facilitates bridgebuilding.

The prophets positioned the people of God within God's story. They offered the people of the old-covenant community the right perspective on reality. The prophets' ministry was the Lord's bid to call the people of Israel to understand and live their identity as a covenant community. Much of what they said, therefore, relates well to God's people today and enables us to understand and live our identity as a covenant community. The prophets invite God's people to *look back* to his salvific acts, *look up* to admire his greatness, *look around* to see the needs of others, and *look forward* to his intervention in judgment and salvation. For each of these

8. Thompson, "Community Oracles," 42.

directions, we can see a significant degree of overlap between the old-covenant community and the new-covenant community.

*Look back.* The prophets often took the people on a trip down memory lane. Isaiah, for instance, begins by reminding the people of Israel that they are the Lord's children (1:2). The Lord reared (1:2) and provided (1:3) for them from their infancy as a nation. In doing so Isaiah was reminding Israel of the Lord's care for them throughout their history. This was typical of the prophets. The ultimate evidence of the Lord's goodness and faithfulness, and, therefore, the primary focus of the prophets, was the exodus event. The liberation from the slavery of Egypt, the miraculous crossing of the Red Sea, the hazardous journey through the desert, and the entrance into the promised land, were the highlights of God's salvific acts. This was the great Old Testament salvation story the old-covenant community were frequently invited to bring back to memory. The purpose, however, was not nostalgia. Remembering their past served the dual purpose of motivating them to obedience in the present and to foster hope for the future. This invitation to the covenant people to look to the past to celebrate and respond to God's great salvation is relevant to us. Redemption, ransom, freedom from slavery, and deliverance are all themes that apply to us too. Indeed their relevance for us is heightened since we look back to a greater exodus and to a greater salvation story (cf. Rom 6:5–14; Col 1:13–14; Gal 5:1). This salvation story motivates our obedience and fuels our hope for the future. Therefore we can gladly respond to the prophets' invitation to look back to the Lord's salvation.

*Look up.* The prophets were radically God-centered. They did not only deliver a message *from* God but also *about* God. They reminded the people of his greatness. They refined and enlarged their view of God. Malachi, for example, was addressing the people's distorted notion that God did not make a distinction between those who feared him and the arrogantly wicked (Mal 3:13–15). The prophet rebutted this fallacious viewpoint, explaining that the Lord does pay attention to those who fear him in the present (3:16) and will demonstrate the distinction between those who fear and the evildoers in the future (3:17—4:3). Malachi invited the people to look up, gain the right perspective on God and on reality, and live accordingly. This God-centered emphasis runs throughout the prophetic literature. Isaiah begins his prophecy by reminding the people of the Lord's care (1:2), provision (1:3), holiness (1:4), justice (1:7–8), power (1:9), and mercy (1:9). Malachi ends his prophecy by reminding the people of the Lord's attentiveness (3:16), grace (3:17), justice (3:18), fury (4:1), and healing (4:2).

Furthermore, the prophets reminded the people of their privilege and responsibility toward their God. They chastised the people for their lack of obedience (Isa 1:2). They exhorted the people to trust the Lord (Mal 3:16–18). They rebuked the people for their lack of love (Isa 1:4). They called the people to turn back to their God (Isa 1:18–20). In other words, they called the people to appreciate the privilege, and abide by the responsibility, of being in a covenant relationship with the Lord. This covenant had a legal framework, with detailed stipulations; nevertheless, at the heart of it was a deep bond of love and obedience (Deut 6:1–5). It is telling that the first of the two commandments Jesus cites as a summary of the law is: love the Lord your God with all your heart, soul, and mind (Matt 22:37; Deut 6:5). The specific laws that regulated how the people were to relate to their God fell under the bigger banner of loving the Lord their God. This was the essence of the law. This immediately helps us to see the great continuity for us—the new-covenant people. We are unmistakably called to love the Lord our God with all of ourselves. Therefore, the prophetic words that enable us to admire God and call us to respond in love, obedience, trust, faith, and repentance are readily applicable to us.

*Look around.* Similarly, the second commandment Jesus cites to complete his summary of the law is: love your neighbor as yourself (Matt 22:39; Lev 19:18, 34). The original context of this commandment follows a series of specific laws regarding relations with neighbors and especially with the most vulnerable in society: the poor, foreigners, and servants. The Lord cared, and cares, about how his people treat each other and how they treat foreigners. The prophets mirrored this concern and often chided the people of Israel for their injustice. Frequently the Lord rejected the people's expressions of worship because they were tarnished by the mistreatment of the most vulnerable in their society (Isa 1:10–17). The Lord's exhortation to love our neighbors remains a responsibility for the new-covenant community. Indeed, even the specific attention for the most vulnerable is echoed in the New Testament (Jas 1:27).

To further grasp the relevance for us of these last two directions we have considered, it is worth considering how the prophets describe the new covenant's relationship with the law of Moses. Jeremiah 31:33 says: "I will put my law within them, and I will write it in their hearts." Ezekiel 36:27 says: "I will put my Spirit within you, and cause you to walk in my statutes and be careful to obey my rules." Moreover, in looking forward to the new covenant the prophets were hearkening back to the words of Moses. Moses anticipated a time when the Lord would circumcise his people's hearts so they would love him fully (Deut 30:6) and obey his commands (Deut 30:8). Moses, Jeremiah, and Ezekiel, therefore, all saw the law as pertinent for new-covenant believers. This does not mean we are under the law of Moses (cf. Rom 6:14–15; Gal 5:18) or that the law applies to us in the same ways it did within the theocracy of Israel. Nevertheless, these descriptions prevent us from considering the law as unimportant for us. The law is relevant to us; indeed, it is written in our hearts. The Lord calls and enables us to live out this law engraved in our hearts which is summarized with the two great commandments—love the Lord your God with all of yourself and love your neighbors as yourself. This understanding further confirms the pertinence of the prophets' words for us.

Furthermore, although the prophets were covenant-enforcers they did not go after the people on technicalities or the fine print but on the deeper matters, the core of the law. If anything, the people were often satisfied to display a superficial adherence to the law and neglect the essence of the law (Hos 6:4–6). The specific commandments were the outworking of the people's love for God. Without this love, adherence to the commandments was worthless. The prophets, therefore, were less interested in the letter of the law and more interested in the essence of the law. The famous summary in Micah 6:8 is another way to capture the essence of the law the Lord required and which the prophets sought to enforce: "He has told you, O man, what is good; and what does the Lord require of you but to do justice, and to love kindness, and to walk humbly with your God?" For this reason, the prophetic exhortations to look up and look around ring through history and reach us today.

*Look forward.* The prophets also invited the old-covenant community to look to their future. Just as the purpose of looking to the past was not nostalgia, so too the purpose of looking to the future was not curiosity. The prophets spoke about their future to bring transformation in the present. Isaiah described imminent judgment (1:7–8) to provoke immediate repentance (1:18–20). Awareness of tomorrow should make you walk in the right direction today. The prophets often announced both judgment and salvation. As we have noted throughout, these imminent and localized future events point forward to greater eschatological and global future events. The judgment of Samaria and Jerusalem thus warn us of the ultimate day of God's judgment. The descriptions of blessings and restoration anticipate the ultimate day of God's salvation. Indeed, the prophets often intermingled the description of God's intermediate interventions in history with God's final intervention at the end of history. The purpose of looking to the future judgment was to warn the people to return to the Lord. The purpose of painting a picture of future blessing was to offer hope to those who were discomforted and to incentivize obedience by promising the reward. We see these goals in Malachi's final disputation. He invited the postexilic community to look ahead to the ultimate day of reckoning. For the evildoers, the day will be like a burning furnace and will reduce them to stubble and ashes (4:1, 3). For those who fear and serve the Lord, it will be a day when the sun of righteousness will rise with healing in its wings and they will leap like calves from the stall (4:2). What a contrast! This contrast crystallizes the distinction between the righteous and the wicked, between who serves God and who does not serve him (3:18). This vivid picture of the future functioned as a powerful warning for the wicked to repent. It also offered hope to those who were discouraged in their service to the Lord and thus invigorated their obedience.

These effects of looking to the future are relevant today. The biblical writers often, and unashamedly, describe the future blessing and reward to incentivize obedience (Phil 3:14; Col 3:23–24). Similarly, they announce judgment to bring transformation in the present (2 Cor 5:10; Heb 2:1–4). The announcement of judgment is also a warning to those who have not yet come to Christ (Acts 10:42–43; 17:30–31). Moreover, awareness of the severity of future judgment also cultivates our appreciation, knowing that Christ took upon himself the judgment that belongs to us (Isa 53:4–6). In all these cases we see how the invitation to look forward strengthens our identity and elicits our obedience as God's covenant people.

These directions the prophets invite us to look at show us the continuity that exists between the old-covenant community and the new-covenant community. The river is not too wide. We can apply the prophetic message to us. Therefore, without neglecting or undermining the distance that does exist, we can build the bridge. Indeed, this link between the two covenant communities is the strongest bridge we can and should build.

## Shaky Bridges

At times it may be possible to build a bridge from the biographical information of the life of the prophets to individuals today. Preachers frequently build and cross this bridge when preaching the prophets. The prophets were examples of faithfulness, perseverance, patience, obedience, faith, and courage. They were men of faith who spoke in the name of the Lord and remained steadfast for many years in the face of intense opposition. No wonder James invites us to take the prophets as examples (Jas 5:10; cf. Heb 11:32–38). We have a lot to learn from them.

However, this valid and well-traveled bridge is not as solid as it may appear for three reasons. First, drawing connections between the prophets and individuals is often difficult due to the significant differences that exist between the role the prophets played in their day compared to the role we are called to live out today.[9] Second, this bridge can only be built from a limited section of prophetic literature. The prophetic books are anthologies of oracles interspersed with few biographical details. The focus is on the message of the prophets more than on their lives. This should be reflected in our preaching. Third, even when biographical information is given, the *primary* purpose of these details is to complement and advance the *message* of the books rather than inviting us to emulate the prophets. Consider, for example, Jeremiah, a prophet who frequently shared autobiographical information. The Lord told him to buy land in his hometown with the Babylonians at the door, ready to invade Judah (Jer 32). Would you obey and buy land in a warzone? Jeremiah did. He is a great example of obedience. However, if our preaching of Jeremiah 32 focuses primarily on the prophet's obedience we risk missing the function of this episode within the framework of the book. With the Babylonians looming, Jeremiah bought land in a warzone to convey the assurance that the Lord would bring his people back after the exile. The Lord's promised deliverance was sure. You could bank on it! The prophet delivered this message with his words and displayed it with his life. Therefore, we can build and cross a bridge between the prophets and individuals today; however, we need to be aware this can be a shaky bridge. We must proceed with caution and ensure we are not violating the function of the biographical information within the prophetic books.

9. As we noted in chapter 3, we do see similarities between the role of the prophets and the role that preachers have today. However, the parallels between the prophets and most other believers are significantly fewer.

A bridge that instead we should *not* attempt to build and cross is the bridge between Israel and our nation. We cannot claim our country is God's treasured possession (cf. Mal 3:17). Israel was in a unique and national covenant relationship with the Lord. Our nations are not! The distance is too big to bridge.

## BUILD THE BRIDGE

Once we have assessed the distance (the river to cross) we can build the bridge. The key to this phase is to translate the contextualized prophetic message (i.e., the *textual truth*) into a *timeless truth*. We need to strip the prophetic message from its timebound garments. This can be tricky, yet it is essential to bridge the gap from the prophetic world to our world. The following guidelines direct the transition from the *textual truth* into the *timeless truth*. The timeless truth should agree with the rest of Scripture, apply to New Testament believers, and be anchored to the preaching text.

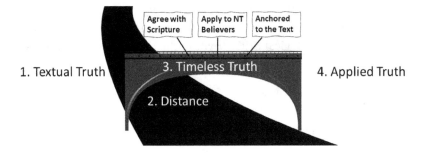

## Agree with the Rest of Scripture

Scripture corroborates Scripture. This guideline is crucial to ensure the truth that emerges from our study of the passage is accurate. If it is, it will agree with the rest of the biblical revelation. Therefore, we must compare the *textual truth* with the grid of Scripture and refine it accordingly. This is achieved by asking questions: Does the truth I have identified correspond with the teaching of the rest of Scripture? What are the other primary passages in Scripture that deal with the same subject matter of my text? Do these other passages certify, clarify, or modify the textual truth I have found in the passage? Engaging with these questions enables us to have confidence that what we are preaching is not only anchored to our passage but also in line with the rest of Scripture. This guideline falls under the umbrella of systematic theology since its goal is to systematize the textual truth with the rest of the teaching of Scripture on the same topic.

When we compare our passages in Isaiah and Malachi to the grid of Scripture, no major component requires modification. The testimony of Scripture is that rebellion is a serious matter before the Lord and merits judgment. This corresponds with the textual truth we discovered in Isaiah's opening oracle. Scripture also teaches throughout that, despite appearances, the Lord pays attention to those who fear him, and one day the difference between the faithful and the wicked will be crystal clear. The rest of Scripture corroborates Malachi's final oracle.

Note that this process should refine or complete, not overturn or overrun, the truth of the passage. If we struggle to reconcile the textual truth with the grid of what the rest of Scripture says, then there are two possibilities: either our identification of the textual truth is flawed or our grid of what we think the rest of Scripture teaches is defective. In these cases, we must continue to work hard until we see how our text accords with the rest of Scripture. Patience and humility are the key virtues that protect us from shortcutting this process and squeezing our textual truth into our rigid theological grid. Privilege the text over your theological system, even if this involves admitting you do not have a perfectly squared theological system.

## Apply to New Testament Believers

The timeless truth should apply to New Testament believers. This guideline overlaps with the previous one, but its specific focus is to ensure we are overcoming the covenantal distance. A bridge usually rises to an apex before descending on the other side. Often, to transition from the textual truth to the timeless truth, we need climb up from the specifics of the text to broader, more general language. Sunukjian and Robinson[10] call this process climbing up the "ladder of abstraction" to find "language that not only describes what is happening in the text, but that is also sufficiently broad to describe similar things that might occur in different centuries or cultures."[11] Timeless! We climb until we reach the apex, the timeless truth that applies to New Testament believers. An effective check to ensure the

10. Robinson, "Heresy of Application," 308.

11. Sunukjian, *Invitation to Biblical Preaching*, 51–52.

success of this process is to articulate the timeless truth in the present tense. When we shift from the past tense of the textual truth to the present tense, we have identified the timeless truth. It is timeless because the truth now does not just apply to the original biblical audience but also to the contemporary world.

A key part of rising toward the apex is to consider how the textual truth relates to Christ. When we do this, we are better positioned to know how it applies to New Testament believers. Pelton, a keen Christocentric preacher, exhorts us to move from the textual truth (which he calls the "textual big idea"[12]) to the timeless truth relevant to New Testament believers (which he calls the "canonical big idea"[13]) by exploring "how the canonical center of Scripture—the gospel and its implications—completes the meaning of the preaching portion and makes it true for the church."[14] Whether or not you make an explicit reference to Christ, how the textual truth relates to Christ, and through him to New Testament believers, is the decisive factor in formulating the timeless truth. This guideline falls under the umbrella of biblical theology since its goal is to trace how the textual truth progresses through the various stages of salvation history.

Applying this guideline to Isaiah's lawsuit requires skillful bridge-building. The river is wide because Isaiah's announcement of judgment does not apply to us today in the same way as it applied to Judah. Land invasion and desolation were curses of the Mosaic covenant (Deut 28). Judah's local and national judgment, however, foreshadow the final and universal judgment all rebels deserve—that we deserve! This understanding begins to bridge the distance between Judah in Isaiah's day and the church in our day. However, we also know by the progress of revelation that those who are in Christ are no longer under judgment (John 3:18). Therefore, whilst the descriptions Isaiah offers of rebellion match the rebellion we frequently see in us, by the grace of God in Christ we are spared the judgment we merit. Indeed, it is the book of Isaiah that explains the reason for this. One of the metaphors Isaiah employed to describe sinfulness was a pervasive and grave disease. "The whole head is sick, and the whole heart faint. From the sole of the foot even to the head, there is no soundness in it, but bruises and sores and raw wounds; they

12. Pelton, *Preaching with Accuracy*, 18.
13. Pelton, *Preaching with Accuracy*, 19.
14. Pelton, *Preaching with Accuracy*, 19.

are not pressed out or bound up or softened with oil" (Isa 1:5–6). Isaiah resumes this language in his most famous chapter to describe the forgiveness and salvation we find in Christ—the suffering servant: "But he was pierced for our transgressions; he was crushed for our iniquities; upon him was the chastisement that brought us peace, and with his wounds we are healed" (Isa 53:5). The textual truth's journey through the progress of revelation, and in particular through Christ, completes the meaning of Isaiah 1 for the church.

*The timeless truth of Isaiah* 1:2–9: Rebellion against God is ungrateful, personal, ugly, and merits judgment. Yet because Christ took upon himself our rebellion we are forgiven, empowered, and called to live as obedient children.

The distance between us and Malachi's disputation is narrower. The primary task is simply to climb up the ladder of abstraction by removing the timebound garments and transition into the present tense.

*The timeless truth of Malachi* 3:13—4:3: The notion that it is vain to serve the Lord is false. The Lord not only pays attention to those who serve him, he also promises one day he will show the distinction between those who serve him and the wicked by acting in judgment and salvation.

## Anchored to the Preaching Passage

The *timeless truth* must be anchored to our preaching passage. This final guideline may appear redundant. After all, we derive *timeless truth* from the *textual truth*, which in turn is the result of careful study of the preaching passage. Why then include this guideline at this stage of the process? I include it because of a risk I sometimes see in my own sermon preparation. Once I compare *textual truth* with the grid of Scripture and I trace its progress throughout salvation history, the product (i.e., the *timeless truth*) can end up far removed from the preaching passage. We can end up losing our *textual truth* in the intricate web of systematic and biblical theology. When this happens, the *timeless truth* can either become an encompassing and sophisticated theological proposition or a broad and simple statement. In both cases it bears little resemblance to the *textual truth* we discovered in our passage. Therefore, it is wise that after we do our theology bit we verify that the *textual truth* is still evident, and indeed is the driving factor, in the *timeless truth*. The link between the two ought to be organic and indissoluble. To achieve this, I find Duvall and Hays's advice about the *timeless truth* (which they call "theological principle"[15]) astute. "Select the theological principle that is as specific as possible while still general enough to apply to us as New Testament believers."[16] The timeless truth of Isaiah's opening oracle should not become: "Due to Christ's substitutionary death and vicarious sacrifice on the cross, those that have repented and received him as their Savior and Lord and have been regenerated by the Spirit of God have been cleansed from their sin to walk in sanctity of life by the power of the Spirit." That statement buries the *textual truth* under a pile of New Testament concepts and theological jargon. Conversely, the timeless truth of Malachi's closing oracle should not become: "God will judge the wicked and save the faithful." Overtheologizing (as with the first example above) and overgeneralizing (as with the second example) move the timeless truth far away from the textual truth. Climb up the ladder of abstraction only as much as is strictly necessary.

## APPLY THE TRUTH

Once we have built the bridge, we need to cross it and carry the timeless truth to our world. We need to apply the truth to our lives and the lives of our listeners. Application is often the Achilles' heel of many preachers. This difficulty derives not only from the lack of specific training in this area but also from the lack of clarity regarding what constitutes a good application. Should the application be general or specific? Practical or theological? Forceful or subtle? I find a strong application has two primary characteristics: it is text-driven and life-changing.

### Text-driven

Back to the text! A strong application derives directly from the preaching passage. Indeed, it should match the application embedded in the text. As Davies demonstrates, Scripture comes to us preapplied. Application, therefore, comes primarily from listening carefully to Scripture since it

15. Duvall and Hays, *Grasping God's Word*, 43, 201.
16. Duvall and Hays, *Grasping God's Word*, 201.

"isn't something that we bring to the Bible, it is something that we derive from it."[17] Our application should be much more, and much more careful, than a series of inferences we derive from the timeless truth. Our application should be the contextualization of the purposefulness of the preaching passage.

Remember, Scripture is not a series of abstract propositions but divine truth intermingled with, and directed to, a real-life context. While this can be a challenge because it requires us to identify and remove time-bound garments, it is also a significant help in determining application. The real-life context gives us a concrete picture of the abstract truth. It shows us what the timeless truth looks like applied to specific people in specific circumstances. These specific people and specific circumstances, though distant from us, are analogs to us in many ways. Therefore, when we consider the response the prophets wanted to elicit back then, we are on track to determine the response we want to achieve today. Part of our study of the passage should involve discovering how the truth the prophets announced applied, or was meant to apply, to the lives of their listeners. Viewed this way, application is not an unsafe afterthought disconnected from the text, but rather the product of careful exegesis of the text. Exegesis yields application. Therefore, once we have built the bridge by identifying the timeless truth, we do not abandon our preaching passage. Rather, we travel back and forth across the bridge multiple times to ensure we are carrying the application with us.

The purpose of Isaiah's lawsuit oracle was to elicit repentance. He confronted Judah with the gravity of their rebellion and the reality of God's judgment in order to call them to return to the Lord and to honor him by living obediently. This response that is implied in our passage is made explicit in the immediate context (Isa 1:18–20). This is the application we must maintain and mirror. As we noted, we read Isaiah's words through the lens of Christ. When we do this, we will certainly be comforted to know he has paid the price for our rebellion. It is right and appropriate to rejoice in this great truth. However, this should not be done to the detriment of the strong word of exhortation and warning embedded in the passage. The purpose of Isaiah's words is to confront us with the ugliness of our sinfulness so we will repent and return to the Lord. To channel this applicative thrust, when I preached this passage, I invested most of my time exploring Isaiah's vivid descriptions of our sinfulness

17. Davies, *Get Preaching*, 22.

(rebellious children, foolish animals, disrespectful subjects, and pervasive disease). The force of these metaphors shamed us and caused us to repent deeply. I did conclude the sermon with the good news that, due to Christ, our brokenness is met with forgiveness—by his wounds we are healed. However, I ensured this crucial element did not overturn the summons to repentance but rather strengthened it.

Remaining on the same original applicative trajectory also reduces the risk of deriving our application from some peripheral aspect of the passage. This strong connection between text and application allows us to weave the application throughout the sermon rather than just tacking it on as an appendix. This will maximize the potency of the application as our hearers see that the application derives directly from the text.

Malachi's purpose in his final disputation was to rebuke, exhort, and comfort those who were serving the Lord by rebutting the false notion that serving the Lord is pointless. If we follow this trajectory we are staying on track, and we will be able to weave the application throughout the sermon. Note in the following outline how the applicative thrust runs throughout the sermon and is text-driven.

> *Introduction*: Has serving the Lord ever felt pointless to you? Maybe we have never said it outright, but the thought has crossed our minds and crept into our hearts and left us discouraged. We can be tempted to give up!
>
> *Historical context*: The people of Judah in Malachi's day felt this temptation . . .
>
> I. *The Lord exposes and condemns the fallacious idea that serving him is pointless* (3:13–15)
>
> II. *The Lord pays attention to those who serve him* (3:16)
>
> III. *The Lord will reward those who serve him*
>
> > a. They will be his treasured possession (3:17–18)
> >
> > b. They will bask in the healing warmth of the sun of righteousness (4:2a)
> >
> > c. They will leap with joy like calves released from the stall (4:2b)
>
> IV. *The Lord will judge the wicked* (4:1, 3)
>
> *Conclusion*: The Lord sees and rewards those who serve him. It is not pointless! Do not give up!

## Life-changing

A strong application must aim at making a difference in people's lives. The timeless truth must not remain an abstract proposition but must make an impact in our world. Application can fail to make a difference in people's lives for at least two reasons.

First, our application can fail because it is not big enough. In the goal to be practical, we can risk reducing applications to a list of things we ought to do and a list of things we ought not do. We focus on the external rather than the internal, the minutiae rather than the core. This will not bring about true transformation; rather, it risks leading our people down a path of superficial adherence or, even worse, a path of legalism. Scripture deals with ultimate, not frivolous, matters. The prophets were not lightweight boxers dancing around, landing a series of harmless jabs. They were heavyweights that delivered knockout blows. The prophets exposed deep-rooted sins, urged repentance, warned of judgment, fostered faith, nurtured hope, and exhorted obedience. Therefore, our application should not settle for the superficial but should go after the deepest needs of our people. When this happens, as Robinson explains, "flint strikes steel. The flint of someone's problem strikes the steel of God's word, and a spark emerges that can set that person on fire for God."[18] So aim big. Scripture challenges us, exhorts us, woos us, shakes us, and we should do the same in our application. Filling hearts with the deep-set conviction that the Lord sees and rewards those who serve him has a significantly greater chance of being life-changing than offering five tips to reduce the temptation of giving up in the incoming week. Applying the prophets, therefore, involves bringing to bear the force of heavyweight punches upon us today. However, boxers are only effective if they strike. This leads us to the second reason why applications can fail.

An application can also fail to be life-changing because it lacks specificity. This does not contradict the previous reason. I am not advocating minutiae but specificity. I am not suggesting replacing heavyweight punches with harmless jabs. Rather, I am highlighting the need to land our heavyweight punches. We need to preach big, but then we need to show how ultimate realities transform daily lives. As Duvall and Hays highlight:

---

18. Robinson, "Blending Bible Content and Life Application," 299.

> If we never suggest ways to make our applications specific, people may not know exactly how to live out the message of the Bible in the down and dirty of real life. Don't be afraid to make specific suggestions. People don't just need to know *what* to do; they also need to know *how* to do it. We not only have to offer biblical insight; we also have to offer them skills and wisdom for living out that insight.[19]

Therefore, when exhorting our people to obey we need to show them what obedience looks like in the different spheres of life (family, work, church, etc.). When exposing deep-rooted sin we need to help them spot specific sins (pride, greed, sloth, lust, etc.) they may be overlooking or tolerating. Landing heavyweight punches requires insightful knowledge not only of Scripture but also of our people. I find the best place to start with this is my own life. What difference does the timeless truth make, or should it make, in my life? What does that look like? Considering how the timeless truth transforms my life helps me guide—or better, still shepherd—others to see how the same truth transforms their lives.

For example, Isaiah 1 shows us the ugliness of our sinfulness. The passage deals with weighty matters. Heavy punches! When I preached this passage, in order to land this weighty message in our lives I associated Isaiah's language about sin in general with specific sins we struggle with. I used the following specific sins: When you don't pray, you slam the door shut in your Father's face (rebellious children, v. 2); when you waste God's money on yourself, you are biting the hand that feeds you (foolish animal, v. 3); when you are more concerned about your reputation than his kingdom, you are turning your back on your King (disrespectful subjects, v. 4); when you gossip about others and call it sharing, you are cleaning raw wounds with a muddy towel (pervasive disease, vv. 5–6). The specificity of these examples did not trivialize the seriousness of sin, they just brought Isaiah's words much closer to home. They brought us to repentance by showing us the ugliness of sin in our lives. They also showed us what living obediently looks like in some specific areas of our lives.


## PREACH THE PROPHETS!

Bridge-building is not easy. It requires exegetical study, theological reflection, and pastoral sensitivity. Knowing and thinking through the

---

19. Duvall and Hays, *Grasping God's Word*, 241 (italics original).

mechanics is a good start, but bridging the gap from the world of the prophets to our world is not an easy task. Yet it is the preacher's task. The prophets played a critical role in revealing God's plan of salvation for the church. They occupy a significant proportion of the biblical canon, similar in size to the entire New Testament. Therefore preachers who desire to be faithful to God's word and God's church will preach the prophets. As preachers it is our duty to take on this significant construction project so as not to deprive the church of the wealth and depth of the prophetic message. The best way to develop a desire to preach the prophets is to travel over to and spend time in their world. Once we experience God speaking to us through the prophets, we will want to build a bridge to enable our people to experience it too. The best way to develop our bridge-building skills is to start building. Preaching the prophets with a desire to be a faithful conduit will equip you, encourage your people, and honor God. Kaiser, who has been building bridges for many years, testifies of the privilege and power of preaching the words of the prophets: "To preach these words faithfully is to unleash for God's people direction, comfort, and a hope that surpasses every other expectation that mortals could ever imagine or aspire to on planet earth."[20] Preach the prophets!

20. Kaiser, *Preaching and Teaching from the Old Testament*, 119.

# APPENDIX A

## Types of Parallelism

| Type | Explanation | Example | Reference |
|------|-------------|---------|-----------|
| Synonymous | The second line restates the idea found in the first line. | Rejoice greatly, O daughter of Zion! Shout aloud, o daughter of Jerusalem! | Zech 9:9 |
| Antithetic | The second line contrasts the first line. | Seek me and live; But do not seek Bethel, | Amos 5:4–5 |
| Synthetic | The second line expands the idea expressed in the first line. | Woe to the wicked! It shall be ill with him, For what his hands have dealt out shall be done to him | Isa 3:11 |
| Climactic | The subsequent lines both restate and develop the initial idea, thus combining synonymous and synthetic parallelism. | Fear not, for I am with you; Be not dismayed, for I am your God; I will strengthen you, I will help you, I will uphold you with my righteous right hand. | Isa 41:10 |
| Chiastic | The sequence of ideas is presented and then repeated in reverse order like a mirror effect: ABBA, ABCCBA, etc. | Make the heart of this people dull, And their ears heavy, And blind their eyes; Lest they see with their eyes, And hear with their ears, And understand with their hearts. | Isa 6:10 |

# Bibliography

Achtemeier, Elizabeth. *Preaching from the Minor Prophets*. Grand Rapids: Eerdmans, 1998.

————. *Preaching from the Old Testament*. Louisville: Westminster John Knox, 1989.

Adam, Peter. *Speaking God's Words*. Downers Grove, IL: InterVarsity, 1996.

Alexander, Desmond T. *From Eden to the New Jerusalem: An Introduction to Biblical Theology*. Grand Rapids: Kregel Academic, 2008.

Alter, Robert. *The Art of Biblical Poetry: Revised and Updated*. New York: Basic, 2011.

Alter, Robert, and Frank Kermode, eds. *The Literary Guide to the Bible*. Cambridge: Harvard University Press, 1987.

Archer, Gleason L. *A Survey of Old Testament Introduction: Revived and Expanded*. Chicago: Moody, 2007.

Arnold, Bill T., and Bryan E. Beyer. *Encountering the Old Testament: A Christian Survey*. 3rd ed. Grand Rapids: Baker Academic, 2015.

Arthurs, Jeffrey D. "Pathos Needed." In *The Art & Craft of Biblical Preaching*, edited by Haddon Robinson and Craig Brian Larson, 591–95. Grand Rapids: Zondervan, 1996.

————. *Preaching as Reminding: Stirring Memory in an Age of Forgetfulness*. Downers Grove, IL: InterVarsity, 2017.

————. *Preaching with Variety: How to Re-create the Dynamics of Biblical Genres*. Grand Rapids: Kregel, 2007.

Ash, Christopher. *The Priority of Preaching*. London: Christian Focus, 2010.

Augustine. *De Doctrina Christiana*. Edited and translated by R. P. H. Green. Oxford: Clarendon, 1995.

Bailey, Kenneth E. *Jesus through Middle Eastern Eyes: Cultural Studies in the Gospels*. Downers Grove, IL: Intervarsity, 2008.

Barnett, Paul. *The Second Epistle to the Corinthians*. Grand Rapids: Eerdmans, 1997.

Baxter, Richard. *The Reformed Pastor*. Edinburgh: The Banner of Truth, 2007.

Beale, G. K., and D. A. Carson, eds. *Commentary on the New Testament Use of the Old Testament*. Grand Rapids: Baker Academic, 2007.

Berding, Kenneth, and Jonathan Lunde, eds. *Three Views on the New Testament Use of the Old Testament*. Grand Rapids: Zondervan, 2008.

Berlin, Adele. *The Dynamics of Biblical Parallelism: Revised + Expanded*. Grand Rapids: Eerdmans, 2008.

Biola University. "Haddon Robinson: Preaching into the Wind: Q&A – National Ministry Conference." *YouTube*, July 9, 2012. 54:37. https://www.youtube.com/watch?v=73NUZyajnzQ.

Block, Daniel I. "Preaching Ezekiel." In *Reclaiming the Old Testament for Christian Preaching*, edited by Grenville J. R. Kent et al., 157–78. Downers Grove, IL: InterVarsity, 2010.

Boda, Mark J., and J. Gordon McConville, eds. *Dictionary of the Old Testament Prophets*. Downers Grove, IL: InterVarsity, 2012.

Bodey, Richard Allen. *Inside the Sermon: Thirteen Preachers Discuss their Methods of Preparing Sermons*. Grand Rapids: Baker, 1991.

Brand, Chad O., ed. *Perspectives on Israel and the Church: 4 Views*. Nashville: B&H, 2015.

Bright, John. *The Authority of the Old Testament*. London: SCM, 1967.

Brooks, Phillips. *Lectures on Preaching*. New York: Dutton, 1877.

Brueggemann, Walter. *Preaching from the Old Testament*. Minneapolis: Fortress, 2019.

———. *The Prophetic Imagination*. 2nd ed. Minneapolis: Fortress, 2001.

Bullinger, E. W. *Figures of Speech Used in the Bible: Explained and Illustrated*. Eastford, CT: Martino, 2011.

Calvin, John. *Institutes of Christian Religion*. Grand Rapids: Eerdmans, 1989.

Carlson, Robert A. *Preaching Like the Prophets: The Hebrew Prophets as Examples for the Practice of Pastoral Preaching*. Eugene, OR: Wipf & Stock, 2017.

Carson, D. A. *The Gospel According to John*. Grand Rapids: Eerdmans, 1991.

———, ed. *The Scriptures Testify about Me: Jesus and the Gospel in the Old Testament*. Nottingham, UK: InterVarsity, 2013.

Carson, D. A., and John D. Woodbridge, eds. *Hermeneutics, Authority, and Canon*. Grand Rapids: Zondervan, 1986.

———, eds. *Scripture and Truth*. Grand Rapids: Baker, 1992.

Chalmers, Aaron. *Interpreting the Prophets: Reading, Understanding and Preaching from the Worlds of the Prophets*. Downers Grove, IL: InterVarsity, 2015.

Chapell, Bryan. *Christ-Centered Preaching: Redeeming the Expository Sermon*. 2nd ed. Grand Rapids: Baker Academic, 2005.

———. *Christ-Centered Sermons: Models of Redemptive Preaching*. Grand Rapids: Baker Academic, 2013.

Chisholm, Robert B., Jr. *Handbook on the Prophets*. Grand Rapids: Baker Academic, 2009.

Cicero, Marcus Tullius. *Cicero on Oratory and Orators*. Edited and translated by J. S. Watson. Carbondale: Southern Illinois University Press, 1986.

Clowney, Edmund P. *Preaching and Biblical Theology*. London: Tyndale, 1962.

———. "Preaching Christ from Biblical Theology." In *Inside the Sermon*, edited by Richard Allen Bodey, 57–64. Grand Rapids: Baker, 1991.

———. *Preaching Christ in All of Scripture*. Illinois: Crossway, 2003.

———. *The Unfolding Mystery: Discovering Christ in the Old Testament*. Phillipsburg, NJ: P & R, 1988.

Cullman, Oscar. *Christ and Time: The Primitive Christian Conception of Time and History*. Translated by Floyd V. Filson. Philadelphia: Westminster, 1950.

Davies, Gwilym. *Get Preaching: Application*. Ross-shire, UK: Christian Focus, 2020.

Davis, Andrew M. *Christ-Centered Exposition Commentary: Exalting Jesus in Isaiah*. Nashville: B&H, 2017.

Davis, Dale Ralph. *The Word Became Fresh: How to Preach from Old Testament Narrative Texts*. Ross-shire, UK: Christian Focus, 2012.

DeGreef, Wulfert. *The Writings of John Calvin: An Introductory Guide*. Louisville: Westminster John Knox, 2008.

DeRouchie, Jason S. *How to Understand and Apply the Old Testament: Twelve Steps from Exegesis to Theology*. Phillipsburg, NJ: P & R, 2017.

———, ed. *What the Old Testament Authors Really Cared about: A Survey of Jesus' Bible*. Grand Rapids: Kregel Academic, 2013.

Dodd, Charles Harold. *The Apostolic Preaching and Its Developments*. London: Hodder and Stoughton, 1970.

Duvall, J. Scott, and J. Daniel Hays. *Grasping God's Word: A Hands-on Approach to Reading, Interpreting, and Applying the Bible*. Grand Rapids: Zondervan, 2012.

Edwards, Jonathan. "The Excellency of Christ." In *The Works of President Edwards*, 5:535–66. 10 vols. New York: S. Converse, 1829.

Edwards, Jonathan, "Sinners in the Hands of an Angry God. A Sermon Preached at Enfield, July 8th, 1741." Edited by Reiner Smolinski. *Electronic Texts in American Studies* 54. https://digitalcommons.unl.edu/cgi/viewcontent. cgi?article=1053&context=etas.

Fee, Gordon D., and Douglas Stuart. *How to Read the Bible for All It's Worth*. 4th ed. Grand Rapids: Zondervan, 2014.

Feinberg, John S., ed. *Continuity and Discontinuity: Perspectives on the Relationship between the Old and New Testaments*. Westchester, IL: Crossway, 1988.

Fokkelman, J. P. *Reading Biblical Poetry: An Introductory Guide*. Louisville: Westminster John Knox, 2001.

Forsyth, Mark. *The Elements of Eloquence: How to Turn the Perfect English Phrase*. London: Icon, 2019.

Geisler, Norman L. *Christ: The Key to Interpreting the Bible*. Chicago: Moody, 1975.

Gentry, Peter J. *How to Read & Understand the Biblical Prophets*. Wheaton, IL: Crossway, 2017.

Gibson, Scott M., ed. *Preaching the Old Testament*. Grand Rapids: Baker, 2006.

Girdlestone, R. B. *The Grammar of Prophecy: A Systematic Guide to Biblical Prophecy*. Grand Rapids: Kregel, 1955.

Goldingay, John. *Key Questions about Biblical Interpretation: Old Testament Answers*. Grand Rapids: Baker Academic, 2011.

———. *Models for Interpretation of Scripture*. Toronto: Clements, 2004.

Goldsworthy, Graeme. *The Goldsworthy Trilogy: Gospel & Kingdom, Gospel & Wisdom, and The Gospel in Revelation*. Milton Keynes: Paternoster, 2011.

———. *Preaching the Whole Bible as Christian Scripture: The Application of Biblical Theology to Expository Preaching*. Nottingham, UK: InterVarsity, 2000.

Gooding, David. *The Riches of Divine Wisdom: The New Testament's Use of the Old Testament*. Coleraine, UK: Myrtlefield House, 2013.

Gordon, Robert P., ed. *The Place Is Too Small for Us: The Israelite Prophets in Recent Scholarship*. Winona Lake, IN: Eisenbrauns, 1995.

Gowan, Donald E. *Theology of the Prophetic Books: The Death & Resurrection of Israel*. Louisville: Westminster John Knox, 1998.

Green, Joel B. *How to Read Prophecy*. Leicester: InterVarsity, 1984.

Greidanus, Sidney. *The Modern Preacher and the Ancient Text: Interpreting and Preaching Biblical Literature*. Grand Rapids: Eerdmans, 1988.

———. "Preaching Christ." *Calvin Theological Seminary Forum* (Spring 2003) 3–4. https://www.calvin.edu/library/database/crcpi/fulltext/csf/spring2003.pdf.

———. *Preaching Christ from the Old Testament: A Contemporary Hermeneutical Method.* Grand Rapids: Eerdmans, 1999.

Grudem, Wayne A. *Tyndale New Testament Commentaries: 1 Peter.* Nottingham, UK: InterVarsity, 1988.

Gundry, Stanley N., and Darrell L. Block, eds. *Three Views on the Millennium and Beyond.* Grand Rapids: Zondervan, 1999.

Gundry, Stanley N., and Alan Hultberg, eds. *Three Views on the Rapture: Pretribulation, Prewrath, or Posttribulation.* Grand Rapids: Zondervan, 2010.

Gundry, Stanley N., and C. Marvin Pate, eds. *Four Views on the Book of Revelation.* Grand Rapids: Zondervan, 1998.

Hardy, H. H., II. *Exegetical Gems from Biblical Hebrew: A Refreshing Guide to Grammar and Interpretation.* Grand Rapids: Baker Academic, 2019.

Hays, J. Daniel. *The Message of the Prophets: A Survey of the Prophetic and Apocalyptic Books of the Old Testament.* Grand Rapids: Zondervan, 2010.

Hays, J. Daniel, et al. *An A-to-Z Guide to Biblical Prophecy and the End Times.* Grand Rapids: Zondervan, 2007.

Hays, Richard B. *Echoes of Scripture in the Gospels.* Waco, TX: Baylor University Press, 2016.

House, Paul R. *Old Testament Theology.* Downers Grove, IL: InterVarsity, 1998.

Humes, James C. *The Sir Winston Method: The Five Secrets of Speaking the Language of Leadership.* New York: Morrow, 1991.

Jackman, David. *Teaching Isaiah: Unlocking Isaiah for the Bible Teacher.* Ross-shire, UK: Christian Focus, 2010.

Johnson, Dennis E. *Him We Proclaim: Preaching Christ from All the Scriptures.* Phillipsburg, NJ: P & R, 2007.

Kaiser Jr., Walter C. *Back Toward the Future: Hints for Interpreting Biblical Prophecy.* Eugene, OR: Wipf & Stock, 1989.

———. *The Christian and the "Old" Testament.* Pasedena, CA: William Carey Library, 1998.

———. *Hard Sayings of the Old Testament.* Downers Grove, IL: InterVarsity, 1988.

———. *The Majesty of God in the Old Testament: A Guide for Preaching and Teaching.* Grand Rapids: Baker Academic, 2007.

———. *Preaching and Teaching from the Old Testament: A Guide for the Church.* Grand Rapids: Baker Academic, 2003.

———. *Preaching and Teaching the Last Things: Old Testament Eschatology for the Life of the Church.* Grand Rapids: Baker Academic, 2011.

———. *Toward an Exegetical Theology: Biblical Exegesis for Preaching & Teaching.* Grand Rapids: Baker Academic, 2007.

———. *Toward an Old Testament Theology.* Grand Rapids: Zondervan, 1978.

Keller, Timothy. *Preaching: Communicating Faith in an Age of Sceptism.* London: Hodder and Stoughton, 2015.

Kent, Grenville J. R., et al., eds. *Reclaiming the Old Testament for Christian Preaching.* Downers Grove, IL: InterVarsity, 2010.

Köstenberger, Andreas J., and Richard D. Patterson. *Invitation to Biblical Interpretation: Exploring the Hermeneutical Triad of History, Literature, and Theology.* Grand Rapids: Kregel Academic, 2011.

Kugel, James L. *The Idea of Biblical Poetry: Parallelism and Its History*. London: John Hopkins University Press, 1998.

Kuruvilla, Abraham. *Privilege the Text: A Theological Hermeneutic for Preaching*. Chicago: Moody, 2013.

Langley, Ken. "When Christ Replaces God at the Center of Preaching." *Journal of the Evangelical Homiletics Society* 9.1 (March 2009) 53–84. https://journal.ehomiletics. org/wp-content/uploads/jehs_09-1_mar_2009.pdf.

Lanham, Richard A. *A Handlist of Rhetorical Terms*. 2nd ed. Berkeley: University of California Press, 1991.

Larson, Craig Brian, ed. *Prophetic Preaching*. Peabody, MA: Hendrickson, 2012.

Lausanne Movement. "Bible Exposition: Ephesians 3 – John Piper (Part 2) - Cape Town 2010." *YouTube*, September 26, 2011. 22:38. https://www.youtube.com/watch?v=1a5V1O4M4rU.

Leggett, Donald A. *Loving God and Disturbing Men: Preaching from the Prophets*. Toronto: Clements, 2003.

Leith, Sam. *Words Like Loaded Pistols: Rhetoric from Aristotle to Obama*. New York: Basic, 2012.

Logan, Samuel T., Jr., ed. *The Preacher and Preaching: Reviving the Art*. Phillipsburg, NJ: P & R, 1986.

Long, Thomas G. *Preaching and the Literary Forms of the Bible*. Philadelphia: Fortress, 1989.

Long, V. Philips. "The Art of Biblical History." In *Foundations of Contemporary Interpretation: Six Volumes in One*, edited by Moisès Silva, 287–429. Grand Rapids: Zondervan, 1996.

Longenecker, Richard N. *Biblical Exegesis in the Apostolic Period*. Carlisle: Paternoster, 1995.

Longman, Tremper, III. "Literary Approaches to Biblical Interpretation." In *Foundations of Contemporary Interpretation: Six Volumes in One*, edited by Moisés Silva, 95–192. Grand Rapids: Zondervan, 1996.

Luckenbill, Daniel David. *Ancient Records of Assyria and Babylonia: Volume 1—Historical Records of Assyria from the Earliest Times to Sargon*. 2 vols. Chicago: University of Chicago Press, 1926.

———. *Ancient Records of Assyria and Babylonia: Volume 2—Historical Records of Assyria from Sargon to the End*. 2 vols. Chicago: The University of Chicago Press, 1927.

McCartney, Dan, and Charles Clayton. *Let the Reader Understand: A Guide to Interpreting and Applying the Bible*. 2nd ed. Phillipsburg, NJ: P & R, 2002.

McComiskey, Thomas Edward. *The Covenants of Promise: A Theology of the Old Testament Covenants*. Grand Rapids: Baker, 1985.

McConville, J. Gordon. *Exploring the Old Testament: A Guide to the Prophets*. Downers Grove, IL: InterVarsity, 2002.

McGuigan, Brendan. *Rhetorical Devices: A Handbook and Activities for Student Writers*. Smyrna, DE: Prestwick House, 2007.

McMickle, Marvin. *Where Have All the Prophets Gone?: Reclaiming Prophetic Preaching in America*. Cleveland: Pilgrim, 2006.

Merkle, Benjamin L. *Discontinuity to Continuity: A Survey of Dispensational and Covenantal Theologies*. Bellingham, WA: Lexham, 2020.

Moody, Josh, and Robin Weekes. *Burning Hearts: Preaching to the Affections*. Ross-shire, UK: Christian Focus, 2014.

Moore, Thomas Verner. *The Prophets of the Restoration: Haggai, Zechariah and Malachi*. New York: Carter & Brothers, 1856.

Morris, Leon. *Tyndale New Testament Commentaries: 1 Corinthians*. Leicester: InterVarsity, 1995.

Motyer, Alec. *A Scenic Route through the Old Testament*. London: InterVarsity, 2016.

Mounce, Robert H. *The Essential Nature of New Testament Preaching*. Eugene, OR: Wipf & Stock, 2005.

Moyise, Steve. *Jesus and Scripture: Studying the New Testament Use of the Old Testament*. Grand Rapids: Baker Academic, 2010.

———. *The Old Testament in the New: An Introduction*. 2nd ed. London: Bloomsbury T. & T. Clark, 2015.

Murray, David. *Jesus on Every Page: 10 Simple Ways to Seek and Find Christ in the Old Testament*. Nashville: Nelson, 2013.

Negev, Avraham, ed. *Archaeological Encyclopedia of the Holy Land*. Jerusalem: Jerusalem Publishing House, 1972.

Niehaus, Jeffrey Jay. *God the Poet: Exploring the Origin and Nature of Poetry*. Wooster, OH: Weaver, 2014

Nogalski, James D., and Marvin A. Sweeney. *Reading and Hearing the Book of the Twelve*. Atlanta: Society of Biblical Literature, 2000.

O'Brien, Julia M. *Challenging Prophetic Metaphor: Theology and Ideology in the Prophets*. Louisville: Westminster John Knox, 2008.

Packer, J. I. *God Has Spoken*. Downers Grove, IL: InterVarsity, 1979.

———. "Why Preach." In *The Preacher and Preaching: Reviving the Art*, edited by Samuel T. Logan Jr., 1–29. Phillipsburg, NJ: P & R, 1986.

Pelton, Randal E. *Preaching with Accuracy: Finding Christ-Centered Big Ideas for Biblical Preaching*. Grand Rapids: Kregel Ministry, 2014.

Piper, John. "My Pastor Uses Pre-Made Sermons – Should I Be Concerned?" *Desiring God*, April 4, 2016. Audio interview. 9:42. https://www.desiringgod.org/interviews/my-pastor-uses-pre-made-sermons-should-i-be-concerned.

Poythress, Vern S. *God-Centered Biblical Interpretation*. Phillipsburg, NJ: P & R, 1999.

Pritchard, James B., ed. *The Ancient Near East: An Anthology of Texts & Pictures*. Princeton: Princeton University Press, 2011.

Rata, Tiberius. "Covenant." In *Dictionary of the Old Testament Prophets*, edited by. Mark J. Boda & J. Gordon McConville, 99–105. Nottingham, UK: InterVarsity, 2012.

Robertson, O. Palmer. *The Christ of the Prophets*. Phillipsburg, NJ: P & R, 2008.

Robinson, Haddon W. *Biblical Preaching: The Development and Delivery of Expository Messages*. 3rd ed. Grand Rapids: Baker Academic, 2014.

———. "Blending Bible Content and Life Application." In *The Art & Craft of Biblical Preaching*, edited by Haddon Robinson and Craig Brian Larson, 294–99. Grand Rapids: Zondervan, 1996.

———. "The Heresy of Application." In *The Art & Craft of Biblical Preaching*, edited by Haddon Robinson and Craig Brian Larson, 306–11. Grand Rapids: Zondervan, 1996.

Ryken, Leland. *How to Read the Bible as Literature. . . and Get More Out of It*. Grand Rapids: Zondervan, 1984.

———. *Words of Delight: A Literary Introduction to the Bible.* 2nd ed. Grand Rapids: Baker Academics, 1992.

Ryken, Leland, and Tremper Longman III, eds. *A Complete Literary Guide to the Bible.* Grand Rapids: Zondervan, 1993.

Sandy, Brent D. *Plowshares and Pruning Hooks: Rethinking the Language of Biblical Prophecy and Apocalyptic.* Downers Grove, IL: InterVarsity, 2002.

Sandy, D. Brent, and Ronald L. Giese Jr. *Cracking Old Testament Codes: A Guide to Interpreting the Literary Genres of the Old Testament.* Nashville: B&H, 1995.

Schreiner, Thomas R. *The King in His Beauty: A Biblical Theology of the Old and New Testaments.* Grand Rapids: Baker Academic, 2013.

Selvaggio, Anthony. *The Prophets Speak of Him: Encountering Jesus in the Minor Prophets.* Darlington, UK: Evangelical, 2013.

Silva, Moisès, ed. *Foundations of Contemporary Interpretation: Six Volumes in One.* Grand Rapids: Zondervan, 1996.

Smith, Gary V. *Interpreting the Prophetic Books: An Exegetical Handbook.* Grand Rapids: Kregel Academic, 2014.

———. *The Prophets as Preachers: An Introduction to the Hebrew Prophets.* Nashville: Broadman & Holman, 1994.

Smith, Steven W. *Christ-Centered Exposition Commentary: Exalting Jesus in Jeremiah and Lamentations.* Nashville: B&H, 2019.

———. *Recapturing the Voice of God: Shaping Sermons Like Scripture.* Nashville: B&H, 2015.

Spurgeon, Charles Haddon. "Christ Precious to Believers." *The Spurgeon Archive.* https://archive.spurgeon.org/sermons/0242.php.

———. "The Desire of All Nations." *The Spurgeon Archive.* https://archive.spurgeon.org/sermons/3442.php.

Stott, John, R. W. *Between Two Worlds: The Art of Preaching in the Twentieth Century.* Grand Rapids: Eerdmans, 1982.

Stuart, Douglas. *Old Testament Exegesis: A Handbook for Students and Pastors.* 4th ed. Louisville: Westminster John Knox, 2009.

Sunukjian, Donald R. *Invitation to Biblical Preaching: Proclaiming Truth with Clarity and Relevance.* Grand Rapids: Kregel, 2007.

Sweeney, Marvin A. *The Prophetic Literature.* Nashville: Abingdon, 2005.

Thompson, Andrew. "Community Oracles: A Model for Applying and Preaching the Prophets." *Journal of the Evangelical Homiletics Society* 10.1 (March 2010) 31–57. https://journal.ehomiletics.org/wp-content/uploads/jehs_10-1_mar_2010.pdf.

Tisdale, Leonora Tubbs. *Prophetic Preaching: A Pastoral Approach.* Louisville: Westminster John Knox, 2010.

Troxel, Ronald L. *Prophetic Literature: from Oracles to Books.* Chichester: Wiley-Blackwell, 2012.

Tucker, Gene M. *Form Criticism of the Old Testament.* Philadelphia: Fortress, 1976.

Vanhoozer, Kevin J. *Is There a Meaning in This Text?: The Bible, the Reader, and the Morality of Literary Knowledge.* Grand Rapids: Zondervan, 1998.

Virkler, Henry A., and Karelynne Gerber Ayayo. *Hermeneutics: Principles and Processes of Biblical Interpretation.* 2nd ed. Grand Rapids: Baker Academic, 2007.

Von Rad, Gerhard. *The Message of the Prophets.* London: SCM, 1982.

———. *Old Testament Theology: Volume Two.* 2 vols. Edinburgh: Oliver and Boyd, 1970.

Waltke, Bruce K. *The Old Testament Theology: An Exegetical, Canonical, and Thematic Approach*. Grand Rapids: Zondervan, 2007.

Walvoord, John F., and Roy B. Zuck, eds. *The Bible Knowledge Commentary: Minor Prophets*. Colorado Springs: Cook, 2018.

Ward, James, and Christine Ward. *Preaching from the Prophets*. Nashville: Abingdon, 1995.

Watson, Wilfred G. E. *Classical Hebrew Poetry: A Guide to its Techniques*. Sheffield: JSOT, 1986.

Westermann, Claus. *Basic Forms of Prophetic Speech*. Cambridge: Lutterworth, 1991.

Wilson, Paul. *Preaching as Poetry: Beauty, Goodness, and Truth in Every Sermon*. Nashville: Abingdon, 2014.

Wright, Christopher J. H. *Knowing Jesus through the Old Testament*. Downers Grove, IL: InterVarsity, 1992.

———. *Sweeter than Honey: Preaching the Old Testament*. Carlisle: Langham Preaching Resources, 2015.

CPSIA information can be obtained
at www.ICGtesting.com
Printed in the USA
LVHW081619251122
733989LV00008B/649